To Keep and Bear Arms

Who shall stand guard to the guards themselves?

JUVENAL

That the Subjects which are Protestants may have Armes for their
defence Suitable to their Condition and as allowed by Law.

ENGLISH BILL OF RIGHTS, 1689

A well regulated Militia being necessary to the security of a free State,
the right of the people to keep and bear Arms,
shall not be infringed.

AMERICAN BILL OF RIGHTS, 1791

To Keep and Bear Arms

The Origins of an Anglo-American Right

J OYCE L EE M ALCOLM

H ARVARD U NIVERSITY P RESS
Cambridge, Massachusetts
London, England

This book has been digitally reprinted. The content
remains identical to that of previous printings.

First Harvard University Press paperback edition, 1996

Library of Congress Cataloging-in-Publication Data

Malcolm, Joyce Lee.
To keep and bear arms :
the origins of an Anglo-American right /
Joyce Lee Malcolm.
p.   cm.
Includes bibliographical references and index.
ISBN 0-674-89306-9 (cloth)
ISBN 0-674-89307-7 (pbk.)
1. United States—Constitutional law—Amendments—2nd.
2. Firearms—Law and legislation—United States—History.
3. United States—Constitutional history.
4. Firearms—Law and legislation—England—History.
I. Title
KF4558 2nd.M35   1994
344.73'0533'09—dc20
[347.30453309]   93-26710
CIP

FOR MY FATHER,
JACOB NEWIRTH SITRIN,
WHO LOVES LEARNING

Contents

Preface

THE right of ordinary citizens to possess weapons is the most extraordinary, most controversial, and least understood of those liberties secured by Englishmen and bequeathed to their American colonists. It lies at the very heart of the relationship between the individual and his fellows, and between the individual and his government. For obvious reasons few governments have ever been prepared to grant such a privilege. Nor was it the "true, ancient, and indubitable right" the English Bill of Rights pretended. The right was born in 1689 with its inclusion in that document and perpetuated, with modifications, in the American Bill of Rights a century later. Today it is a right in decline. Other Anglo-American rights have been broadened since the eighteenth century, and new ones added, whereas the right of individuals to have weapons is viewed as an anachronism. Englishmen no longer have this right, and it is under vigorous assault in the United States.

Few of our rights have attracted the historical attention they deserve, and the right of citizens to have weapons is no exception. In Britain, where the subject has not been controversial, it has been a casualty of benign neglect. In the United States, by contrast, the recent debate over gun-related violence has drawn scholarly attention to the Second Amendment guarantee of the "right of the people to keep and bear arms"—but that attention has revealed a sorry state of affairs. The language of the Second Amendment, considered perfectly clear by the framers and their contemporaries, is no longer clear. Changed circumstances and long years of indifference have made it difficult to reconstruct the philosophy behind the right, let alone ascertain with any confidence the intention of its drafters. Add to these obstacles the absence of studies by English constitutional historians, the unfortunate chasm between the fields of English and American history, and the tendency of Americans to stress their nation's originality, and the result is a lack of basic information about its origins and much misinterpretation. Nor has the attention it has succeeded in attracting been especially helpful. As the focus of a highly emotional controversy, the subject has attracted more belligerents eager to furnish ammunition for their viewpoint than scholars prepared to analyze and inform.

This book is not intended to add fuel to a sufficiently hot American fire. Rather, it is meant to shed light in places very dark indeed. As a scholar of seventeenth-century English history, I am particularly curious about the evolution of this extraordinary right. Why did Englishmen, led by the so-called governing classes, conclude that such a dangerous public freedom was necessary? What caused them to add it to the list of thirteen "true, ancient, and indubitable" liberties in 1689? How was this "ancient" right applied? Once all this is made plain, or at least plainer, what can it tell us of the intentions of the American framers in appending an even broader right to their new constitution?

Information garnered about these and related questions offers benefits beyond tracking the origins of a liberty, valuable as that is. An analysis of this information adds another dimension to our picture of English life, politics, and constitutional development in the turbulent seventeenth century. Just as important, the results set the American controversy over the meaning of the Second Amendment, and the wisdom of an individual right to have weapons, upon a foundation of fact. And, more generally, the enterprise affords the rare opportunity to chronicle the evolution of a right.

The right to be armed occupied no mean place among other liberties. A glance backward reveals the importance formerly attributed to the armed citizen in Anglo-American constitutional thought. Even a century ago both conservative and liberal statesmen and theorists regarded the armed citizen as crucial to the maintenance of limited government and individual liberty. Clearly they lacked our confidence in what the American founders liked to call "parchment barriers." According to Thomas Macaulay, the Englishman's ultimate security depended not upon the Magna Carta or Parliament but upon "the power of the sword."[1] To his mind "the legal check was secondary and auxiliary to that which the nation held in its own hands . . . the security without which every other is insufficient." England's greatest jurist, William Blackstone, believed that private arms undergirded the constitutional structure. His list of rights in the first chapter of his work *Commentaries on the Laws of England* was followed by the admission: "In vain would these rights be declared, ascertained, and protected by the dead letter of the laws, if the constitution had provided no other method to secure their actual enjoyment."[2] As an added protection, he explained, there were "auxiliary rights." The fifth and last auxiliary right, meant to protect all the others, "is that of having arms for their defence . . . It is, indeed, a publick allowance under due restrictions, of the natural right of resistance and self preservation, when the sanctions of society and laws are found insufficient to restrain the violence of oppression."[3]

The notion that an individual right to have weapons was essential to limited government was more complex than this, however. It involved the conviction that there must be civilian control of the sword, and it grew out of a particular attitude toward citizenship and government, self-defence, the citizen army and the professional army, obedience and resistance. Taken together it is the reflection of a congeries of seventeenth-century prejudices and experiences remote from the lives of modern Britons and Americans, yet instrumental in shaping the constitutions that have served them well.

The historian venturing into this area faces a host of difficulties. First, the shoulders of other historians, upon which seventeenth-century scholars can ordinarily stand, are absent. Fundamental work is lacking, and the occasional studies that impinge upon the subject are scattered over the fields of legal, political, and social history, as well as political theory. Second, the records can be stubbornly silent about the motives behind critical aspects of the topic, such as the Game Act of 1671, which made it illegal for most Englishmen to keep firearms. Lastly, with few exceptions, only the brave or foolhardy dare bridge the Atlantic to follow the transmission of ideas and liberties from mother country to colonies. As a specialist in English history, albeit an American, I cautiously attempted the leap. My aim in exploring that critical era has been to open up the subject to further research, not to pretend to exhaust it.

What follows is not traditional legal history. In investigating the origins of this right, I have been concerned to cast as wide a net as possible. This was essential not only because the subject overlaps many separate fields, but because all legal and constitutional history is best understood in context; indeed, where direct evidence is deficient, there is no satisfactory alternative but to dredge clues from the context.

The primary focus of this book is the transformation in the seventeenth century of an often onerous duty into a right. The chronological analysis is interrupted by a chapter in which I examine the availability of firearms and the actual enforcement of weapons restrictions, and another where I scrutinize the drafting of the arms article in the English Bill of Rights and its subsequent interpretation. In the final chapter I explore the transmission of the right to be armed to America and the impact of the English experience on the events leading up to, and including, this addition to the American Bill of Rights. While the impact of classical republican and Enlightenment thought on the American foun-

Preface

ders is clear and well documented, the English influence on the Second Amendment is the missing ingredient that has hampered efforts to interpret its intent correctly.

Although I have not had many scholarly shoulders to stand upon in undertaking this research, I have benefited enormously from the generosity of many institutions and the advice and encouragement of many scholars and friends. A research fellowship from the National Endowment for the Humanities enabled me to embark upon this project. Research fellowships from the American Bar Foundation, the Bunting Institute at Radcliffe College, the Liberty Fund, and a Mark DeWolfe Howe research grant and visiting fellowship from Harvard Law School provided the leisure and academic resources to complete the research and much of the writing.

I am indebted to many individuals. I should especially like to thank John Kenyon, whose provocative comment about the Game Act of 1671 in *The Stuart Constitution* set me thinking about this topic, and who very kindly read and commented on the manuscript that resulted. Herbert Johnson boldly agreed to review the section on American history to save me from pitfalls and errors. Grateful thanks are also due many friends and colleagues for their patience, confidence, unflagging encouragement, and inspiring example. Of these I particularly wish to thank Sir Geoffrey Elton. John Morrill has been consistently gracious in sharing his extensive knowledge of seventeenth-century England despite an always hectic schedule, and David Underdown has been a valued friend since I began my doctoral dissertation. I would also like to thank Robert Cottrol, Raymond Diamond, and Donald Lutz for permitting me to read copies of their articles prior to publication.

Nearer to home, I have been no less fortunate. My secretary, Mary Daly, readily tackled the painstaking task of converting the entire manuscript to a computer format, greatly simplifying the final stages of the work. There is little I can say to adequately thank my immediate family: my son Geordie, whose lifetime has coincided with this endeavour; Mark and Lisa, who endured a similar preoccupation when I was at work on my first book, *Caesar's Due;* and above all my husband, Neil, for listening, advising, reading, and generally putting up with a companion engrossed in a complex and time-consuming task. Any errors that remain in the text are my own.

To Keep and Bear Arms

Quotations are cited exactly as in the sources, except that the more unusual abbreviations have been extended. Dates are given in Old Style, though the year is taken as beginning on January 1.

CHAPTER ONE

A People Armed

THE right of citizens to be armed not only is unusual, but evolved in England in an unusual manner: it began as a duty. From the proverbial "time out of mind" Englishmen had a duty to be armed. Like most duties it was often resented and, in this instance, commonly regarded as onerous, if not dangerous. Yet, at a crucial moment in English history, when the governing classes seized a rare opportunity to draw up a bill of rights, this long-standing and unpopular duty was transformed into a right. Its development as a duty was quite natural, as a right far more complex.

The decentralization and disorder of the Middle Ages made popular participation in local peacekeeping the most practical means of maintaining order. The authority of the Crown had increased substantially by the sixteenth and seventeenth centuries, but its limited financial resources led to the continuation of a practice that had, among other benefits, the virtue of being cheap. Similarly, the difficulty and expense of maintaining permanent armies and popular hatred of mercenaries compelled the Crown to rely instead upon citizen-soldiers to defend the realm. Both policies involved considerable risk, since English subjects would have to be armed and trained to arms. What surprises is not the use of these medieval expedients, but their persistence into modern times—that the arms pressed into the hands of the general population as the most practical means of ensuring public quiet remained there. Indeed, the Crown's attempt late in the seventeenth century to shift to less perilous methods of maintaining order provoked the political nation to claim for all Protestants a right to have weapons. That right played a major role in the evolution of limited government.

It was during the seventeenth century that this transformation of a duty to have arms into a right took place. To understand why it occurred then, indeed why it occurred at all, we must focus upon that pivotal era. The seventeenth century is deservedly famous for its periodic and unprecedented political turmoil. It was a time of urgent concern with the boundaries of subjection and sovereignty and the obligations of government and religion. Yet the setting in which most Englishmen lived and worked remained in many respects unchanged by the upheavals in church and state. England was, and remained, overwhelmingly rural, with most of its people clustered in small villages of less than 500 persons. It was a society dominated by a landed aristocracy but comprising many prosperous independent farmers—England's famed yeomen—and increasing numbers of merchants, professionals, and craftsmen, the "middling sort." The great majority of Englishmen, however, were small freeholders or tenant farmers.[1] Although civil war would loosen the aristocracy's grip on power, they dominated Parliament at the end of the century as they had at its start. With the exception of the civil war years, ordinary Englishmen were not noticeably more enthusiastic about their police duties in 1689 than in 1600. But against this background of sameness was a foreground of turmoil in which a man's ability to have weapons assumed grave significance. Before investigating the complex forces that would produce this transformation, one must examine the Englishman's traditional role as peacekeeper.

England would not have a standing army until late in the seventeenth century, or a professional police force until the nineteenth century. From "time out of mind," therefore, the Englishman had been obliged to add to his other civic duties the dangerous chore of law enforcement.[2] His first responsibility was to defend himself. He was also expected to protect his family and his property against attack. It was assumed he would have the means at hand to do this, and he was held legally blameless for any harm inflicted upon his assailants. As a popular seventeenth-century guidebook for justices of the peace explained: "If Thieves shall come to a Man's House, to rob or murther him, he may lawfully assemble company to defend his House by force; and if he or any of his company shall kill any of them in defence of Himself, his Family, his Goods or House, This is no Felony, neither shall they forfeit any thing therefore."[3]

It is natural to expect a man to defend himself and his loved ones, but the Englishman was obliged to protect his neighbour as well. From at least the early Middle Ages, whenever a serious crime occurred villagers, "ready apparelled," were to raise a "hue and cry" and, under the supervision of the local constable or sheriff, pursue the culprit "from town to town, and from county to county" on "pain of grievous fine."[4] In addition, the law made residents of a parish liable for compensating a victim of a robbery or riot committed in their parish for half of his loss. The development of firearms made the pursuit of culprits an increasingly dangerous obligation. Late in the seventeenth century—a heyday of highway robbers—Parliament attempted to modify collective responsibility. As one member argued, when the law was first established "men had not the use of fire-arms; nothing but clubs and pitchforks; and the thieves might have been stopped."[5] But the bill failed and the obligation remained.

Another police duty placed upon the people was the keeping of watch and ward. Town gates were closed from sundown until sunrise, and each householder was required to take his turn keeping watch at night or ward during the day. The watch was to be carried out "by men able of body, and sufficiently weaponed."[6] Widows and householders of unsound body had to hire a substitute. During times of war or unrest the number of watchers was usually doubled.[7] Anyone who failed to stand watch was liable to be put in the stocks or presented at quarter sessions. As in the case of hue and cry, the obligation caused concern and even resistance by the second half of the seventeenth century. Growing numbers of men and women from all classes were cited for refusal to perform their duty.[8]

Beyond the local peacekeeping tasks of "hue and cry" and "watch and ward," all able-bodied men were bound to help the sheriff put down riots as members of his *posse comitatus*. By the seventeenth century the trained bands of the militia were generally summoned for this task, but the duty to serve on a posse continued, and posses were not uncommon during the Civil War.[9]

A man's civic responsibility to help keep the peace stretched beyond his village and even beyond his county. He owed his sovereign service in the militia. Such service was a source of both pride and vexation. The English liked to boast that they were "the freest subjects under Heaven" because, among other things, they had the right "to be guarded and defended from all Violence and Force, by their own Arms, kept in their own hands, and used at their own charge under their Prince's Conduct."[10]

Of course, they were seldom actually pleased at having to serve in the militia, and to do so at their own charge, but militia service appears to have been an integral part of English life from early times. With the exception of the first years of Norman rule, Anglo-Saxon, Norman, Angevin, Lancastrian, and Tudor kings chose to trust their subjects with arms and to modify and supplement the militia if need be, rather than to abolish it.[11] So keen were monarchs to develop a citizen-army that by 1252 not only freemen but the richer villeins were ordered to be armed, and in the years that followed unfree peasants were included as well. "The state in its exactions," F. W. Maitland wrote, "pays little heed to the line between free and bond, it expects all men, not merely all freemen, to have arms."[12] These acts formed the basis for Edward I's great Statute of Winchester of 1285, which organized the military might of the realm.[13] For much of English history, therefore, the emphasis was on extending and fixing the obligation to keep and supply militia weapons, not disarming Englishmen. It was not who was supposed to be armed, but who was to pay for the arms, and where subjects were bound to battle, that became the chief sources of contention by the seventeenth century.[14]

All able-bodied men between the ages of sixteen and sixty were liable for militia service, but from 1573 it had become the practice to select small groups of men, commonly known as trained bands, for special training.[15] Such service was not popular, and the duty tended to devolve upon the poorer farmers and less prosperous craftsmen. During the seventeenth century at least 90,000 men served in the trained bands of England and Wales at any one time.

The militia was financed by a tax levied on anyone with any income, even the clergy and the poor. Poor men were usually grouped in such a way that several families might be jointly responsible for "finding" a single piece of military equipment, whereas, at the opposite end of the economic scale, a wealthy landowner might be responsible for producing a mounted man fully equipped, complete with pay in his pocket to last him some thirty days. Although the clergy contributed to the militia, they were not expected to fight. After the English Reformation Catholics were in a similar position, expected to contribute but not to participate. Unlike their fellow subjects, Catholics were not allowed to keep their militia weapons at home.

This seventeenth-century militia was not the flexible force English kings of the time required. A thicket of obligations and customs spelled out each county's military duties and the use the King might make of its militia. The militia was first and foremost a defensive force and could not be taken out of the realm. Members were even reluctant to leave their own counties. As commander-in-chief of the militia the King decided when to call out the trained bands and what their task was to be. However, it was the local magnates—lords lieutenant, deputy-lieutenants, and lower-ranking officers—who were responsible for carrying out royal orders. Their power to interpret or misinterpret royal wishes should not be underestimated.[16] For their part, rank-and-file militiamen were unreliable when called upon to put down internal riots whenever their sympathies lay with the rioters.

The militia, therefore, could serve to some extent as the King's hammer against either an invader or the great magnates, and an inexpensive hammer at that, but it afforded both the aristocracy and ordinary subjects some control over royal policy. And, of course, it necessitated the arming and training of a very large portion of the population.

With the development during the seventeenth century of professional, well-drilled armies on the Continent, English kings were tempted to abandon the militia in favour of a professional force.[17] But the impact of these large military establishments on their home states struck the English as appalling. The greatly increased cost to a country that maintained such an army, and the enhanced power the fighting force gave the ruler, frequently led to a fatal loss of its parliament's political authority. According to Michael Roberts, European parliaments sometimes granted their ruler permission to maintain a force they knew might sap their freedom because "in the last resort the Estates had rather sacrifice a constitutional principle, and retain the security afforded by a standing army, than risk the appalling sufferings and crushing financial exactions which, as the experience of the Thirty Years' War had shown, awaited the militarily impotent or old-fashioned."[18] Parliament had to appropriate the monies for such a project, and its members were well aware of the means for control the militia afforded them and the danger inherent in royal command of a permanent, professional soldiery. It was a longstanding antipathy. King John had been obliged by Magna Carta to remove "all alien knights, crossbowmen, sergeants and mercenary soldiers" from the kingdom, and fear of mercenaries and standing armies persisted into the seventeenth century, inciting and exacerbating seventeenth-century confrontations between the Crown and Parliament.[19] Unless there was war or the immediate danger of it, Parliament was unwilling to vote the necessary funds for a force of any substantial size. As an island nation, the English could cling to principle with less risk and deny their king this dangerous tool.[20] The Crown had little option but to maintain the militia as an effective fighting force.

The English subject's duty to defend himself and his country may have been a source of power and cause for civic boasting—indeed, pamphleteers during the sixteenth, seventeenth, and eighteenth centuries grew increasingly exuberant in their praise of the militia concept—but it was more likely to be regarded as a nuisance by the man called upon to participate. Not only was he put to the expense of obtaining and maintaining the weapons the law required, but he might have to devote several days, possibly longer, to musters and military duty. Just as irksome were the mandatory practice sessions, for the King insisted that the people be expert in the use of the arms they were obliged to possess. Villages were instructed to maintain targets or butts at which local men were to practice, first with the longbow, later with the musket. It is obvious from the number of statutes and proclamations which reiterated these orders that both maintenance of targets and practice sessions were often neglected. An act of Henry VIII, for instance, specified "that butts be made . . . in every city, town, and place, According To The Law of Ancient Time Used, and that the said inhabitants, and dwellers in every of them, be Compelled To Make and Continue Such Butts, upon pain to forfeit, for every three months so lacking, twenty shillings. And that the Said Inhabitants Shall Exercise Themselves With Long-Bows In Shooting At The Same, and elsewhere, in holy days and other times convenient."[21] By the time this was enacted, firearms had begun to replace the longbow. The same act, therefore, permitted lords, knights, esquires, gentlemen, and the inhabitants of every city, borough, and market-town "to have and keep in every of their houses any such hand-gun or hand-guns, of the length of one whole yard . . . to the intent to use and shoot the same, at a butt or bank of earth only . . . whereby they and every of them, by the exercise thereof . . . May The better Aid And Assist To The Defence of This Realm, When Need Shall Require." This was an admission on the King's part of the popularity of firearms amongst his subjects and their use in armies on the Continent.

In the meantime the Crown continued to encourage the use of bows and arrows, with Henry VIII reminding every family to provide each son, at the age of seven, with a bow and two shafts and to see to it that the child knew how to use them. Failure to do this meant a fine of 6s. 8d. for each month the family neglected its civic duty.[22] The stiffness of the fine was obviously meant to underline the Crown's seriousness in this matter.

In the years preceding the Civil War the fortunes of the militia fluctuated wildly. As might have been expected, military duties were executed with alacrity when danger threatened, but at other times both officials and citizens tended to become lax, if not derelict. Complaints of neglect echo down the years. A jury at the Court of Hustings in May 1569 presented the grievance: "There is to much bowling and to little shoting."[23] On another May day ninety-one years later, the Court Leet of Lyme issued a presentment that there had been no butts in the parish of Lyme Regis for three months past.[24] Accordingly that town was fined twenty shillings and ordered to set up targets before the Court next convened or pay a further twenty-shilling fine. It is difficult to be certain, however, whether the relatively small number of such cases meant that military duties were attended to, or that there was little taste for enforcing them. The latter seems more likely, since long intervals passed when the militia was not mustered at all. With the exception of the civil war years of the mid-seventeenth century, the period between 1589 and 1660 was marked by a general disinterest in things military.[25]

The responsibility for the decline in military preparedness during the early part of the seventeenth century lay less with a generation accused of having "fallen from Charity to impiety" than with a king, James I, who was a genuine man of peace; a period of ten years free from the menace of invasion; and an alteration of the militia law. In a far-reaching act that explicitly revived or repealed a number of Tudor statutes, James repealed Philip and Mary's statute of 1557/8 mandating weapons assessments for the militia, and he failed to revive the companion statute that set out a schedule for musters.[26] A jurisdictional dispute between county justices of the peace and the militia lieutenancy and a desire to revise the assessment system were apparently behind this repeal.[27] The precipitate lapse of existing militia legislation was an impetuous blunder. It had the effect of reinstating the 300-year-old Statute of Winchester! There was understandable consternation and confusion when the Crown continued to appoint lords lieutenant, to order annual musters, and to impose militia taxes on the strength of the royal prerogative alone rather than existing law. Complaint was less than it might have been, however, since the schedule of militia musters was pared down considerably.[28]

The situation changed abruptly, as did the level of complaints, with the succession of James's son, Charles I. Charles was eager to make the militia a creditable fighting force. To accomplish this he planned to modernize the militia, to standardize its equipment, and to introduce the latest European military tactics. Since Englishmen had an intense distaste for professional armies, any attempt to improve their militia ought to have been especially welcome. Indeed, during the early years of Charles's reign their fears of standing armies soared as news filtered back to England of the terrible depredations on the Continent resulting from the Thirty Years' War. The army Charles raised as England's contribution to that struggle added to the antiarmy sentiment, for, when Parliament failed to provide adequate financial support, the King billeted his soldiers in private homes and funded the force through expedients such as forced loans.

Yet unpopular as professional armies were, the manner in which the militia operated was also criticized. Until 1630 the King's so-called exact militia was financed by a rating system that was, and was perceived to be, highly inequitable.[29] The sudden shift in royal expectations for the militia was itself a problem. Coming as Charles's program did after a period of exceptional laxity, it aroused a storm of protest among local officials and militiamen alike.

Tact and patience might have overcome the reluctance of Charles's subjects to pay increased military taxes and of local officials and the militia to shoulder new tasks. Yet tact and patience were qualities Charles lacked. Matters were made still more difficult because of the dubious legal authority the King possessed to impose any changes in the militia. Since the expiration of the militia statute of 1558 there was no legal provision for the militia apart from ancient statutes; that is, there existed no statutory obligation to pay new assessments, provide arms, or attend musters. In 1628, when the Crown finally decided to introduce a militia bill into Parliament, both the King and his militia program were in bad odor. In the general chaos that terminated that session the bill was lost. To continue his program, Charles had little option but to impose it on the strength of his prerogative rights and prerogative enforcement of the lapsed militia legislation of 1558, dubious claim indeed for a sharp increase in militia taxes and strict punishment of defaulters.

Opposition from local officials and militiamen had grown so intense by the 1630's that in contrast to the King's high expectations, the militia had reached what a scholar of its history described as "a low ebb."[30] No wonder Robert Ward, the author of *Animadversions of Warre*, a handbook for military men published in 1639, seemed near despair as he proclaimed the virtues of the militia and pleaded for increased understanding on the part of trained band members: "They doe not consider how deeply every man is interested in it, for if they did, our yeomandrie would not be so proud and base to refuse to be taught, and to thinke it a shame to serve in their owne Armes, and to understand the use of them; were they but sensible, that there is not the worth of one peny in a Kingdome well secured, without the due use of Armes, and that the Gospell, which is the Garland of our Kingdome, cannot prosper and flourish but under the shadow of the sword."[31]

Far more renowned writers, of course, had long championed the militia. Machiavelli's works, with their strong preference for a citizen militia over other types of military force, had been familiar to educated Englishmen from the reign of Elizabeth. *The Art of War* had been translated into English in 1560, with editions in 1573 and 1588, and *The Discourse* and *The Prince* in 1636 and 1640 respectively, by which time they were already well known. And though there was much else in Machiavelli to instruct, provoke, and amaze, John Pocock finds that "the rigorous equation of arms-bearing with civic capacity is one of Machiavelli's most enduring legacies to later political thinkers."[32] It is always difficult to gauge the influence of any writer's views. Lois Schwoerer cautions that "it is impossible to say" how widely Machiavelli's works were read, although Felix Raab assures us that by the early seventeenth century their influence had spread well beyond their actual readers.[33] England's Sir Walter Raleigh, however, had pointed out that it was a basic principle of a tyrant "to unarm his people of weapons, money, and all means whereby they resist his power."[34] And Sir Thomas More, in *Utopia,* advocated the training of both men and women for the protection of their homeland and their friends.[35]

Yet Robert Ward's plea makes it abundantly clear that in 1639, notwithstanding the encomiums of any number of political philosophers, most Englishmen did not consider themselves privileged to serve in a militia. In fact, they resented the military demands made upon them by their government. It took war and revolution to change their minds.

The obligation to own and be skilled in the use of weapons does not, of course, imply that there were no restrictions upon the type of weapon owned or the manner of its use. Before elaborating on the restrictions, one must address the distinction between a duty and a right. In brief, a duty is an obligation, a right an entitlement. Certain duties entailed the exercise of particular powers and privileges. The Englishman's peacekeeping obligations required him to own and use weapons. But he had no explicit *right* to have weapons for either peacekeeping or self-defence. Five hundred years of performing a duty did not automatically transform that obligation into a right. And though Englishmen often tended to transform long-standing custom into entitlement, that did not happen in this instance. No claim was made for a right for Englishmen to be armed either in Magna Carta or in subsequent listings of English liberties before 1689.

Until the Civil War, restrictions on ownership of weapons were few and not especially onerous.[36] During the sixteenth century, when firearms began to come into common use, the Crown attempted to place guns under special control. Two statutes, one passed late in the reign of Henry VIII, the other during the reign of his son Edward VI, laid down the basic restrictions upon the use of firearms in force during the seventeenth century. The act initiated by Henry VIII in 1541—the same act that reiterated the requirement for militia practice—was primarily intended to limit ownership and use of two concealable weapons frequently employed in crime, the handgun and the crossbow.[37] The preamble complained of the use of handguns and crossbows by robbers and noted with regret that enthusiasm for firearms had led "divers gentlemen, yeomen and servingmen . . . [to] have laid apart the good and laudable exercise of the long-bow, which always heretofore hath been the surety, safeguard and continual defence of this realm of England, and an inestimable dread and terror to the enemies of the same."

To correct both states of affairs the law restricted the use of crossbows and handguns (any firearm with a barrel less than one yard in length) to persons with a yearly income from land of at least £100. No one possessed of less than that income was to ride about carrying a crossbow bent or a gun charged, except in time of war or in going to and from musters. No gun was to be shot within a quarter mile of a city, borough, or market-town unless at a target or in defence of one's house or person. Conversely, the law was careful to specify that not only gentlemen, but yeomen, servingmen, the inhabitants of cities, boroughs, market-towns, and those living outside of towns could certainly "have and keep in every of their houses any such handgun or handguns, of the length of one whole yard" for target shooting. It was hoped that through such practice gun owners might "the better aid and assist to the defence of this realm, when need shall require." The act of Edward VI merely banned the use in firearms of quantities of small pellets, then referred to as "hail shot," as dangerous to life and limb and highly destructive of wildlife.[38] It also prohibited the shooting of a handgun within city or town precincts except at a target.

The crimes of possessing a handgun when not qualified or of using hail shot were misdemeanours usually punished by loss of the weapon in question or a fine. In some instances, as in the case of a Nottinghamshire labourer found guilty of "shooting with hailshot" in 1621, the defendant was fined twenty shillings and bound "not to shoot again for seven years."[39] Clearly there was no intention of preventing even someone guilty of wrongful use of a gun from ever using one again. The privilege of shooting was merely withdrawn for a certain period, usually, in fact, for much less than seven years.

The Court did, however, remain uneasy about the widespread availability of firearms, and there were at least two attempts by Tudor monarchs to monitor or control them. In 1553 Edward VI ordered "all persons who shoot guns" to register their names with their local justice of the peace. But by the early seventeenth century a popular legal guide for justices took note of the 1553 requirement to "quaere if this be now in use."[40] In 1569 Elizabeth's Privy Council proposed that the government, rather than the members of the militia, store militia firearms. When the idea aroused widespread opposition from local officials it was withdrawn.[41] Indeed, when guns for the militia were in short supply, the officials of Kent suggested not more, but less government control, and advocated unlimited use of guns for hunting.[42]

It is apparent that the regulations in effect before 1640 did not interfere with the basic duty of the English people to keep arms for the defence of themselves, their neighbours, or the realm. The Crown, through its exclusive right to make saltpetre and gunpowder, retained the potential for limiting the supply. But not until the reign of Charles I, when distrust of the King was increasing and monopolists had made gunpowder scarce and expensive, did this seem a real danger. And when it did, Parliament was quick to act.

Although the general public was free to have arms, because there was no *right* to have weapons the government always had the power to disarm any individual or class of individuals it considered dangerous to the peace of the realm. This was the case with English and Welsh Catholics, who had been regarded as potential subversives since the English Reformation and suffered a variety of civil liabilities. Like other subjects, they were assessed for a contribution of arms for the militia, but they were not always permitted to keep these weapons in their homes. Nevertheless, Catholic families were presumed to have weapons on hand for their self-defence. During periods of extreme religious tension or imminent invasion, the purchase of weapons by Catholics was viewed with suspicion. But it was the stockpiling of arms, even the rumour of stockpiling, rather than the possession of weapons for self-defence, that caused their neighbours' anxiety.[43] What is significant and ominous in the arms restrictions imposed on Catholics is not that they put a large group at a disadvantage, but that they set a precedent by singling out a section of the community as *potentially* dangerous and legally disarming them.

There were reasons other than those of state for restricting the use of firearms. Chief among these was the protection of that pastime dear to the hearts of the English aristocracy and to the stomachs of the rural population, the pursuit of game. Although it forms a very separate thread in the fabric of English arms use, it was a strand that was to become thoroughly and purposely entangled in the effort during the Restoration period to disarm the greater part of the English population. For that reason the impact of the hunt upon the use of firearms, and its distinct and lively history, must be examined.

To Samuel Johnson it seemed remarkable that "hunting was the labour of the savages of North America, but the amusement of the Gentlemen of England."[44] In truth, hunting would have been the labour of ordinary Englishmen no less than North American "savages" had not the English aristocracy demanded exclusive rights to the sport. Far more was at stake for the aristocracy than a selfish desire to monopolize their favourite amusement. They viewed common folk armed to keep the peace as an unfortunate necessity, but common folk armed to hunt as an unnecessary, unacceptable menace. Thus, the upper classes sought exclusive rights to the sport not only, as they claimed, to preserve game animals but to curtail the opportunity for common men to go about armed. This was achieved through the passage of game acts that imposed a property qualification on hunting and prohibited those who failed to meet it from using, and in some instances even owning, hunting equipment.

Justification for such blatantly inequitable legislation involved a carefully nurtured double standard, according to which the local squirarchy in pursuit of a hare were practicing "a Recreation for Kings and Noblemen," healthy and honourable in every way, whereas local labourers in pursuit of the same small beast were "very bad Christians . . . of little or no Worth . . . loose, idle, disorderly and dissolute Persons" destined to ruin themselves and their families by neglecting useful employment and likely to turn to highway robbery and burglary.[45]

The subject would be of only passing interest were it not for the fact that in 1671, in the guise of an act to protect wildlife, Parliament passed the first law in English history that took from the majority of Englishmen the privilege of having firearms. The lengths to which the upper classes were prepared to go, ostensibly to guard their hunting prerogative, and the drastic impact of their efforts on the right of Englishmen to possess arms, make plain that far more was involved than what William Blackstone regarded as "a most Princely diversion and exercise."[46]

The mixed motives for passage of game laws were recognized by William Holdsworth in his classic compilation, *A History of English Law*. Holdsworth pointed out that game legislation proceeded on many different bases, one of which was "the principle that assemblies for the purposes of hunting and sport gave opportunities for riot and disorder."[47] William Blackstone listed four chief grounds for passage of game laws:

1. encouragement of agriculture and improvement of lands

2. preservation of several species

3. prevention of idleness and dissipation in husbandmen

4. prevention of popular insurrections and resistance to the government by disarming the bulk of the people

The last was, he conceded, "a reason oftener meant than avowed by the makers of Forest or Game Laws."[48]

The very first game act to set a property qualification upon hunting was passed in 1389 in response to the great social uprising of that time. According to the act, all laymen having an annual income from land of less than 40s., and clergymen having less than £10 per year, were forbidden to hunt or to keep hunting dogs and hunting equipment. Its preamble admitted that it was meant to hinder "divers artificers, labourers, and servants" from assembling under pretence of hunting to conspire against their superiors. When Henry VII came to the throne after years of civil turmoil, one of the measures he employed to maintain quiet in the countryside was a severe game act. This act made deer hunting with disguises or at night a felony. Coke, in the *Institutes,* expressed outrage at "this new and ill penned Law" that was at odds with the old forest statutes, "by which no man might lose either life or limb for killing a wild beast."[49] By Queen Elizabeth's reign humane judgments had reduced her grandfather's law to a nullity.

Because the English legal and military system required the general public to assume a variety of police and military functions, no game act until that of 1671 actually removed from the common people the privilege of owning arms. Rather, these acts simply prohibited the use of weapons for hunting.

With the accession in 1603 of James I, there was a dramatic change in the hunting laws and in the rigor with which they were enforced. Within the first six years of his reign—in 1604, 1605, and 1609—no less than three new game acts were passed. These acts altered the property qualification needed to hunt far more materially than any act in the preceding two centuries; made it illegal for unqualified persons to keep coursing dogs, sell game, use guns, crossbows, or other devices to take game; and brought some poaching cases before the kingdom's highest courts, including the Court of Star Chamber.[50] The law of 1609 also empowered officials with a warrant to enter homes and barns to search for dogs, nets, and prohibited hunting devices.

James demanded strict enforcement of the game laws and, as a study of the Stuart "game prerogative" makes clear, "had taken into his own hands the task of providing for a strict preservation of the game throughout the country."[51] From the time he arrived in England, he began to appoint aristocrats as his gamekeepers, granting them broad powers to enforce the law.[52] In many cases these powers went beyond the bounds of the statutes, as the royal gamekeepers were given jurisdiction over large areas of private property and even entire counties. James's motives were undoubtedly mixed: he was not only a hunting zealot but a man obsessed by fear of a violent attack upon his person.

Charles I was just as suspicious of his subjects as his father had been and just as keen to protect game. In addition, he viewed royal forests and his game prerogative as an untapped source of revenue. It is this last motive that led to an exacerbation of popular hostility toward game parks and game laws and demonstrated his subjects' potential for armed protest.

Charles set three schemes in motion to turn royal forests into gold: 1) disafforestation of some royal parks and forests for cultivation or sale; 2) expansion of royal forests to their ancient boundaries; and 3) revival of ancient forest law in order to profit from fines.[53] These policies aroused tremendous opposition, with entire communities, from the poorest cottagers to the largest landowners, banding together to fight the Crown program. Ancient forest laws were draconian in many respects. A farmer within a designated forest area, for example, was not permitted to protect his crops from deer and other game. Any extension of royal forests would seriously impinge upon the rights of all those who fell within the broader bounds. However, disafforestation, or the removal of a royal forest from forest status for the purpose of its enclosure and sale, might leave hundreds of poor residents without a means of subsistence. The widespread riots that resulted, among the worst the kingdom would experience before the Civil War, vividly demonstrated the English villager's capacity for taking up arms and provide confirmation of the availability of firearms among the rural population even before the Civil War. The scale of these riots impressed the aristocracy as well as the Crown with the potential for popular, armed revolt.

A disafforestation scheme that threatened the livelihood of thousands of small farmers and poor villagers, for example, led to large-scale riots over vast regions of southern and western England, striking in particular the counties of Wiltshire, Dorset, Hampshire, Gloucestershire, Worcestershire, and Rutland. In his study of these uprisings, Eric Kerridge was particularly impressed by how well the people in these areas were "versed in the arts of organising irregular military bands."[54] Residents of the eighteen townships within Braydon Forest entered into a compact, and large bands composed of every social class, armed with muskets and "illegal" weapons—presumably handguns—travelled from place to place terrorizing agents of the enclosers and levelling fences. When the sheriff of Wiltshire attempted to put a stop to the disorder, he was met by a determined force of some 1000 men, fully armed and in disguise.[55]

Riots in Dean Forest in Gloucestershire that same year were no less serious. In one riot alone some 500 residents, armed with muskets and pikes, pulled down the hated enclosures. In Gillingham Forest rioters were so "numerous, well-armed, and resolute" that the sheriff of Dorset was powerless to stop them.[56] The trained bands were of little aid to the authorities since they refused to take action against their neighbours.

Charles I's forest and game policy resulted in wholesale poaching as well as riots. In Windsor Forest resentment against the revival of forest courts and forest laws led Surrey gentry to encourage mass daytime poaching of royal deer, with poachers hunting in companies as large as eighty or one hundred.[57] Where there was not such mass poaching the new, strict enforcement of forest law led to a great increase in the deer herd, which posed its own threat to forest residents. The people of Berkshire complained to the county Grand Jury "against the innumerable red deer in the Forest, which if they go on for a few years more, will neither leave food nor room for any other creatures in the Forest."[58] When the situation failed to improve, country people, in a "riotous and tumultuous manner," slaughtered more than a hundred deer and threatened to pull down the pales around the forest lodge to release the rest.[59]

By the time the Civil War broke out in 1642 popular feeling against royal forest and game policy was intense. In the chaos of wartime the common people took their revenge. Enclosures were destroyed, in some cases not to be erected again until late in the eighteenth century, and royal deer and other game were slaughtered, often to the last animal.

Charles I's forest policy had a significant impact on the history of the people's right to have arms, and it offers insight into seventeenth-century arms ownership. By heightening popular feeling against private forests and game laws, it led to massive destruction of game and game preserves, which both the Crown and the aristocracy would be eager to restore at the first opportunity. Equally ominous, the riots were a vivid demonstration of the common people's access to firearms and their ability to arm and organize quickly.

CHAPTER TWO

Bearing Arms through War and Revolution

T HE crisis of confidence between Charles I and his subjects drew the attention of all parties to the issue of control of the sword. Of course, general unease over the distribution of weapons had never been far beneath the surface—the King did not trust his citizen-army; his subjects did not trust him with a professional army; and the aristocracy tolerated arms in the hands of the common people with misgivings. But the collapse of trust that split the government and the years of war and disorder that followed exposed and sharpened these apprehensions. The era, therefore, bears close examination for the heightened tensions it produced, the lessons learned, and the expedients devised.

On August 12, 1642, Charles I declared war on his English opponents and called upon his subjects to join his army at Nottingham.[1] Before the most alarmist Englishman had any inkling that civil war lay in his future, however, political upheavals in Scotland and Ireland had done much to change attitudes toward the importance of personal arms and a citizen militia.

The revolt of the Scots in 1639, known as the First Bishops' War, taught Charles and his English subjects a variety of useful lessons about the power of the sword. The Scots took to arms in opposition to the King's attempt to impose the Anglican prayer book upon their Presbyterian church. Charles responded by drawing together a massive army and navy to teach the rebels their duty. Many Englishmen disliked the King's "high church" policy, his Catholic queen, and his leniency toward the Catholics, and they heartily sympathized with the Scots. Moreover, as one future parliamentarian recalled, Englishmen were "sensible of the oppressions they themselves lay under; and how dangerous to the people of England a thorow success against the Scots might prove."[2] Others were simply angered by the demands for monies to meet the military costs of the campaign.[3]

Public resistance became nearly universal. Landlords connived with their tenants to avoid taxation and, when forced to supply equipment, gave the army the worst weapons they could find. Many militiamen drafted into the army, disliking their mission, gave vent to their prejudices on the march north. They threw open enclosed fields, emptied jails, chopped down the new church altar rails installed on the orders of Archbishop Laud, and attacked officers they suspected of being secret Catholics. Others deserted at the first opportunity and returned home. When the Crown tried to discipline offenders it often found local officials reluctant to act. Charles's loyal councillor Thomas Wentworth, Earl of Strafford, detected in the army assembled to fight the Scots "a generall disaffection to the King's service."[4] Not surprisingly, the King "found it necessary to entertain the first overture of a treaty."[5]

It was not the Scots, therefore, but Charles and his English subjects who were taught a lesson. Charles learned, to his chagrin, that militiamen forced to fight for an unpopular cause were unreliable, local officials were unlikely to enforce unpopular policies, and the militia structure yielded an inefficient and ineffectual field army. Many Englishmen, however, were heartened by these "flaws" in the system and by the power of public opinion, if not to dissuade the King from his course, to eventually drive him from the field of battle. They had explored avenues of passive resistance and of outright disobedience and rediscovered the virtues of a militia system composed of their friends and neighbours. The true helplessness of the Crown when local officials, local people, and local militia presented a united front was obvious.

The costs of the Bishops' War forced Charles to summon a parliament for the first time in eleven years. When its members insisted upon a discussion of grievances before granting new monies, Charles lost his temper and dissolved it. War with the Scots broke out again, and the King managed to establish a ceasefire only by agreeing to pay the Scots some £850 a day until a permanent settlement could be reached. Willing or not, Charles had to call another parliament and to work with it.

Among the grievances that members of the famous Long Parliament addressed when they assembled in November 1640, none more graphically betrayed the breakdown of trust between Crown and people than the unprecedented attack on the ancient royal monopoly over production of gunpowder. Monopolies of such everyday commodities as soap, salt, and wine were regarded as illegal and were resented for the restrictions they imposed on trade and the higher prices that resulted. The gunpowder monopoly, however, was undoubtedly a royal prerogative. But

Charles's opponents were suddenly struck by the potential it gave the Crown to render the people defenceless.

Even the King's friends admitted that "many men suffered" from the way in which the monopoly had been managed.[6] Nevertheless, his defenders maintained that the gunpowder prerogative was a "considerable" and necessary right of the King, "as it restrained that precious and dangerous commodity from vulgar hands" and "brought a considerable revenue to the Crown."[7] While they denied that the King had any intention of disarming his enemies, Charles's supporters argued that those opposed to the monopoly meant to arm the people, "that thereby they might be sure to have in readiness a good stock in that commodity, against the time their occasions should call upon them."[8] It is interesting that the King's defenders conceded the intention of keeping gunpowder, "that precious and dangerous commodity," out of "vulgar hands."

The King's opponents raised grave objections to the continuation of the royal monopoly. Sir John Colepeper deemed it "a great grievance, that enhancing the price of gunpowder whereby the Trained Bands are much discouraged in their exercising," while Sir John Clotworthy branded the monopoly no less than "a project for disarming of the kingdom."[9]

The authors of the Long Parliament's infamous catalogue of complaints, the Grand Remonstrance, cited the gunpowder monopoly separately from other monopolies and accepted the contentions of its harshest critics. They indicted it as "the desperate design of engrossing all the gunpowder into one hand, keeping it in the Tower of London, and setting so high a rate upon it that the poorer sort were not able to buy it, nor could any have it without licence, thereby to leave the several parts of the kingdom destitute of their necessary defence, and by selling so dear that which was sold to make an unlawful advantage of it, to the great charge and detriment of the subject."[10] To calm the public, Charles agreed to surrender his monopoly and, in August 1641, approved "An Act for the free making saltpetre and gunpowder within the kingdom." A blow had been struck for access to ammunition, and an important prerogative of the Crown over the power of the sword was removed.

Another event that emblazoned upon the English consciousness the need for civilian control of weapons occurred only a few weeks after passage of the act ending the royal monopoly on gunpowder. In October 1641 Catholics in Ireland revolted and massacred thousands of Protestant men, women, and children.[11] Panic that an Irish invasion was imminent swept across England.[12] Haunted by nightmares of being murdered in their beds, and with their king a hesitant and uncertain protector, Englishmen took matters into their own hands. They disarmed local Catholics in house-to-house searches, confiscated any weapons they found, and put many Catholics in jail or summarily ejected them from town. The merest hint that a local Catholic was purchasing horses or accumulating weapons brought his neighbours—often aided by local trained bandsmen—to his door, where the search for arms frequently deteriorated into a sack of the premises. In Bristol, only a few hours sail from Ireland, it was reported that citizens kept watch "in arms day and night to prevent the surprising of the City by the Irish rebels," while residents of Yorkshire and Staffordshire began to carry weapons when they went about their chores or to church.[13]

The break between King and Parliament came in a dispute over control of the sword. Command of the trained bands unquestionably belonged to the Crown, but a majority in Parliament and a substantial proportion of their constituents feared that Charles might use an army mobilized to suppress Irish rebels against them instead. When the King refused to grant control of the militia to Parliament, that body took the extraordinary step of declaring the King's refusal unsatisfactory and its own militia ordinance in effect.

The militia controversy, with its clear issue of control of the sword, was a barometer of popular trust. A royal councillor judged that of all issues then in debate, "the militia was the argument which they [the parliamentarians] found made the deepest impression in the people."[14] Despite the King's undoubted military prerogative, the public was inclined to agree with Parliament.

This contest over the militia set off an unseemly scramble for militia arsenals and control of the trained bands. The Crown and Parliament began by vying for the great arsenals of the kingdom, while townsmen sought to protect and strengthen their local militia supplies.[15] A London newspaper observed that "contention for the publique Magazen hath beene the first blowne sparke in other Counties."[16]

Once they had secured the militia weapons the royalists and the parliamentarians handled them very differently. The royalists confiscated militia arsenals and the weapons of individual militiamen for the use of a field army. Charles's difficulties with the militia during the Bishops' War and his unpopularity had persuaded him to circumvent the militia and establish a field army based upon the institution of the commission of array, a system that had not been used for over a century. Commissioners of array, unencumbered by militia restrictions, could tax, recruit, and move their troops freely. But this emphasis on the removal of men and materials for a central army, which left the localities vulnerable, ran counter to the desire of villagers for local self-defence. The parliamentarians, in contrast, permitted local militia to retain their weapons and join field armies for limited campaigns. This was one of the reasons royal commissioners of array encountered far more resistance than they or their monarch had foreseen.[17]

How did the English civilian fare once the initial scramble for men and weapons was over and civil war under way in earnest? Was he the disarmed and defenceless prey of roving armies? Although some trained bandsmen and some civilians were disarmed, a great many Englishmen managed to keep weapons for personal protection throughout the war. Indeed, from 1642 through 1646 the quantity of arms in the kingdom soared. Early shortages were soon overcome as each side financed a flourishing arms industry. Royalist manufactures centered on Oxford, where 35 barrels of gunpowder were produced weekly, and Bristol, which turned out a ton of musket shot, 200 muskets, and 30 pairs of pistols a week.[18] In Weymouth another factory produced 900 weight of match a week for the Crown. In a conflict in which 1000 men constituted a considerable force, these figures are significant.

There were times, of course, when rampaging troops disarmed civilians or when civilians summoned to musters failed to bring any weapons. In these last instances it is difficult to ascertain whether those summoned had no weapons or were merely afraid any arms they brought with them would be confiscated. In August 1642, for example, one of the King's leading officers, Sir Ralph Hopton, and his colleagues summoned a posse to Modbury in Devon, "hoping," Hopton wrote later, "to have found it like that they had seene in Cornewall, consisting of Regiments of foote well armed (though in farr greater numbers) whereof at that tyme they had great occasion."[19] To his consternation Hopton "found it far otherwise, for though there appeared a great concourse of people, yett it was rather like a great fayre then a Posse, there being none but the Gentlemen that had any kind of armes or equipage for warr." In this instance we must believe either that the men of Cornwall were far better armed than those of Devon, or that since the royalists had acquired a reputation for forcible seizure of arms, those who attended the posse unarmed left their weapons at home. The latter seems more likely. But in 1644, Parliament ordered the consortium of eastern counties known as the Eastern Association to raise 20,000 men with guns, who appeared "in so naked a posture that to employ them [was] to murder them." In this case it is more difficult to determine whether they had arms at home.[20] Parliament had not been disarming men who appeared at musters, and there were complaints that the Essex recruits were in need of coats, clothes, and shoes, as well as weapons. All that can be said with certainty is that Parliament thought 20,000 men *with guns* could be raised.

But there are reasons for concluding that many, if not most, common people had arms throughout the Civil War. It seems probable that in a period of extreme peril men who had weapons would prefer to keep them at home, rather than risk their confiscation. If they had no firearms they would very likely make every effort to secure some. In this regard, evidence exists that the weapons of both armies were being "lost" or illegally sold. Both sides resorted to repeated warnings against soldiers "spoyling and losing arms," a clear indication that the abuse was widespread. Regulations for the army of the Eastern Association and other parliamentary forces required officers to make good any horses and weapons lost under their command, unless they could prove the losses had occurred in battle.[21] On the royalist side a proclamation of March 1643 referred to "insufficient satisfaction" obtained from earlier proclamations against losses of military weapons and ordered all Crown officers to turn in a detailed account of the number and quantity of arms of every regiment.[22]

Although some weapons were genuinely lost, others were probably carried home by deserters or sold to civilians. To halt this abuse the parliamentary committee of Stafford made it a crime for a civilian to purchase a weapon from a soldier. This committee also conducted house-to-house searches for concealed arms and sharply warned civilians that "all that shall buye any without license shall be esteemed Malignants . . . and so shall those that know of any such and do not within 24 houres disclose it to the Governour or Committee, and who shall convey or consent to convey anie out of the Towne shall be punished in a higher measure then the former."[23]

The many occasions during the war when armed civilians came to the aid of neighbours, or volunteered to help a field army for a particular skirmish, give further proof of widespread private ownership of firearms. In 1642 thousands of armed country men defended Manchester, Cirencester, and other cities threatened by royalist recruiters or troops. Many men unwilling to leave their farms and homes to join a field army willingly aided their party when an incident occurred in their neighbourhood.[24]

As the war dragged on, country people became increasingly exasperated by the seemingly endless disorder and taxation. From the beginning of the conflict groups of neighbours had joined to defend one another, and now they began to meet more often to discuss their own needs and ideas for ending the war. Finally, a group of 1500 Shropshire farmers announced their determination to obey neither King nor Parliament but "to stand upon their own guard for the security of their persons and estates." The "peaceable army," or club movement, grew until some fifteen counties and thousands of civilians were involved.[25] Some of these volunteers were eager but ill-equipped to confront the warring armies— wielding only pitchforks and clubs—but thousands of others came with muskets and birding guns. They came into conflict with both warring parties. Thousands of clubmen attacked Hereford after its royalist governor sent his soldiers to collect double the usual tax monies. An officer of Parliament from whom these clubmen sought help reported that they numbered between 15,000 and 16,000 and were equipped with "at least 6 or 7000 muskets and other fire armes."[26] If this estimate is accurate, a sizeable number of the so-called clubmen, between a third and a half, had firearms. Armed civilians, even those fairly well organized, are seldom a match for trained troops, but the English clubmen demanded and received respect. Their refusal to contribute men and money to the royal party helped seal its fate.

During the campaign of 1645, when the club movement was in its heyday, the royal cause met with a series of disasters from which it had not the strength or popular support to recover. In June, Charles's armies were decisively beaten at Naseby by the combined force of a parliamentary field army, the New Model, commanded by Fairfax and Cromwell, and a Scots army. When the fighting was over that day the royal army had lost all its infantry, all its guns, most of its baggage train, and every single regimental battle standard. As one historian summed it up, "the disaster was total."[27] A month later the remaining royal field army was crushed at Langport, and the following spring Charles surrendered to the Scots.

Charles's captors found themselves in the ironic position of needing his agreement to legitimize a settlement to the war. Months of fruitless negotiation and dissention followed, as Charles successfully employed the tactic of delay to divide his enemies. The majority in Parliament were soon at odds with members of the New Model Army, who came to see themselves as the true representatives of the people entitled to play a pivotal political role. After a series of royalist uprisings in 1648 known as the Second Civil War had been suppressed, the radicals and the army purged Parliament of its more moderate members. The remaining members of what became known as the Rump Parliament tried and executed

Charles Stuart for treason, then abolished the monarchy and the House of Lords.[28]

With the execution of their king on January 30, 1649, Englishmen embarked upon an experiment in republican government intended to secure the "antient and fundamental Laws and Liberties" of the realm. However, to preserve the aims of the English Civil War during a period of insecurity, its victors found that they had to deny the rights they had meant to protect. In this instance their problems were obvious: there was constant fear that royalists would gather sufficient men and weapons to launch a counter-revolution, or that the exiled heir would try to regain his throne with outside aid. With the Commonwealth threatened by internal insurrection and foreign invasion, the new rulers had ample excuse to maintain a large standing army. Thus, to "save" the revolution and protect the rights of Englishmen, the New Model Army, Parliament's force of seasoned and politically conscious veterans, remained on foot. And the country that had always depended upon an impromptu militia found itself supporting a standing army respected and feared throughout Europe. In such difficult times what became of the duty and privilege of bearing arms? Did the old traditions survive new circumstances?

The new government's most urgent tasks, the restoration of order and the prevention of counter-revolution, were exceedingly difficult because by 1649 large numbers of Englishmen possessed private weapons, which they had become accustomed to using as they saw fit. Parliament's approach to the problem was to draw a sharp distinction between friends, the "well-affected," and enemies, "malignants" and "papists." The former, as custom demanded and they expected, retained weapons and were treated with something less than rigor when they misused them. The latter were deprived of the privilege of possessing firearms and were subjected to frequent searches, seizures, harassment, and arrest.

The mass of common people were necessarily treated as "well-affected," and they resumed their former peacekeeping duties. But for the first time in English history they did so under the umbrella of military rule.[29] A force of between 12,000 and 40,000 men was garrisoned in the capital and in major towns across the country. The behaviour of these soldiers, compared with that of contemporary European armies or of English armies between 1642 and 1649, has been characterized as exemplary.[30] Nevertheless, the army was expensive and unpopular and the government carefully controlled its activities and steadily reduced its numbers. The army worked cooperatively with the militia and government supporters. According to the author of a recent study, its garrisons served as centers for magazines of arms, often those collected from county forces at the end of the war, which were distributed to the well-affected during times of emergency.[31]

The Interregnum government was anxious to return to more traditional and less costly methods of peacekeeping. As early as April 1649 it began to frame an act that would strengthen the militia and place it on a sound legal basis.[32] This reconstruction was completed early in 1651. As one guarantee of their loyalty, militiamen were obliged to swear allegiance "to the Commonwealth of England, as it is now Established, without a King or House of Lords."[33] The government had sufficient confidence in the militia to call upon it to fight alongside the army during times of crisis. At the battle of Worcester in 1651, for example, up to one-third of the force that defeated Charles II's army of Scots and royalists was composed of militiamen.[34] Although the militia was initially subsidiary to the army, as the size of the army declined it gradually resumed its role as the major form of local defence.[35]

The new militia was not limited to the traditional role of its predecessors, the suppression of occasional riots and defence against invasion. Rather, it was used as a police force whose primary function was the prevention of subversion. This was reflected in the new militia statute. Whereas earlier militia acts had focused upon military assessment and frequency of musters, the new act dealt with the duties of the trained bands in unprecedented detail. To protect the government, the militia was specifically authorized to "search out and repress" conspiracies, and to secure, disperse, or imprison "the parties whom they finde to be especially active and dangerous."[36] But militia operations extended beyond the restraint of potential conspirators. Its members were ordered "to disarm and secure . . . all Papists, and other ill-affected persons that have of late appeared, or shall declare themselves in their words or actions against this present Parliament, or against the present Government established or have or shall hold correspondency with Charls Stuart, the Son of the Late King, or any of his party." The preamble of the Militia Act indicates that its authors were not only aware of this alteration in function but defensive about it. "It [is] necessary," they began, "that the Commonwealth be put into a posture of Defence, for the Preservation of the Peace and Liberties of the People . . . against the Endeavours, Conspiracies and Practices of divers Parties and Interests, different in themselves, yet united under several specious pretenses, all tending to the utter over-throw of the Safety of the Nation."[37]

The militia's new role was to become even more apparent in 1655. Early in that year, when the very existence of the government seemed in peril, Cromwell appointed leading municipal officials, sheriffs, and army officers in London and the counties to serve as militia commissioners. The new commissioners were given instructions that laid even greater stress on espionage than those of 1651 and treated disarmament and the use of arms with "greater stringency."[38] In an essay on the major-generals, D. W. Rannie found "the interference with individual liberty" of these instructions "serious throughout."[39]

It was therefore the Rump Parliament—that body which had the stomach to bring Charles Stuart to trial—that converted the militia into an instrument for the surveillance and disarmament of its political enemies. And it was this new style of militia that the Cavalier Parliament of the Restoration was to copy and put to use against its authors.

The Interregnum governments from time to time also considered another expedient for peacekeeping that was later adopted by Charles II—the creation of a volunteer, or select, militia. On several occasions proposals were put forward to organize volunteer units supported by local subsidies for protection of specific localities. But although volunteers were invaluable on specific occasions, a full-fledged program of volunteer militia was never instituted.[40]

The new government was prepared to continue using the well-affected for traditional, and even for expanded, police duties, but tact and perseverance were required to cajole them into using their weapons *only* when the state saw fit. In this regard the system of royal and private forests presented an especially ticklish problem. The Civil War had afforded an irresistible opportunity for people living in or near forests and parks to strike a blow against the inequities of the game laws. When the dust cleared in 1646, Parliament found the kingdom's game parks, a symbol of aristocratic privilege, a shambles. The deer had been "universally destroyed" in the royal park at Easthamstead, deer had vanished from New Forest, and all game was gone from Waltham Forest.[41] In some parks even the trees had been destroyed.

Members of Parliament sympathized with the anger of the poachers, but they were not immune to the attractions of the hunt, or unaware of the need to reaffirm class privileges. They compromised by easing the economic complaints of rural residents while preserving class distinctions. An ordinance passed at Parliament's earliest convenience asserted that, "by reason of the great Liberty that several idle and loose Persons at this Time take unto themselves by Guns . . . and other unlawful means, to kill and destroy Game," it was necessary to act promptly, lest it "prove a Destruction to the said Game."[42] No attempt was made to discover who had emptied the parks of game, but justices of the peace were instructed to enforce existing game legislation. Four years later, after Oliver Cromwell had evicted the Rump and become Lord Protector, a statute "against stealing or killing Deer" was passed to stiffen enforcement.[43]

During the 1650's armed residents of the fen country rioted after peaceful petitioning had failed to halt a drainage scheme. Some eighty persons armed with muskets, short pikes, and swords descended on the works and wounded one guard.[44] The Council of State ordered an investigation, but none of the offenders was ever brought before a jury, nor was there any suggestion that the rioters be disarmed.

Although the leaders of the Commonwealth government treated well-affected armed citizens with kid gloves, they were quick to take them off when dealing with potential enemies. The militia was ordered to search the homes of "malignants" and suspected malignants and confiscate any arms they found. Details of royalist plots uncovered by espionage bear witness to the effectiveness of this disarmament. Royalist plotters were forced to import arms or buy them in London and transport them at great risk to the site of an intended uprising. Had the conspirators managed to keep their personal weapons, this would not have been necessary.[45] Furthermore, after a plot failed—and they all did—royalists made every effort to dispose of the weapons lest any be found in their possession.[46] The many references in the records of the royal Court in exile to the "search and disarming of Cavaliers' houses" make plain that royalist fears of being found with weapons were legitimate.

There seems little justification for the assertion of one of Parliament's agents "how easily in a very few daies an army of 20,000 horse and foote might be raised and furnished with all things," but the very ability of the King's party in 1655 to make "so bold an attempt in the middle of the kingdom" provoked a further crackdown on potential enemies.[47] Militia officers were ordered to disarm "all Papists who declare against the present Government, or correspond with or send supplies to Charles Stuart, or any other, tending to the disturbance of the peace, or who raise tumults, and to seize their horses."[48] Officers were also to "exercise espionage on strangers," to confiscate "all stray arms and ammunition," and to reorganize the militia with loyal volunteers. To prevent militia weapons from falling into royalist hands, militia commissioners were warned "to see that all arms of horse or foot, ammunition, war provisions, trophies, etc., be secured in safe places, and inventories taken of them, whether secured or left in the owners' hands, to prevent embezzlement or misconversion, and to have them always ready for public use."[49]

In 1655 Major-General John Desborough and his regiment, with the aid of the West Country militia, were so successful in carrying out their orders that Cromwell divided the rest of the kingdom into nine similar military regions, each under the jurisdiction of a professional officer. The hated institution of major-generals had begun.

Among their duties the major-generals were to ensure that "all Papists and those who assisted the late King have their arms secured in some garrison."[50] Former royalists could keep weapons only if they obtained a special licence. The major-generals went about their work with vigour, the disarming "proceeding briskly in many districts" and so many suspicious persons arrested that there were complaints of lack of space for prisoners. For their part, the major-generals complained of being over-worked.[51] The crackdown in the counties was thorough but not simultaneous—"the Majour Generalls' occasions not permitting them to bee in accion att one tyme"—and the government feared that some of its enemies had escaped to London.[52] In 1656, therefore, the London Council appointed commissioners to execute the new militia instructions and issued a proclamation against the wearing of daggers and "pockett pistolls."[53]

The installation of major-generals may not have provoked James Harrington's famous book, *Commonwealth of Oceana,* but its appearance in 1656 was particularly timely, with its insistence upon the need for a republic to have an armed citizenry and its condemnation of government by an army. According to John Pocock, Harrington was the first to state "in English terms" the thesis that "only the armed freeholder was capable of independence and virtue."[54] Harrington argued that power must be related to property and property to military tenure, hence "citizens who do not defend themselves abandon a vital part of their power and virtue."[55] Pocock believes that Harrington's most enduring legacy is his portrait of the proprietor of land "autonomous in his own defence," the union of "ballots and bullets, arms and counsels . . . the agrarian warrior and freeman."[56]

Oceana was avidly read and discussed in the years immediately following its publication. Many pamphlets published before the Restoration testify to the impact of Harrington's ideas.[57] Yet it is uncertain how influential these notions were once the republican experiment was over. After 1660 the works of republicans were banished from the Bodleian Library, and Harrington's proposals for models of government were "reputed no better than whimsical and crack-brained."[58] In *English Democratic Ideas in the Seventeenth Century,* G. P. Gooch concludes that the writings of the Interregnum republicans "found few students and fewer converts" among the next generation.[59] Yet, experience was doubtless a more potent teacher than any number of theoretical treatises. And the generation that had lived through the Interregnum did not need political theorists to remind them of the connection between the possession of arms and political power.

Three years after the installation of the major-generals everything changed. On September 3, 1658, the anniversary of his glorious victories at Dunbar and Worcester, Oliver Cromwell died. The Council of State chose as his successor his son Richard, "a meek, temperate, and quiet man," judged by Lucy Hutchinson among others as not possessed of "a spirit fit to succeed his father, or to manage such a perplexed government."[60] As it happened, he never really managed the government, for actual power was in the hands of the army generals. The Rump Parliament, that remnant of the Long Parliament summarily ousted by Oliver in 1653, was recalled to fill the political vacuum.

Members of the Rump had excellent reasons for feeling insecure. They were singularly unpopular, even with Londoners, their legitimacy as a government was questionable, their actual power problematic. When they learned that supporters of the Stuarts were planning another series of revolts, they quickly adopted measures designed to monitor and control the weapons of the realm. In fact, within a month of convening in May 1659 they appointed a committee to investigate the activities of London gunsmiths suspected of selling weapons to "malignants" and created a committee for intelligence. While these measures were not unusual in the circumstances, on July 22 the Rump passed a truly extraordinary measure: "An Act for the Householders to Give an Account of Lodgers, Horses, Arms, and Ammunition," the first attempt to list every weapon in the realm.[61] All householders within the cities of London, Westminster, and nearby suburbs were given one week in which to present their local constable with a list of persons lodging with them and "a true and perfect list of all Arms or Ammunition, as also all Horses" in their own or their lodgers' possession. Householders living outside London and its suburbs were permitted twenty-five days to submit a similar list to their local militia commissioner. Failure to submit a list or submission of an erroneous one was punishable by imprisonment without bail in the common jail until a fine, not to exceed fifty pounds, was paid. A reward was offered to anyone who informed militia officers of unreported arms or ammunition. If, upon examination of the lists, the authorities found "just cause of suspicion and danger to the Commonwealth," or that arms were owned by anyone "who ought not by Law to use or have such Arms," they could confiscate the weapons. The act was to continue in force until December. A new militia act was also passed that July, but it was the act for the immediate listing of persons and weapons that was without precedent.

Carrying out the terms of the new act was a massive task. In light of the Rump's unpopularity and the speed with which lists were to be returned, it is legitimate to query whether the census of arms was ever produced. The evidence is scanty and inconclusive. There had been a shortage of arms among royalist plotters even before the new crackdown. John Mordaunt, one of the exiled Court's leading agents in England, had already warned Charles that lack of weapons jeopardized plans for armed risings during August: "And truly, Sir, we have not foot armes sufficient for those numbers of men (which) will appear in your quarrell . . . for such armes wee allwayes depended to have had them from your Majestie."[62] Charles replied that his friends "ought not to be deterred by want of arms," because once they captured Bristol it could supply them. But he did promise to send arms as soon as he received the money to purchase them.

By late July, however, when the Rump's new arms control program should have been in full swing, there were conflicting reports of its progress. Parliament's agents in the Welsh border counties, a region full of disaffected gentry, admitted that the search for weapons had been a failure.[63] In other areas, however, many known suspects had been interrogated and disarmed. Dr. William Denton, a close friend of the Verney family, advised Colonel Henry Verney to comply with the new law and send in the list of his horses at Stowe, "for it cannot be safe . . . to shuffle it off."[64] Denton had already sent in his own list, and he wrote to Sir Ralph Verney that "offensive . . . Persons, Armes, and horses are secured in divers counties."[65] Among the Verney papers is a list, dated August 15, 1659, of the names of Ralph Verney's family, including servants and the arms delivered up.[66]

There seems to have been fitful compliance with the new law. Suspects aside, the general listing of private weapons does not seem to have been carried out. A captain stationed at Norwich on the east coast reported hearing "daily of the buying up of arms." A similar report reached the Court in exile. One writer claimed that "thousands of arms are bought daily, some for the King, some for the Fifth Monarchy men, but none are seized."[67] Captain Edmund Waring wrote from Shrewsbury that he doubted the persons named to the new militia would even serve.[68]

Despite its efforts, the Rump failed to prevent a series of uprisings in August; it did, however, manage to cling to life through a combination of its own diligence, army power, and the sheer incompetence of its opponents. During the most successful uprising, led by George Booth, the western city of Chester was captured and held for a short time. The insurrections convinced the powerful general John Lambert to come out of retirement. He rapidly lost patience with the Rump's antimilitary attitude and forced it to dissolve in October. With no Parliament, generals vying for power, radical sects threatening to impose their own brand of order, and royalists determined to bring back monarchy, the realm seemed on the verge of anarchy.

At this juncture George Monck, general of the army of occupation in Scotland, called for the restoration of the Rump, and in return was named commander-in-chief by its Council of State. On January 1 he marched his troops across the border at Coldstream. En route to London he was confronted by armies of greater size but encountered no resistance. Upon his arrival in the capital, he recalled not only the Rump but those Presbyterian members of the Long Parliament who had been excluded in 1648. This body, to the great joy of the people, voted for the election of a new, "convention parliament," to convene on April 25, 1660.

Cavaliers were not permitted to vote or to serve in the Parliament, but many did so. The overwhelming sentiment among its members and their constituents was for a return to monarchy. Against this wave of emotion the frantic efforts of some members to impose restrictions upon Charles before admitting him to the throne were unavailing. The majority insisted that no time should be lost discussing such matters, for until Charles was installed the realm was vulnerable to attack and insurrection. Caution was brushed aside with disdain. With grateful thanks, members of the Convention Parliament prepared for the re-establishment of the Stuart dynasty.

The kingdom that Charles II returned to rule was volatile but eager for order, well armed but anxious to be obedient. A political honeymoon lay ahead, during which a proud people's customary rights were protected only by the King's good sense and the anxious hands of the new and very reactionary Parliament. Of the welter of political theories, causes, experiences, and experiments to which Englishmen had been subjected during the civil wars and the Interregnum, the one indelible legacy of these years, remembered even at the height of Restoration euphoria, was what C. H. Firth described as "a rooted aversion to standing armies and an abiding dread of military rule."[69]

CHAPTER THREE

The Dissidents Disarmed

W A R and its aftermath had altered the distribution of weapons in England and the attitude of its citizens toward their control. The public had become convinced of the need for personal weapons for self-defence and practiced in organizing armed resistance. Government use of weapons had also changed. During the Interregnum a new type of militia had emerged whose chief mission was the surveillance and disarming of the regime's political opponents. Nonetheless, popular attachment to the militia as an institution was stronger than before the Civil War, because experience of the alternative, a professional army, had been so disagreeable. Abhorrence of permanent military establishments had grown among those of all political persuasions. Also, the chaotic months before Charles II's return had created one additional dilemma for the new king: the distribution of weapons was overwhelmingly in his subjects' favour. The Court had to retrieve substantial, if not dominant, control of the sword if royal government and royalist power were to be successfully restored.

From his vantage point on the Strand, John Evelyn watched the resplendent procession that escorted Charles II through his capital and marvelled that "such a Restauration was never seene in the mention of any history, antient or modern, since the returne of the Babylonian Captivity, nor so joyfull a day, and so bright, ever seene in this nation."[1] The reception that awaited Charles II when he entered London on May 29, 1660, was probably the most wildly enthusiastic, and surely the most exquisitely ironic, ever accorded an English monarch. Among the crowds shouting and weeping as he passed were hundreds who had watched the execution of his father some eleven years earlier, who had cheered every victory of his executioners. Thousands of others, former supporters of the Crown during the Civil War, had made their peace with Charles's opponents and prudently withheld aid from the Prince during his long years of exile. Only once his restoration seemed assured had they leapt self-righteously onto the royal bandwagon. The crack army regiments that dutifully flanked the King and his retinue that day as they rode from Dover to London were drawn from the republican army, "that very army," Evelyn remarked, "wich rebelled against him." Moreover, those members of Parliament who had brilliantly orchestrated Charles's return, "without one drop of bloud" and without a single prior restriction on his power, had, in their eagerness to exalt monarchy, inadvertently elevated Parliament. Parliaments might be merely the King's "great council," but this Parliament had made a king! Its members might humbly receive him on their knees, but no one knew better than their cynical young monarch the true fragility of his position.

To his credit, the so-called merry monarch immediately capitalized upon the euphoria to correct his father's mistakes and establish a more absolute monarchy. This proved to be a wise move, for even as skeptical a king as Charles Stuart could scarcely have guessed how quickly there would be "a new revolution in the general affections of the people." Within two years he would be informed of "universal" disaffection, and within seven years his most famous civil servant, Samuel Pepys, would muse: "It is strange how . . . everybody do now-a-days reflect upon Oliver and commend him; what brave things he did, and made all the neighbor princes fear him; while here a prince, come in with all the love and prayers and good liking of his people, who have given greater signs of loyalty and willingness to serve him with their estates than ever was done by any people, hath lost all so soon, that it is a miracle what way a man could devise to lose so much in so little time."[2] Fortunately for Charles programs were in place before his popularity seriously waned that would protect him from such popular fickleness and restore to the monarchy much of the power of the sword.

Popular enthusiasm for the return of Charles Stuart and relief at the reestablishment of monarchy were genuine enough, as most Englishmen anticipated a return to the good old days and the good old constitution. But no regime could have easily mended the political and religious dissension or satisfied the sharply conflicting expectations. Presbyterians and more radical Protestant dissenters, for example, relied upon the King's generous pardon and promise of religious toleration, while former royalists wanted prompt recompense for years of hardship endured on the King's account and the pleasure of punishing those who had lorded it over them since the old king's surrender. These former royalists were the first to become disenchanted.[3]

The gravest problem facing the Court, however, was not disappointed "friends" but potential enemies. To make his reign secure Charles had to retrieve the power of the sword, but this had to be done with tact to avoid offending his allies or betraying his distrust of a well-armed public. In particular, it was difficult to crack down on suspicious subjects without seeming to violate his generous promise to forgive and forget.

The situation at the time of Charles's arrival was particularly perilous. His subjects were well armed and volatile, and the country abounded with former enemies. Yet he had neither a loyal military establishment nor the means or monies to establish one. Indeed, when his men opened the public arsenals they discovered insufficient firearms and equipment to arm three thousand men.[4] When the King was informed of this severe shortage of arms, his first care purportedly was to conceal it, "that it might not be known abroad or at home, in how ill a posture he was to defend himself against an enemy."

Charles picked his way through this host of problems so deftly and purposefully that it seems naive to believe his solutions were really *ad hoc*. Although he was not given to philosophizing about his theory of kingship, Charles had lengthy firsthand experience of the powerful French and Spanish monarchies as a model, and his father's unhappy relations with English parliaments as a warning. He also had the long and tedious years of exile during which to plan how to reestablish and strengthen the English monarchy. Whether his intentions went beyond merely securing his throne, however, has been the subject of considerable debate.[5] Several anonymous blueprints survive among his government's papers that spell out procedures for the creation of an absolute monarchy in England. It is instructive to examine these suggestions because all lay great stress on the need for royal control of both weapons and military power and suggest how this might be achieved.

A work entitled "Rebellion subdued makes the King more King and the subject more subject" set out a series of rules to help the King keep his subjects passive; among these was the suggestion that every tenant of the Crown provide specific men and arms for a militia, "so by this meanes his Majesty may at all tymes and upon all occasions, be supplied with his owne and not need the tribute of the people, which he cannot obtain from a parliament, but for the same he must sell, and part with some rich and pretious branch of his prerogative to inlarge ther insatiable freedom."[6] The author of two essays sent to the Duke of Buckingham in 1662 warned the King that he had "ye Wolffe by ye Eares," for if he "doe not destroy" the power of the Commons, "it will devour him,

Crown, Dignity, and all."[7] After all, the power that "brought in may cast out . . . if the power and interest be not removed." Not only the common people but also the lords were seen as a menace: "A Prince cannot be safe, or his crowne fixed, where Lords and Commons are capable of revolt, and this both or either be, till he be Absolute." To achieve this the "proper and only way, and to be safe, is with Armies. Mony and Armes must be had." The King must realize that "it is not the splendor of precious stones and gold, that makes Enemies submit, but the force of armes. The strength of title, and the bare interest of possession will not now defend, the stres will not lye there, the sword is the thing." These essays stress the necessity for royal control of weapons and military power free from parliamentary control. Charles did not need anonymous treatises to convince him that the old quarrel between Crown and commoners was merely "hid in ashes." He may never have aspired to the sort of absolute monarchy these essayists extolled, but he immediately turned his attention to the strategy they suggested: control of the weapons of the realm.

Charles urgently needed to establish a large, efficient, and thoroughly loyal militia. This was no simple matter, for the only militia statutes passed since James I revoked the Tudor militia acts in 1604 were invalid because they had been enacted without royal approval. A new act was essential, but it was *the* issue most likely to raise difficulties, even in a parliament as eager to please as that of 1660. Control over the only permanent military organization in the realm had been the immediate provocation for civil war. A new militia act would have to clarify the extent of royal, as opposed to local, control of the militia; the methods and level of taxation for militia equipment; and the legitimate use of the trained bands.

Wrangling over a new militia bill began prior to the King's return. A group of more cautious MPs were determined to prevent Charles "from interfering with the militia" for at least five years.[8] But the House of Lords approved a militia bill only to have it emphatically rejected by the Commons because it contained provision for martial law, a feature members fiercely opposed.[9] As a result, when Charles arrived there was no valid militia act, and little likelihood of one in the near future.

The King, with his security in jeopardy, was not about to wait for such statutory niceties. There are assertions that, faced with this predicament, Charles toyed with the idea of retaining the 60,000-member republican army, but the force's reliability was doubtful at best, and it was estimated that so many of its soldiers were disaffected that "it was not safe to administer a general purgation."[10] In any case, the King's staunchest allies in Parliament were keen to dismantle an expensive military establishment whose past accomplishments they had ample reason to abhor. The alternative was to use the militia, even without statutory authority.

Within ten days of his triumphant arrival Charles was reported to be "settling the militia in all counties under Lords Lieutenants," with "the unanimous advice" of his Privy Council.[11] No one publicly questioned the King's right to do so, but he was obviously on shaky ground, relying upon his prerogative powers alone for authority to tax and muster men. He could establish a working militia, but his subjects might refuse to accord it the respect of a legal body, and Parliament could always undercut it. This may, in fact, have been the underlying reason Parliament, in the face of unremitting royal pressure and endless talk of the danger of revolution, was content to wait two years before passing a militia act. Clearly, despite their eagerness to please the King, both the Convention Parliament which welcomed the restoration of monarchy and the Cavalier Parliament that succeeded it harboured lingering doubts about royal absolutism. The militia was the litmus test of their trust, and they managed to keep final control of it in their own hands.

In any event Charles promptly selected lords lieutenant, who were instructed to choose deputies of known loyalty. His Privy Council perused lists of nominees for deputy lieutenants during July and made the final selections.[12] Once their staff was selected, militia officers were urged to organize, equip, and muster their regiments as quickly as possible. There is ample evidence that they followed orders and went about their tasks during the summer months very conscientiously.

In the absence of a new militia act, the general assumption was that the King would settle the militia in "the old accustomed way."[13] The militia had been fundamentally altered during the Interregnum, however, and what was "custom" had become blurred. Left to his own devices, Charles opted for two major departures from the militia of his father and grandfather. First, although he retained the old organization and methods of assessment, his militia's duties copied those devised for the militia of the Interregnum, allowing for extensive police powers to disarm anyone judged dangerous to the peace of the kingdom. In July Charles instructed his lieutenants to deploy their men to monitor the "motions" of "suspected" persons and to prevent such persons from meeting privately.[14] If those of "suspected or knowne disaffection" to the Crown managed to get "any store of arms into their hands," the weapons were to be seized at once and employed for the use of the trained bands. Although its task was similar, Charles's militia was more arbitrary than its predecessors. The Interregnum militia required three or more commissioners to disarm suspects, and the militia act passed in March 1659/60 had raised this number to five. Charles's instructions, however, were so vague on this point that any militia officer on his own initiative could disarm anyone. Moreover, it was clear that the phrase persons of "suspected or knowne disaffection" would be translated to include anyone prominent for his support of the Interregnum governments or a follower of other than the established church—the very individuals the King had supposedly pardoned. In fulfilling its mission, the militia employed tactics which were rough indeed.

Although it was essential that Parliament pass a militia act as quickly as possible in order to confirm the King's right to command that force, to establish a method of assessment, to excuse the militia's actions and exonerate those who had carried them out, and, above all, to end the confusion over the legality of the militia itself, it was more than a year after Charles's return before the body completed even a temporary measure. The preamble of "An Act declaring the sole right of the Militia to be in the King; and for the present Ordering and Disposing the same" of July 1661 sheds some light on the activities of the militia during the period before the act's passage. In it Parliament justified the militia and its methods on the grounds that "during the late usurped governments, many evil and rebellious principles have been distilled into the minds of the people of this kingdom, which unless prevented, may break forth to the disturbance of the peace and quiet thereof."[15] Specifically, the act noted that since June 24, 1660—less than a month after Charles's return—"divers persons suspected to be fanaticks, sectaries or disturbers of the peace have been assaulted, arrested detained or imprisoned, [by the militia] and divers arms have been seized and houses searched for arms." Parliament apparently felt it incumbent upon them to justify these measures and exonerate the officers and men involved.

Charles's second and more original innovation was the creation of a separate corps of self-supporting volunteers, or private soldiers, as large as the regular militia. As the King explained to his lords lieutenant, many persons "out of affection to our service and the peace of their Countrey in these vnsettled times may voluntarily offer (for the present) assistance above their proportions."[16] These persons were to "understand that we shall take very well such seasonable expressions of their affection to vs, and the Kingdome." Volunteers were to be arranged in troops and provided with officers to drill them. To ensure that "the greater number of Persons of Quality may be engaged in the service," the volunteer troops were to be smaller than regular militia units.

It was an ingenious scheme. It provided Charles with a nationwide army of royalist stalwarts independent of the ordinary militia with its thicket of restrictions. This army was also likely to be more zealous in the suppression of dissent and more prepared to take on tasks the regular militia would find objectionable. The volunteer regiments made it possible for large numbers of former royalists to assume a position that could gratify their egos and give them some power over their old opponents. Best of all, the volunteer force doubled the size of the militia at no cost to the Crown or the general population. It therefore freed Charles from the necessity of appealing to Parliament when he needed additional troops. By providing the King with an independent military force, it fulfilled the recommendation of one plan for a more absolute monarchy: "By this means his Majestie may at all tymes and upon all occasions, be supplied with his owne and not need the tribute of the people, which he cannot obtain from a parliament, but for the same he must sell, and part with some rich and pretious branch of his prerogative to inlarge ther insatiable freedom."[17] The King's creation of this volunteer army, of course, betrayed his distrust of the regular militia, despite efforts to make it reliable. It also implied distrust of Parliament and his belief that a sizeable police apparatus was needed to safeguard his government.

The main features of the volunteer army—its size, longevity, duties, and relationship to the regular militia—demonstrate the vital role its creator had mapped out for it. The first full instructions sent to the King's lords lieutenant had asked that, in addition to a militia, they organize regiments of volunteers. Numerous references in their subsequent correspondence testify to the seriousness with which they followed these instructions. The Earl of Exeter, lieutenant for Northumberland, for instance, wrote Secretary Nicholas in August: "As to the King's instructions concerning volinters, I have beene as industrious as I could, and have listed I beleeve 100 good men within my owne liberty of Peterborouw Soake . . . they will muster as a troop this week; as volinters under me to serve his Majesty."[18] He intended to recruit the eastern part of his county next and had already selected an officer to do the same in the west. Eventually he hoped to have three troops of volunteer horse "which will give a check to those which looke after devisions and disturbing the cuntry and incouragement to Honest men." There was even a degree of competition among lieutenants in raising volunteers. Some officers sprung into action only after learning that another lieutenant had recruited more men. The emphasis, at least during 1660, was upon raising volunteer cavalry rather than infantry, perhaps because of the greater mobility of cavalry and its greater appeal for aristocrats.

The result of energetic recruitment was a volunteer corps of impressive size. For every county muster list in which the regular and volunteer troops are distinguished, the volunteers are at least as numerous as the regulars, and in some cases more so.[19] Since the regular militia of England and Wales ordinarily numbered some 90,000 men, the volunteers were intended to be at least that number. Together the two bodies constituted a formidable force.

Official instructions stated that volunteer troops were a temporary expedient, to be used only from time to time. The Council declared that their mission was "to be in readiness upon any extraordinary occasion," just "for the present."[20] In fact, "extraordinary occasions" became very frequent, especially when unpleasant duties such as disarming fellow citizens were involved. And, despite the Crown's claim that the volunteers were needed only during "these doubtfull tymes," the men were still on duty in 1667, some seven years later. They might have continued serving even longer had not the entire militia establishment been permitted to decline after that date.

An examination of the activities of Charles's police force makes it clear that he preferred the volunteers to the regular militia, not only because he could use them without paying for their services and burdening local taxpayers, but because they were more trustworthy. In October, when the Earl of Winchelsea, lord lieutenant of Kent, instructed a deputy to "list what voluntiers you can," the deputy was at the same time to confiscate the weapons of his regular militia: "Lastly, both for horse and foot you may now preceed to disarme according to the powers in these instructions: but you must bee very secret in it, and quick, that none may have time, or notice to embessell their Armes."[21] The Court granted lieutenants discretion to disarm the regular militia. Government control of militia weapons had been recommended in a treatise written at this time to assure the King that "they may be vsed for and not against him."[22] Winchelsea seemed to have been worried about arms in general circulation and instructed his officers: "If you heare of great numbers of Armes you may seize them and in case you heare of meetings of armed persons in very great numbers you may use your discretion in disarming them."[23] The armed persons, it seems, did not even have to be of doubtful loyalty, and the decision to confiscate weapons was left to the judgment of a single deputy lieutenant.

The size, novelty, and activities of the volunteer corps led to uneasiness, even among the King's friends. In January 1661, a month rife with talk of plots and the occasion of Venner's uprising, the House of Commons was considering drafting a protest "against raising volunteer horse."[24] There is no record that any such protest was actually made.

The volunteers went on to play a pivotal role in strengthening royal control, a role the Court was careful to acknowledge. As one lord lieutenant wrote after his volunteers were praised for their handling of a tricky situation: "I am glad to fynd there is soe true a sense of our voluntier Troopes, whoe have been soe instrumentall in settling the peace of this Countie. I wishe they may have encouragement, for I am sure they well deserve it."[25]

The safety of the King and his government, of course, depended not only upon a loyal and sizeable citizen-police force but also upon the elimination of effective sources of revolt. In this respect the republican army stood out as the single most dangerous source. Few royalists were sufficiently naive to suppose the army's acquiescence in the restoration of monarchy meant it was suddenly a bulwark of royalism. But even if it had been, the force was very costly to maintain and the long years of humiliation at its hands had instilled in royalists and in a large portion of the English population a deep resentment and suspicion of all standing armies. The debates in Parliament made clear its members' distrust of all armies. Mr. Pierepont summed up the attitude of the Commons: "An Army and Parliament Cannot well subsist together but that the Trayne Bands were sufficient."[26] The Lords concurred, experience having convinced them that "the Power of Peerage and a Standing-Army, are like two Buckets the proportion that one goes down, the other exactly goes up."[27]

Dismantling the tough, veteran force was a risky undertaking, particularly since the soldiers were well armed and the King's men, at least at first, were not. Parliament struggled to devise a scheme for what they intended to be "the complete disbanding of the whole army." Because the soldiers would have to be paid off as they were disbanded, a special tax measure was enacted; and to smooth the men's readjustment to civilian life, Parliament passed "An Act for enabling the Soldiers of the Army now to be disbanded to exercise Trades." This statute waived the usual apprenticeship requirements in the case of veterans. Relieving the soldiers of their weapons was perhaps the greatest difficulty of all. Members of Parliament went through several changes of heart about how to handle the matter. General Monck, commander of the army, suggested that the soldiers keep their weapons until the moment of disbanding, whereupon each regiment would be marched to a convenient place "where the Arms may be secured for his Majesty's Service."[28] There the infantry were to hand over all weapons except their swords, "which are their own," and the cavalry "to deliver up what defensive Arms they have except their horses, Swords, and Pistols." As the time for completing these arrangements approached, Parliament seems to have become less confident that the soldiers would relinquish their arms and contemplated adopting an instruction "touching Satisfaction to be given Troopers disbanded, for their Pistols and Fire Armes."[29] After further consideration, the Commons decided this instruction to pay troops to return their equipment should be "laid aside."[30]

In addition to the problem of retrieving public weapons, members were worried about soldiers riding home with their own weapons and drew up an order "that no private Soldier, being disbanded, ride or travel with any Fire-Arms, upon Pain of losing his said Arms, and of imprisonment during his Majesty's Pleasure."[31] But after some discussion about the dangers of travel the order was amended to permit soldiers to retain arms for two weeks after disbanding. Members also suggested that the King issue a proclamation to put into effect the ancient acts against riding armed, but no such sweeping proclamation seems to have been issued.[32] Despite this painful ambivalence toward them, the soldiers disbanded quietly. The receipt of back pay doubtless sweetened their transition to civilian life. The only hitch in the steady disbandment of the army, in fact, was the sporadic manner in which tax monies became available to pay off the regiments. For this reason, the disbanding took more than a year.

Charles prudently left Parliament to devise the means of dismantling the republican army. His views on the subject of standing armies, however, were at odds with those of the MPs. Provided that the force was loyal, Charles was keen to have a permanent, professional army. As early as August 1660, while Parliament debated the best way of dismantling the army, and while his militia and volunteers were being raised, the King secretly planned a new army of 6000 to 8000 men.[33] The foundation for this force was carefully laid. Three days before Parliament was due to adjourn, an amendment was tacked onto the disbandment bill which stated that all soldiers were to be cashiered "except such of them, or any other, as his Majesty shall thinke fit otherwise to dispose and provide for, at his own Charge." This permitted the King to keep as large an army as he could afford. It ran counter to Parliament's goal to eliminate the army and was obviously rushed through at the last minute for strategic reasons. A second manoeuvre came in the form of a polite request from the King that the regiments assigned to his brothers, the Dukes of York and Gloucester, and Monck's own men be the last to be cashiered. The Houses agreed to two seemingly innocuous additions that were to prove of great importance in the establishment of a new, permanent army.

The Dissidents Disarmed

Charles II's professions and policies in the early months of his reign were plainly at odds. The King spoke often and passionately of his desire for harmony and reconciliation, and of his wish to forget the divisions of the past. But his anxious administration broadcast every hint of a plot and exploited the tension to bear down upon all likely opponents. The King might claim to forgive enemies for past disloyalty, but by asserting that not he, but they, refused to be reconciled and were forever plotting his downfall, he could easily exempt them from his grace. So far from forgiving enemies it became the maxim: "It is impossible for a Dissenter not to be a rebel."[34]

The Crown's technique was nicely illustrated in the addresses of the King and Lord Chancellor at the final session of the Convention Parliament on December 29, 1660. Charles congratulated members for passage of a statute based upon his own declaration of pardon, calling it this "happy Act of Indempnity and Oblivion . . . this excellent Building, that creates Kindness in Vs to each other; and Confidence in Our Joynt and Common Security."[35] He swore to observe it to the letter and vowed that "if any person should ever have the boldness to attempt to persuade Me to the contrary, he will finde such an Acceptation from Me, as he would have, who should persuade Me to burn Magna Charta, cancel all the old Laws, and to erect a new Government after My Own invention and appetite!" Whereas the King assured his subjects of his readiness to forgive, Clarendon emphasized differences. His speech following the King's stressed Charles's disappointment that the Militia Act, that "great bone of contention during the late ware," had been left as uncertain as they found it, "and consequently a foundation of new differences." The King would organize the militia anyway, to prevent the disorders that "many apprehended might arise upon the disbanding [of] the Army." Members were advised to "keep themselves in such a Posture, as may disappoint any seditious designs which are now on foot . . . there cannot be too much vigilance to frustrate those designs." The King himself had set an example of vigilance, taking care that "many suspected and dangerous persons" had been "lately clapped up." "It was," the Chancellor concluded, "high time to look about."

No one could accuse the Crown of failing to look about. It remains a matter for conjecture whether the Court was truly alarmed or whether it meant to create such a fear of revolution that repressive measures could be justified. The answer is probably both. In addition to worries about the impending disbandment of the army, there were the imminent dissolution of the Convention Parliament itself and serious difficulties with the militia. In the absence of a valid militia act many people had refused to participate or contribute their assessed arms, and numerous recruits appeared at musters without their weapons. On December 14 the Privy Council informed all lords lieutenant of the problem: "Divers of his Majesties subjects exempte themselves from being of the trayned bandes in most of the countyes of this kingdome for reasons not to be allowed. And others refuse to appear or to send their horses and armes to the muster, being onely summoned whereby his Majestys service is much obstructed and great mischieefe may proceed from that neglect if not prevented."[36] The Council ordered the lieutenants to put the statutes from Queen Mary's reign concerning attendance at musters into effect and "to proceed according to lawe against all such as shall neglect or refuse a business of that consequence to the safety and welfare of this kingdome." The legal basis for this action was most doubtful.

Even before this problem with the militia had become serious, and when the dissolution of Parliament was still three months away, the Crown began to clamp down on the use of arms. On September 29 a royal proclamation was issued, "For Suppressing of disorderly and unseasonable Meetings, in Taverns and Tipling Houses, And also forbidding Footmen to wear Swords, or other Weapons, within London, Westminster, and their Liberties." The official explanation was that "mischiefs have frequently hapned, and are likely to Ensue" from servants sporting weapons in the capital.

There were other mischiefs afoot in the form of plots. Early in December the government claimed to have evidence of a plot by former soldiers whose objective was to seize the King and Tower, kill the Queen-Mother and all Frenchmen in the kingdom, and restore Parliament. The evidence concerned Major White, "a mean fellow" who allegedly attempted to corrupt one of the underporters of Whitehall palace—a former army comrade—who reported him to the authorities. Several lists of names were found in White's chambers. On this meager evidence leading republicans throughout the country were "clapped up," among them former major-generals Overton and Desborough, and Major Rainborough. A special joint committee of Lords and Commons was created to improve security, but it seldom met, perhaps because, as Secretary William Morrice noted, "nothing is come into more light concerning the plot, which hath set many into an ambiguity and suspence of judgment on which side the plot lies."[37]

The Privy Council took steps of their own, however. They expressed horror at "the great number of arms which hath been lately and are dayly brought and transported out of the Citys of London and Westminster, and of the dangerous consequences the same produce." On December 14 they issued an order to all gunsmiths to report to the Ordnance

Office with a complete list of all the weapons they had produced in the past six months, as well as the names of the customers who had purchased them.[38] Henceforth gunsmiths were to report to the Master of the Armoury every Saturday night with a record of their manufactures and sales for the week. A form of firearms registration had been introduced.

Three days later a royal proclamation ordered all discharged officers and soldiers and "other Persons that cannot give a good Account for their being here" to leave London within two days and to remain no closer than twenty miles from the the city in the future.[39] Two days afterward a dispatch to lords lieutenant throughout the realm warned them that "severall persons of those principles of known disaffection to us your government have furnished themselves with quantities of arms and ammunition as may justly give suspition that it is with design to disturb the peace and tranquillitye of this our kingdome."[40] The militia was ordered to search "in all suspected places for armes and ammunition and where any quantity of either be discovered in the house of any person disaffected to us above what reasonably may be beleeved necessary for his safety and defence," they were to be confiscated. These actions had been set in motion before the King and the Chancellor greeted that final session of the Convention Parliament with their messages of forgiveness and suspicion respectively.

The Crown's repressive measures caused dismay, especially since the public generally regarded the plot that occasioned them as insignificant or nonexistent. Their skepticism was justified. The accused were released six months later without a trial. In his address to Parliament the Chancellor had been defensive. He admitted that "the persons engaged in that conspiracy were only the lees of the people" but argued that "small beginnings ought not to be neglected."[41] One gentleman summed up the situation as it appeared on Christmas Day: "Whether there was any such Plott att all I cannot learne however there is Abundance troubled upon that Account, as well here as in other places."[42] The government had made certain that there would be "Abundance troubled upon that Account."

Fears for the future troubled many Englishmen that Christmas and certainly justified the Court's attack of nerves. The observer cited above remarked that once Parliament was dissolved there was no certainty when another would be summoned. "Some," he noted, "conceived it wilbe longe err any will be thought of." Others judged that it was the monarchy, not Parliament, that faced extinction, and they wagered that "the government will not last a year."[43]

Although some plots were imagined, others were quite real. At least fifty religious zealots were indeed plotting revolution. On January 6 a band of Fifth Monarchists led by a cooper named Thomas Venner sallied out into the streets of London to launch the prophesied fifth universal monarchy of the world under the direct rule of Jesus Christ.[44] They shot a bystander and a local official and managed to seize St. Paul's before the militia and royal guards arrived.[45] The rebels fought fiercely until all were killed or wounded. Venner himself suffered nineteen wounds but miraculously lived to stand trial.

After initial consternation, public reaction was relatively mild, as men were struck more by the "madnesse and unwarrantable zeale" of the rebels and their insignificant numbers than by any real threat to the Crown. Pepys wrote in his diary how he was awakened on the morning of January 9 by cries that "the Fanatiques were up in armes in the City."[46] He had seized his pistol and raced outdoors. He was later amazed to learn that the rebels were "not in all above 31 whereas we did believe them (because they were seen up and down in every place almost in the City, and had been in Highgate two or three days, and in several places) to be at least 500."

When Parliament convened, the Chancellor made clear in his opening address that the government regarded the uprising with utmost seriousness. Clarendon referred to it as "the most desperate and prodigious Rebellion . . . that hath been heard of in any Age" and warned: "Let no Man undervalue the Treason because of the Contemptibleness of the Number engaged in it. No Man knows the Number; but, by the Multitude of intercepted Letters from and to all the Counties of England, in which the Time was set down wherein the Work of the Lord was to be done, by the desperate Carriage of the Traitors themselves, and their bragging of their Friends, we may Conclude the Combination reached very far."[47] He claimed that if not for the courage and industry of the Lord Mayor, "this famous City, or a great part of it, had been turned to Ashes." Nor was that all. "There hath not been a Week since that Time, in which there hath not been Combinations and Conspiracies formed against his Person, and against the Peace of the Kingdom." A study of these plots has detected the government's hand in nearly every one.[48] Clarendon reminded members that their king was very mild and it was up to them to provide laws to protect him. "If the new License and Corruption of this Time hath exceeded the Wickedness of former Ages, that the old Laws have not enough provided for the Punishment of Wickedness they could not foresee or imagine, it will become your Wisdoms to provide new Remedies for new Diseases, and to secure the precious Person of our dear Sovereign from the First Approaches of

Villany; and the Peace of the Kingdom from the First Overtures of Sedition."

In the meantime the royal government had not been lax in shoring up the defences of its "mild" monarch. The Venner uprising had been opportune not only because it gave the government a genuine plot to point to but because it took place on the very day the last two regiments of the republican army were to be disbanded. Given this visible danger, the government retained the regiments and dispatched orders to raise twelve more companies of soldiers and a regiment of cavalry.[49] These troops would form the core of the first English standing army in peacetime. To avoid alarm they were styled "guards" rather than soldiers.

Letters were also rushed to militia officers warning them of the danger of plots "yett undiscovered" and ordering them to disarm all persons "notoriously knowne to be of ill principles or [who] have lately . . . by words or actions shewn any disaffection to his Majestie or his Government, or in any kind disturbed the publique peace."[50] While earlier orders were for such persons to be relieved of arms beyond what was necessary to their defence, the new directives called for them to be totally disarmed. The category of persons who had "by words or actions" demonstrated their disaffection was specific enough, but inclusion of all those "notoriously knowne to be of ill principles" permitted the broadest possible sweep of former republicans and religious dissenters.

These orders appear to have been carried out promptly. The militia remained on full alert throughout January and made hundreds of arrests. By January 8, for instance, the Northamptonshire lieutenants reported that all men of known "evill Principles" had been disarmed and secured "so as we have not left them in any ways of power to attempt a breach of the peace."[51] In Coventry the trained bandsmen and 300 volunteer troops remained in arms all month. In Warwickshire 600 trained bandsmen were in arms, and all other weapons were ordered to be brought to the public magazine for safekeeping.[52] Searches were even made of municipal buildings. A stir was caused when, shortly after the city of Exeter had surrendered 937 musket barrels, a further stock of weapons was discovered "hidden and concealed" in the guildhall.[53] There was debate whether the mayor ought to be summoned to London to account for this cache.

In late March Charles issued a proclamation forbidding transport of arms or ammunition into the countryside without permission from the Master of the Ordnance. Indeed, even lords lieutenant and their deputies had to submit a request if they needed arms and obtain a pass for their shipment.[54] In April disbanded soldiers were ordered to quit London and vicinity for at least a month. The seizure of persons and arms in the capital was so bruskly executed that the King felt constrained to issue a proclamation to soothe and reassure outraged citizens, especially "our good Subjects who were lately of the Army . . . and therein instrumental to Our happy Restauration," that the restrictions on unwarranted search and seizure were still in operation, and the new Act of Oblivion not forgotten.[55] He blamed the enthusiasm of his soldiers for their overstepping the bounds, but explained that since "unreasonable men" of "restless and perverse disposition" had armed themselves in expectation of levying war, it was essential to search out these weapons. Regrettably, during "those late Commotions, several persons have been imprisoned by Souldiers and others, their houses searched, and their Goods taken away without lawful Authority . . . Opprobious words and terms of dissention and discrimination of parties have been used and given to Our great disservice, contrary to . . . the Act of Pardon and Oblivion." Henceforth, he promised that only during extreme emergencies would searches be carried out without the proper warrants.

Charles was somewhat more cautious about searches in the future but, five days after he issued these assurances, the Privy Council ordered militia commanders throughout the realm not only to disarm, but "forthwith to apprehend, secure, and imprison" such "leading persons as you have good grounds to suspect opposite to his Majesty's government."[56] This order was bound to result in the arrest of leading republicans and religious dissenters, whether they had exhibited any opposition to the regime or not. Hundreds of Quakers were arrested and languished in prison for months because their religion was considered dangerous.[57] The rhetoric of reconciliation faded into the background as Crown and Parliament devised "new remedies" for what were dubbed "new diseases."

The new "Cavalier" parliament that met in May—the first elected after the restoration of monarchy—has become notorious for its servility and willingness to strengthen the Crown at the expense of popular liberty. As already noted, however, the Crown did its utmost to goad members into adopting repressive measures. Charles pleaded in his opening address that they be "as severe as you will against new Offenders, especially if they be so upon old Principles," and Clarendon called for the exercise of their "utmost vigilence, utmost Severity."[58] With the help of this Parliament, new laws and royal proclamations tightened the King's hold on the country.

Parliament's very first measure, a new, broader treason act, was followed by measures against public petitions and for censorship. Clarendon claimed to be satisfied with the work of this session and wrote that its members had "pulled up all principles of sedition and rebellion by the roots, which in their own observation had been the ground of or contributed to the odious and infamous rebellion in the long parliament."[59] He noted, in particular, that they had declared "that sottish distinction between the King's person and his office to be treason . . . that the militia was inseparably vested in his majesty, and that it was high treason to raise or levy soldiers without the King's commission."

Indeed, after much debate this Parliament had approved a militia act, albeit one which couldn't have been completely to the King's liking.[60] Members were unwilling to confront the complex and sensitive issues that a permanent militia act required, so this was a temporary measure, due to expire on March 25, 1662. The act contained no provision to transport the militia out of England or to pay it for longer than a month of service, and it prescribed only a mild penalty for disobedience. Hence many constitutional scholars are in agreement that, notwithstanding the act's affirmation of the King's control over the militia, the actual implication was that "the King's prerogative powers for the regulation of the Militia were minimal."[61]

Despite its weaknesses the act had much to commend it from the Crown's point of view. It explicitly declared the "sole right" of the militia, as well as "all forces by sea and land," to be in the Crown. It provided legal authority for the militia Charles had already established and exonerated the rough tactics of his militia officers.[62] Finally, it stated that the militia was to be "exercised, ordered and managed . . . according to such commissions and instructions as they formerly have or from time to time shall receive from his Majesty." This permitted Charles the latitude to employ the militia, at least until March 1662, as he saw fit.

Once Parliament adjourned for its summer recess, the Court, haunted by the spectre of revolt, again sought to clamp down on its opponents. Members had only just returned home when the Council alerted lords lieutenant that men connected with the Interregnum government were once again plotting against the Crown.[63] Councillors claimed to have found "a mutinous spiritt in some persons in this kingdome." The militia was ordered to exercise "more than ordinary rigour and activity . . . have a watchfull eye on the mocions of signall persons" disaffected to the government and "uppon any just grounds of suspicion to disarme them and secure their persons." The trained bands were put on war footing, ready for action at an hour's warning.

A sense of weariness, of *deja vu*, is evident in the reaction to this new alarm. The Earl of Devonshire, lord lieutenant of Derbyshire, reported the new orders to his deputies with the comment: "The persons meant by this letter I suppose are allready known there . . . having been so many several enquiryes after them. But I think it necessary in persuance of these directions that you should very strictly looke into their actions and if by examining them or otherwyse you discover they have any armes, they must be taken from them."[64] And the Earl of Westmorland, who had bragged in January of his swiftness in disarming all those "knowne to be of evill Principles" in Northamptonshire, waited a full month before passing on information of the new alarm to his deputies, and even then he gave no orders for any special watch on suspects.[65]

Parliament may have been willing to shore up the royal defences, but ordinary Englishmen were less anxious about Charles's welfare than about their own. When William Holcroft's Essex militia company gathered in October for a muster, 144 men appeared as ordered, but 192 had defaulted![66] That same month deputies responsible for the western division of Northamptonshire reported the poor results of their muster: "Wee are sory wee cannot give your lordships so good accompt of them as wee desire." Many of the cavalry were unfit, but they found the foot "in a worse condition" because many residents had refused to contribute their assessed arms.[67] There had been problems with the Derbyshire militia all year. Deputies reported "a great willingness to the service," but they hastened to add that "many default especially in the foote, And that in respect of armes." Indeed, one "whole townshippe have appeared and not one arme amongst them. They pretende excuses, and promise a supply."[68] They concluded: "We are my lord extreamely wanting in the many strengths of warr. Armes and money. We have no magazine nor one bullett nor . . . powder, but tried to make shift as we say from hande to mouth."

On occasion, officers were even more reluctant than their troops to spend long days on duty because of yet another false alarm. A deputy complained that when he called an emergency muster of the Scarsdale trained bandsmen, the men appeared, but "none of the deputy lieutenants were willinge to assist me in those partes."[69] It is noteworthy that although members of Parliament were aware of these difficulties—many of them served as militia officers—they were not prepared to pass a permanent militia act that might have corrected the problem.

Before Parliament reconvened, the Crown moved to plug the last free aspect of the arms market—the importation of foreign weapons. On the pretext that the "great Quantityes of Gunnes of all sorts" imported into London had impoverished native gunmakers, and to prevent "any design of Traiterous and factious persons," all importation of weapons or parts of weapons was prohibited.[70]

The Dissidents Disarmed

The Crown now effectively controlled the production and distribution of firearms. Its police establishment kept all "malecontents, fanatics, and sectaries" disarmed and under continuous surveillance. These very measures lost Charles much of his original popularity but failed to ease his government's paranoia. The country and its capital harbored not only subjects who had favoured the Commonwealth and religious dissenters but thousands of disbanded soldiers, some of whom were doubtless as dangerous as the Court claimed. When members of Parliament gathered on November 20 for their new session, therefore, they were treated to a concerted campaign directed against this last group, the veterans. The King greeted the MPs with news that he had found "the general Temper and Affections of the Nation . . . not so well composed." "If you find new Diseases," Charles exhorted them, "you must study new Remedies." Charles had obviously detected new diseases. The following day, egged on by this entreaty and presented with intelligence that "divers malecontents, fanatics, cashiered and disbanded soldiers, and others [had] some design amongst them tending to a breach of the peace," the Commons asked the Lords to join them in urging the King to issue a proclamation "for disarming the disbanded and cashiered Officers and Soldiers; and to command them to depart from, and not to approach within Twenty Miles of this City, for such time as his Majesty shall think fit."[71] Since both the diagnosis of the problem and the remedy for it materialized with such startling rapidity it seems likely that Court physicians had a hand in both.

A week later, the King issued a proclamation ordering all the officers and soldiers of the republican army, whether cashiered or disbanded, and all those men who had ever fought on behalf of Parliament to depart from London within the week and not to come closer than twenty miles of the city before June 24, 1662.[72] During their six months of banishment the former soldiers were not to "weare, use, or carry or ryde with any sword, pistoll or other armes or weapons." This sweeping proclamation caused understandable consternation among veterans, especially among those soldiers who had come from Scotland with Monck. The Commons sympathized and resolved that men who served under Monck "at his coming out of Scotland" and "such as were instrumental in his Majesty's Restitution" should be exempt from the proclamation, but the Lords "could not concur."[73] They protested that "the Proclamation was as large, as with Safety, in this Conjuncture of Affairs, it could extend; his Majesty having granted License to those that had been recommended by the General; and there being some who were not to be trusted." Lords lieutenant were notified of the proclamation and passed the orders on to their deputies. Two days before this proclamation was due to expire, another appeared that extended both the ban and the disarmament an additional six months. There is no record of a proclamation for 1663, but in 1664, 1665, and 1670 similar proclamations were published.[74]

The scope of these decrees is astounding. Not only were the 60,000 men of the republican army of 1660 forbidden to go armed, but so too were all those who had ever fought for Parliament. It is uncertain whether the King's militia and volunteers were willing or able to enforce these edicts, but, at the very least, their effect was to officially deprive a large portion of the male population of the legal right to carry firearms. The Crown no longer felt constrained to humour the veterans. It felt confident enough to admit they were a menace and to treat them as such.

In the course of the year which began with the banishment of the veterans, the Crown completed the apparatus for its control of the realm. Not only had all disturbances been quieted, the Venetian ambassador in London remarked, but "there [seemed] no way for the sectaries to disturb the general repose, owing to the good measures taken and the great vigilance for the safety of the King and people shown by the secretary Bennet."[75] This general repose was no mean accomplishment. Early in the year Sir Henry Bennet, Secretary of State and the King's advisor on internal security, had warned Charles to strengthen his authority "by all the meanes and wayes the Lawe allows you since the dissatisfaction towardes the present government . . . is become soe universal that any small Accident may put us into new Troubles."[76] Moreover, he reckoned the old militia hadn't "vigour enough left in it to meet the present dangers." If the dangers were as great as Bennet argued, it was fortunate for Charles that, in addition to unpopular measures dealing with religious uniformity and a new tax, Parliament finally passed a permanent militia act.

The two Houses were in a self-congratulatory mood at the close of their session in May, as the Speaker of the House informed the King: "We applied ourselves to the settling our great Concern, the Militia," taking care, he said, "to make all Things so certain" that the militia officers "know what to command, and all the People learn how to obey."[77] This long-delayed measure proclaimed, unequivocally, that sole command of the militia was the King's, and it outlined a militia structure similar to that of the past. The police powers of search and seizure that Charles's militia had been practicing were now made lawful. Somewhat less discretion was permitted officers than in the King's present militia, but more than was the case during the Interregnum. Any two deputies could initiate a search for, and seizure of, arms in the possession of any person who, in their judgment, was "dangerous to the Peace of the Kingdom." This definition of who could be disarmed was less precise than in any earlier militia act.

The Dissidents Disarmed

The King and his Council were relieved to have a permanent militia act but feared that the regime might be vulnerable during the transition from the old to the new militia. In anticipation of this changeover the Crown took two further steps to pacify the realm. First, it made use of a new Corporation Act to purge city and town governments of all officials with links to the Interregnum governments of the past. During the summer special commissioners, usually the lords lieutenant, went from town to town ousting officials of doubtful loyalty. In mid-August Lord Northampton wrote that he had just purged Coventry, where he had discharged "only" one alderman, ten councilmen, and one sheriff.[78] That night his associate was "to search their houses for arms and papers." With this housekeeping over he swore in new deputy lieutenants for Coventry, who were ordered to "pursue the Act for settling the Militia." Lord Brereton, chosen to perform the same service for the towns of Cheshire, reported that he had "regulated" the corporation of Chester and at present was in Congleton, "where we finde that towne according to their proportion as rotten as Chester."[79] He guessed, "We shall not finde the other towns much better" but sturdily resolved "to visit as many of them as we can this weeke, that we may have nothing to hinder us from the business of the Militia when it cometh."

The King's second move was to raze the walls of those towns that had been notable for their opposition to his father during the Civil War. In early summer he ordered the lords lieutenant to demolish the walls and fortifications of Gloucester, Coventry, Northampton, Taunton, and Leicester to render them incapable of revolt.[80] Each town's residents were disarmed before they were informed that their walls were to be levelled.

The destruction of Northampton's fortifications was recorded in detail by the Earl of Westmorland. The day before demolition was scheduled to begin his deputies drew the trained bands from the vicinity. Every building in the city was then searched for weapons, and "all such Armes as may be found there in any hands whatsoever" were seized. Public buildings were the first to be searched. Some 200 muskets were discovered in the Town Hall, and a smaller cache was found in the "great" church. These were placed under guard while private homes were canvassed. That done, the county lieutenants arrived, accompanied by four troops of volunteer soldiers. The mayor and the council were then informed that their town walls were to be destroyed. Westmorland reported that they "yielded obedience thereto yett wee dare not say with what countenance of satisfaction because we could not pierce into their harts."[81] In a letter to George Vane, however, he ventured the opinion that the Northampton officials had complied "partly for love but more I think out of fear."[82] His soldiers remained in the town until the walls were completely levelled and only afterward returned the private weapons they had taken. Public arms seem to have been confiscated. The purpose of this exercise was bluntly explained by Lord Northampton, whose own mission was to destroy the defences of Coventry: "I have dismantled this towne of Coventry so far as that it is untenable, and impossible for any that have any skill in Martiall affairs to thinke of it for the future as a place fit to possess in order to a stand, or indeed to hope for conditions."[83] It must have been painfully obvious to the residents of these towns and to their militia that the King did not trust them. With municipal governments purged and walls levelled, the new militia was peacefully installed.

By Christmas of 1662 Charles II had substantially diminished his subjects' ability to rebel. His program to police and disarm all likely dissenters, the Act of Oblivion and Pardon notwithstanding, demonstrated skill, timing, and resourcefulness. Two years after he arrived unarmed to confront an armed and restive nation and a veteran republican army, he had managed to mold trained bandsmen and volunteers into a police establishment of unprecedented size and effectiveness. Using this force Charles had all possible adversaries watched, harassed, disarmed, and in many instances jailed. The foundation of a permanent army had been laid, and the men of Cromwell's army, formerly the pride of England and the terror of Europe, were flattered, disbanded, psychologically disarmed, and then finally deprived of the normal right to carry weapons. Endless alarms of plots provided the excuse to keep the militia on a war footing and to impose restrictions on the production, importation, and movement of arms. Charles had made his regime as impervious as possible to the whims of Englishmen.

All this could not have been accomplished without the cooperation of the royalist gentry. They may have come to regard the danger of revolution as remote, but so long as their own interests coincided with his, they aided the King.[84] They urged him to disarm veterans and acquiesced in his restrictions on weapons and his harassment of those whose past sins had been officially pardoned. The royalist gentry have, with justification, been repeatedly accused of shoring up monarchy by sacrificing the liberties of the people. Indeed, they professed their willingness to part with their privileges, "though they had not many left, for the Public Safety."[85] But they did not relinquish the power of the sword. True, by means of a loophole in the Disbandment Act they permitted the King to have a standing army. But it could only be as large a force as Charles could afford on his own, and no one knew better than they how little he could afford. They had confirmed the royal claim that the militia was "in the King," but since it was staffed by themselves and their peers it was unlikely to carry out royal orders that were not to their liking. Since only a limited amount of money was allotted for the support of the militia, the gentry had final control over any extended *use* of it. Their professions were often servile, but their actions, at least in this respect, were not. James, Duke of York, saw only distrust, not servility, in the behaviour of his brother's parliaments. He later wrote: "The parsimony of the commons, notwithstanding their professions of unlimited loyalty, was evidently intended to keep the King in a state of dependence upon his parliament."[86]

To maintain this state of dependence, members made every effort to ensure the King's reliance upon the militia. They were jealous of any attempt, even in wartime, to expand the royal "guards." A demonstration of their caution occurred in January 1662, when fears of a new plot convinced Parliament that the disbanded soldiers should be banished and disarmed. The Crown had pressed for an expansion of the royal army to meet the new danger, but Parliament quashed the proposal. In their debate on the matter they expressed their distrust of soldiers, no matter whose. Pepys wrote of this incident: "The Lord Chancellor, it seems, taking occasion from this late plot to raise fears in the people, did project the raising of an army forthwith, besides the constant militia, thinking to make the Duke of York General thereof. But the House did, in very open terms, say, they were grown too wise to be fooled again into another army; and said they had found how that man that hath the command of an army is not beholden to anybody to make him King."[87] This comment provides a key to the attitude of the royalist aristocracy. They wanted a king but one who was beholden to them. Ronald Hutton, in his book on the Restoration, concludes that the unifying element within all the political and religious developments of the 1660's was the desire of the gentry to avoid another experience like the civil wars by keeping "Crown, Church, towns, Catholics, dissenters and vagrants all equally within their control."[88] The gentry had permitted the persecution and disarming of their old enemies because they approved of those measures. They had as much to gain from restoration of order as did the King. They sacrificed liberties, but liberties of those they regarded as their enemies. They do not seem to have realized how easily the militia they created and the discretion to disarm could be used against them.

It was the members of Parliament and the classes they represented that, in their own self-interest, would finally wrest weapons from their fellow citizens. In light of this, it is imperative to examine the gentry's behaviour during the Restoration and the reaction of both the Crown and, more important, the common people to their attempt to seize for themselves alone the power of the sword.

The Gentleman's Game

THREATS to freedom sometimes come from unexpected quarters. For seventeenth-century Englishmen the King was *the* expected quarter, and their defences were aimed at protecting their liberties from the Crown. As a shrewd eighteenth-century observer explained, however, though it is "absolutely necessary, for securing the Constitution of a State, to restrain the Executive power . . . it is still more necessary to restrain the Legislative. What the former can only do by successive steps (I mean subvert the laws) and through a longer or shorter train of enterprizes, the latter does in a moment. As its bare will can give being to the laws; so its bare will can also annihilate them: and, if I may be permitted the expression,—the Legislative power can change the Constitution, as God created the light."[1]

Charles II regarded armed subjects as a danger to be contained "by successive steps" and through a "train of enterprizes." But it was the representatives of the people assembled in Parliament on their own initiative who annihilated the privilege of most Englishmen to have weapons and changed centuries of custom almost as suddenly "as God created the light."

It is clear how Parliament accomplished this, but the records are stubbornly silent about why it was done. To grasp why members of Parliament passed the Game Act of 1671, which eliminated that time-honoured privilege, one must place the Game Act in its immediate context and, through a re-creation of members' views of government and society, tease from the tangle of events clues to their motives.

It must have been with immense relief that royalists turned their thoughts from the King's restoration to their own. Exiles back from an impoverished residence on the Continent and victims of dispossession or merely humiliation shared a single-minded zeal to return to the good life, to refurbish their estates, to get on with improvement schemes abandoned years earlier, and above all to resume their domination of the social, economic, and political life of the countryside. For a while this passion to recoup their economic and social status seemed to obliterate all else, most notably any uneasiness about their political liberties. Every warning that political restraints should be imposed upon the new king as a condition of his return was met with rough impatience and cavalierly swept aside in a wave of fervent loyalty. Even the seemingly unobjectionable attempt a week before the King's arrival to enact a bill for "maintaining the just Rights and Privileges of Parliament and confirming the fundamental Laws" received only one reading before Charles's return and was later quietly shelved by the House of Lords.

In stark contrast, considerable attention was lavished upon a bill to ensure that the Long Parliament's abolition of the hated Court of Wards and Liveries and of knight service remained permanent. In exchange for the proceeds from wardship and knight service, members agreed to grant the King the revenues of an excise tax estimated to be worth some £100,000 per year. The fiscal effect of the new arrangement, as one historian points out, was that "in place of income derived from land-owners holding of the Crown, there was substituted an additional tax on beer, cider, and tea, falling on rich and poor alike."[2] This measure, which removed the last vestiges of the aristocracy's feudal obligations to the Crown, sped through the two houses of Parliament. Nothing could more clearly illustrate the priorities of the royalist aristocracy than the different fates of these two measures.

Human nature being what it is, perhaps royalist concerns, heavily skewed toward personal betterment, were only to be expected. After all, not only were their estates and pocketbooks in need of replenishment, but after nearly twenty years every privilege and public office in the gift of the Crown seemed "up for grabs." Decorum as well as political caution fell victim to an unseemly stampede for royal favours. Since much of this scramble for royal gifts had as its object the renewal or enhancement of country privileges, it is not surprising that high on the list of offices to be garnered and projects to be tackled were those relating to the hunt. Above all else, hunting symbolized the life of leisure and privilege the aristocracy had so sorely missed. Moreover, since it was by means of a game act that Parliament prohibited the possession of fire-arms, the approach of the restored king and his followers toward the re-creation of their favourite pastime is of great consequence.

The King shared the general royalist eagerness to return the princely sport to its former luster, and he was aware that, because a game park could be "disparked" when "all the deer etc. are destroyed," both animals and trees had to be replaced quickly.[3] Charles lost no time making his own forests suitable "for a Game of Deer and for the Royal disport," and he spent some £1700 transporting animals to his parks from other English parks and even from Germany. His interest in the sport proved long-standing, for a decade later, shortly before passage of the Game Act of 1671, the royal treasury allocated the impressive sum of £7574 for new fencing for Windsor Great Park.[4] Charles also continued the practice of his father and grandfather, appointing leading councillors to important forest offices and endowing these humble posts with great prestige.[5] To gratify his other supporters Charles also made what have been described as "prodigal grants" of his own parks, and appointed many men to forest offices.[6] It has been suggested that in reviving royal hunting offices the King aimed to counter the local influence of the squirarchy.[7] If this was his intention, it seems to have eluded the gentry who avidly sought such appointments and were immensely pleased when they received them.

In addition to restocking and replanting forests and parks, the King and the aristocracy concluded that game needed more protection. The Earl of Northampton recommended that "now the ruder sort of people in these late times have taken so great libertie that there ought more than ordinary care be taken for the punishing of them."[8] That meant enforcement of the game acts in their full rigor. Despite many more urgent problems during the first weeks after Charles's return, he found time to write letters insisting on strict enforcement.[9] The return of the King and his party clearly meant the return of their favourite country sport, with all the attendant costs to the crops and patience of rural Englishmen.

For those who lived in forest areas, E. P. Thompson found that "the Restoration brought counter-revolution in a score of practical and painful ways."[10] The changes were no less painful for thousands living in open field areas or in the fen country. The collapse of authority during the Civil War had in some instances permitted countrymen to reclaim fields that had been enclosed and to destroy drainage ditches, while the heady days of the Commonwealth, with its more sympathetic, or at least less effective, government, afforded further opportunities for tenants to seize what they felt belonged to them. The triumphant royalists were determined to halt this lawlessness. Counter-revolution meant not only the return of forest law, and the conversion of wardship revenues into a tax on beer and cider, but the relentless renewal of "improvement" projects that had been interrupted by the war.[11] New enclosures mushroomed, especially in the midland counties. Tenants sent formal protests to Parliament and occasionally resorted to force, but could expect little sympathy from MPs or local officials. Enterprising magnates revived schemes for draining the 300,000 acres of fens, a watery world that spread over six counties. Since newly enclosed or drained lands tended to be leased in large parcels to well-to-do tenants, the livelihood of the thousands of small farmers and cottagers who tilled the open fields and fished the fens was at risk. Although historians may argue that in the long run enclosures led to the employment of more labour than they displaced, there is no doubt of the great distress caused in the short run as evicted tenants wandered the countryside looking for "land to be set."[12] The Restoration may have brought joy to the great house, but it brought gloom to the cottage, and a heightened antagonism between lord and tenant that would have important repercussions for the private possession of weapons.

In 1660 the aristocracy's fortunes began to ascend, not only in comparison with their humble neighbours', but in contrast with the King's as well. Even during the honeymoon of sorts that the King enjoyed in the first months after his return, his supporters kept a watchful eye on him and contrived to keep him at a prudent distance from temptation. Their casual attitude toward limiting royal power stemmed less from carelessness or trust than from confidence in their own power. It was a confidence well placed, for not in recent memory had they been so free from Crown control. A generation earlier, Charles I had curbed the power and authority they exercised as local justices by means of his famous Book of Orders, which listed their duties in irritating detail and demanded strict accountability.[13] Moreover, whenever Charles I was displeased with a justice, he could summon the man to appear before Star Chamber, a prospect calculated to terrify even the most self-important country squire. The failure to reestablish Star Chamber after the Restoration has been described as "crucial" in tipping the scales in the gentry's favour. Without it, the only disciplinary tactic left the government was outright dismissal from the commission of the peace, an expedient Charles II seldom felt able to use before 1680.[14]

In addition to the lapse of these old restraints the royalist gentry knew that their king was "beholden" to them and needed their aid to secure his regime.[15] It was they, after all, not the King, who held the power of the sword. As J. H. Plumb pointed out, behind the aristocracy's social, political, and judicial power "lay the sanction of arms, for in the last resort they controlled the militia."[16] No matter how casual they appeared about other powers, they were careful to keep military control in their own hands. The militia bill of 1660 had been rejected because it provided for martial law, which might make them "wards of an army."[17] Two years later their debates on a permanent militia bill revealed the same terror of a standing army, and even of too extensive use of a militia. They rejected a proviso to allow lords to pay a fee of £10 in lieu of providing a horse and armed rider on the ground that "it might prove too great a Temptation to turn all the Horse of England into Money . . . It might give Occasion of Jealousy, as looking to a Standing Force."[18] The Commons hastened to add that in rejecting this proviso they had no "jealousy" of the present age but "looked after what might be."[19] Parliament proclaimed the King sole commander of the militia, but permitted him to raise only a modest £70,000 a year for a maximum of three years to pay trained bands on active duty. Real control of the militia belonged to those who legislated for it, financed it, and staffed its officer corps.

Although Parliament had agreed that the King could raise any soldiers he was able to pay himself (presumably relying on his inability to afford more than a small corps of guards), fears that Charles would expand that corps compelled a royal councillor to reassure Parliament: "I know of nothing that can hinder the King from raising what forces he pleases, if he pays for them himself. My argument is, you are the paymasters; if the occasions of the forces cease, how can any man think you will pay these men that are not employed to the interest you mean they should."[20]

The doubts and precautions that eroded the relationship between the Crown and the aristocracy, few as they seemed at first, led to a honeymoon of startling brevity. As in most relationships, both parties shared in the blame.

For their part, royalists were never as wholeheartedly loyal in practice as in profession. They were as jealous of their rights and privileges as their old parliamentary foes had been; they were rabidly anti-Catholic; and they had an almost pathological fear of professional armies. These three prejudices became twisted in their imagination into a scenario in which a large, royal army would rob them of both their liberties and their religion. In addition to these prejudices, they shared with all Englishmen—and indeed all taxpayers everywhere—a resentment of government taxation.

There is little argument about Charles II's failings; in fact, the harshest indictments against him came from those "who served him longest and knew him best."[21] If the merry monarch was charming, he was also prodigal with his own and the public's money. As head of the Church of England he set a sorry example and was quite unwilling to keep up even the pretence of moral or religious scruples. Charles was openly promiscuous and presided over a Court that shocked his subjects with "an indecency foreign to English standards."[22] Sir George Carteret confided to Pepys that he had reminded the King of "the necessity of having, at least, a show of religion in the Government, and sobriety," but to no avail.[23] Not only was the Court notoriously corrupt but in 1670 Charles became its leader in corruption by secretly selling his friendship and the promise to convert the kingdom to Catholicism to the King of France in return for a pension of some £200,000 a year. Although it was some time before his subjects suspected this duplicity, they were aware of his open tolerance of Catholics at the same time he encouraged the persecution of Protestant dissenters.

Charles tried his subjects in just those areas in which they were most sensitive. He married a Catholic princess of Portugal, arranged a Catholic marriage for his brother when James's Protestant duchess died, permitted great latitude to members of the Catholic faith, and even enlisted Catholics in his royal guards. In contrast to his tolerance of Catholics, Charles's harassment of Protestant sectarians was so vigorous that by 1661 a cleric of the Church of England, no friend to dissenters, would write: "There were great murmurings of discontent . . . especially amongst the Presbyterians, who were unsatisfied for there was no toleration allowed them for the exercise of their religion although his Majestie . . . promised so much vpon the word of a King . . . and by so much the more was their griefe, for they had not so much liberty as the Papists, who were permitted to have their Assemblys and meetings without any contradiction or gainsaying."[24] Royalists agreed with the government's right and duty to persecute dissenters as long as they regarded them as a political threat, but they were most uncomfortable with the lenient treatment of Catholics who they also regarded as a political threat. Once the royalists no longer saw Protestant dissenters as politically dangerous, they were unwilling to permit persecution to continue. Instead they focused their attention entirely upon the Catholic menace.

On the score of standing armies, Charles caused his subjects further anxiety. Just when the republican army was finally disbanded, he created his regiments of "guards." And, as the public feared, these became the core of the first permanent peacetime army in England. Worse, Charles seemed to take advantage of every excuse to expand their numbers, which rose from three regiments at the beginning of 1661 to 8700 men at the accession of James in 1685. Insignificant as Charles's military establishment now appears, the royal guards were, as one member of Parliament put it, "too many to make the people love him, and too few to protect him."[25]

Every unprecedented use of the guards caused public alarm. In 1664

Pepys noted that the King had ordered the hall where a royal ball was to be held guarded by his Horse Guards, "whereas heretofore they were by the Lord Chamberlain or Stewart and their people."[26] "It is feared," Pepys added, "they will reduce all to soldiery, and all other places taken away; and what is worst of all, that he will alter the present militia, and bring all to a flying army." Indeed, the public was so convinced that the King meant to enlarge his army that when Charles declared war on the Dutch in 1665 many people concluded that "the war was made rather for the army, than the army for the war."[27] Nor did the boisterous and arrogant behaviour of the royal guards help matters.[28]

The third and final solvent eroding the good relations between the King and his subjects was taxation. The Crown's legitimate debts, the costs of refurbishing the royal estates and disbanding the republican army, militia costs, and the excise tax to offset wardship revenues all necessitated heavy new taxes.

Parliament was generous at first, but by 1663 the King chided its members: "There hath not appeared that Warmth in you of late, in the Consideration of My Revenue, as I expected."[29] Members reflected the general anger at the costs of the royal government. By 1663 Clarendon found that grumbling in the countryside had reached the point "where the people began to talk with more license and less reverence of the court and the King himself, and to reproach the Parliament for their raising so much money, and increasing of the impositions upon the kingdom, without having done anything for the redress of any grievance that lay upon the people."[30] The following year Clarendon reported that people "expressed their discontents upon the great taxes and impositions which they were compelled to pay and publicly reproached the parliament" for agreeing to taxes in light of "the general want of money" and the "great decay of trade."[31] The economic distress soon reached the manor house with a "sudden fall of rents throughout [the] kingdom, as had never been known before."[32]

Complaints of both the excessive costs of the government and the economic distress of the countryside persisted year after year. In 1667 Pepys commented on the astounding increase in the King's privy purse, which "true English gentlemen do decry," for whereas Charles's grandfather, James I, had spent not over £5,000 per year, the King's father not over £10,000, Charles II spent more than £100,000 in addition to the support of the Duke of York, who had £100,000, and "other limbs of the Royal family, and the guards."[33] In a speech to Parliament on a subsidy bill in 1671, Lord Lucas surveyed the economic results of a decade of Charles's governance with dismay: "There were great expectations at the Restoration of freedom from the heavy burdens of usurpation . . . but now the burdens are increased, and the means of meeting them lessened, there being so little money in the country . . . A few men are growing rich and flourishing, whilst many of those who were imprisoned and sequestered [during the Commonwealth] are left without reward. The pretence of enabling the King to defend the country is not sufficient for so large grants."[34] Lucas was charged with libel for his outspoken criticism but there was a general view that the House of Commons had "met these several years for nothing but to give money."[35]

These grievances led to what Clarendon saw as a "revolution" in the affections of the people. Perhaps because he was part of the regime and would become a victim of the discontent, he exonerated the Crown and ascribed the change in attitude to the perversity of human nature.

> It cannot therefore but be concluded by the standers-by, and the spectators of this wonderful change and exclamation of all degrees of men, that there must be some wonderful miscarriages in the state, of some unheard of defect of understanding in those who were trusted by the king in the administration of his affairs; that there could in so short a time be a new revolution in the general affections of the people, that they grew even weary of that happiness they were possessed of and had so much valued, and fell into the same discontents and murmuring which had naturally accompanied them in the worst times.[36]

Between 1665 and 1667 a cluster of disasters of biblical proportions heightened disenchantment with the royal regime and sharpened anxiety over its use of military power. In response the aristocracy moved to bolster their constitutional, political, and social defences against the Crown. The first of the biblical horsemen to rear its head was War. In 1665 Charles declared war against Holland, Britain's chief trading rival. Although war normally caused subjects to rally round their king, what popular support existed for the Second Dutch War evaporated once the conflict began to take a heavy toll in lives and funds. The deplorable ineffectiveness of the royal administration, which the war exposed, took an even heavier toll on public confidence in the Court.

The war began with a victory for the English fleet, but in June 1666 in a return engagement against the Dutch it suffered grievous losses, with 20 English ships destroyed or taken, 2 admirals killed, another captured, and some 8000 sailors killed, wounded, or captured.[37] Worse was to follow. In 1667, with complaints against the war increasing—"none knowing," as Evelyn explained, "for what reason we first ingagd in this ungratefull warr"—Charles opened peace talks.[38] Under the mistaken assumption that peace would shortly follow, he ordered the ships dismantled and their crews sent home. The Dutch seized the opportunity to send their fleet up the Thames to surprise the English ships in their home port at Chatham. There they sunk vessel after vessel until they ran out of fireships, then departed with the English flagship, *Royal Charles,* in tow. In his study of Charles II's reign, David Ogg summed up the effect of this stunning exploit: "English loss of life was not heavy, but of ships and prestige incalculable. Our fleet had been found in a state of almost complete defencelessness; our blockhouses wanted guns, platforms, and ammunition; some of them had bullets too large for their cannon, and a lurid light had revealed embezzlement and mismanagement in our greatest naval dockyard. But for the defence hastily organized by Albermarle [George Monck] and ably seconded by train bands, volunteers and a few seamen, the English navy might well have been completely destroyed."[39]

To the dismay caused by military humiliation and government mismanagement were added domestic catastrophes. In 1665 the second horseman, Pestilence, arrived. In May, 43 Englishmen died of plague, in June nearly 600, and in September more than 30,000.[40] A year later, in September 1666, as the plague beat a reluctant retreat fresh disaster struck. A fire began in some materials stored in Pudding Lane in London, water supplies were low, the wind brisk, and entire streets of the capital were soon in flames. The population miraculously escaped, but before the fire burned itself out most of the city lay in ashes. No wonder the mood was gloomy. Evelyn recalled 1666 as "a yeare of nothing but prodigies in this Nation: Plague, War, fire, raines, Tempest and Comets."[41] He considered "the late dreadfull conflagration, added to the plague and warr, the most dismall judgments that could be inflicted," which, he added, "we highly deserved for our prodigious ingratitute, burning lusts, dissolute Court, profane and abominable lives."[42] As 1667 dawned, Pepys surveyed the nation's prospects and found "a sad, vicious, negligent Court, and all sober men there fearful of the ruin of the whole kingdom this next year: from which good God, deliver us!"[43]

Popular and parliamentary rage focused, among other issues, on the government's use and misuse of the militia and its funds. The militia's effectiveness as a police and military force had been tested during the war. Its main police function had been to disarm Protestant dissenters and Catholics, the former for fear they would make common cause with the Dutch, the latter after the Great Fire, which many regarded as part of a Catholic plot. The militia's chief military task had been to protect the realm from invasion. Regiments that were amateurish when first mobilized quickly became more expert with continual duty. The militia dealt successfully with small-scale raids and helped deter a major Dutch invasion. Nevertheless, in his study of that force, Western argues, "It became painfully obvious that the rather small job" the militia had been given "was the largest which it was capable of doing."[44] Whether the militia's task was small is debatable, but it was clearly difficult to keep a large militia force on active duty for long. By the spring of 1666, therefore, the Crown had decided to establish a "select militia," a smaller force that could be kept on foot for extended periods during an emergency and recalled when needed. The experiment began in June 1666 with orders for the creation of 3 regiments of horse—some 1500 men— followed almost immediately by orders for creation of an infantry regiment and 17 independent cavalry troops.[45] These soldiers served until September and were recalled when Chatham was attacked in June 1667. Additional men were recruited until the "select militia" numbered 12,000 foot and 3200 horse.[46] They were paid out of regular militia funds. This caused problems because although the government had gotten a large percentage of militia monies, most of it had been diverted to other purposes, and there were serious shortages by 1667.[47]

Both the idea of a "select militia" or "standing militia" and the "embezzlement" of militia funds angered the Commons. Western suggests that the new-modelled militia was resented because some officers of the old parliamentary army had been invited to participate in it.[48] There is reason to believe that many of the soldiers came from the King's independent troops, for, as Western notes, "apparently they already existed as cadres" and commissions to raise them preceded the official order.[49] When the select militia was not on active duty the units continued to exist as cadres. Charles may have hoped to substitute his volunteer regiments for the regular militia and to fund them with monies allocated for it. The resentment against this select militia may have been the jealousy of all standing military forces, as well as fears that it was meant to supplant the regular county militia.

Oddly, at the same time Englishmen were infuriated by the Court's inadequate military preparations, their nightmares of absolute kings governing by standing armies, never far beneath the surface, came up repeatedly in the months that followed. The attack on the King's old chancellor, Edward Hyde, Earl of Clarendon, whose power, defence of the prerogative, and old-fashioned morality had earned him many enemies, is a case in point. The first and most serious charge in the articles of impeachment against Clarendon accused him of having counseled the King "to dissolve this Parliament and to raise a standing army, to pay them with free quarter and contribution and to think no more of future Parliaments, but to govern in an arbitrary way by an army."[50] It was ironic that this accusation, which Clarendon labelled "the most unpopular and ungracious Reproach that any man could lie under," should have been laid at his door, for when the King decided to raise his first troops of guards after Venner's rebellion, Clarendon had been one of only two councillors to advise against it.[51] He was removed from office in June and fled to the Continent in November, leaving behind a petition to the House of Lords protesting his innocence.

The full force of popular fury now fell upon the Crown, with parliamentary investigations into military expenditure and the gross mismanagement that had led to national humiliation. There was a general belief, as Sergeant Maynard put it, that the English had "not been beaten by power and force, but by cheating and cozening."[52] Parliament ignored the fact that its insistence on all troops being quickly disbanded had played a part in Charles's decision to dismantle his navy before a peace agreement had been signed. On the contrary, distrust of the King was such that even after the shortage of troops helped produce a debacle, there was tremendous pressure not to bolster but to abolish the army! Englishmen were more fearful of their own king than of any external threat. When Charles tried to placate public anger by placing twelve newly recruited regiments under the supervision of proven commanders such as Manchester and Fairfax, he only excited fears that he meant to govern by an army. Sir Thomas Tomkins told the Speaker of the House that, since "the country for which he served had a fear of a standing army," the King should be petitioned to dissolve his new forces. This was in July, barely a month after the Dutch destruction of the English fleet. The motion was seconded by Mr. Garroway, although he "thought it not convenient" to move the King to disband the troops before peace had been concluded. With this modification the House voted unanimously to ask the King to disband the army.[53]

By the end of July a peace treaty had been concluded. But fears that Charles would employ any excuse to govern by an army surfaced in parliamentary debates on all sorts of subjects. In December 1667 a general naturalization act was opposed on the ground that "it would draw on the pretence of a standing army to keep so many strangers quiet," and in March of 1668 the same argument was used against religious toleration: "that where toleration was granted point of religion it was necessary that a standing army be established to keep the several opinions in order."[54]

The war had provided a pretext for ordering the disarmament and arrest of suspicious persons within the realm. At Parliament's insistence Catholics, who were seldom defined as "suspicious" by the Crown, were included.[55] Nevertheless, war did not deter Parliament from protecting the access of honest citizens to arms and ammunition. In 1666 the Court introduced a bill into Parliament which alleged that gunpowder had become scarce because it had been "embezzled and transported beyond the seas." The new act intended that "every man that had any gunpowder to sell . . . bring it to the officers of the King's Ordinance and Arms, and that no man should sell any but by a licence first had from them."[56] Members of Parliament generally disliked the bill and were not reassured by the Crown's claim that this new restraint "was not proposed to be general or perpetual, but only when there was a war either at land or sea." They put the bill aside "until there was some better expedient found out to prevent the embezzling and purloining [of] the powder."

Parliament was just as protective of civilian entitlement to arms when it was contending with internal lawlessness. A veritable epidemic of highway robbery made it necessary to devise some means to ensure the safety of travellers.[57] A list of suggestions was drawn up, one of which was "that none ride with firearms." A committee was selected to consider the suggestions and draft a bill. When the bill was reported, the suggested ban on riding armed had been dropped, although members had been assured that no soldier would be permitted to travel with firearms.

From 1667 until April 1671 customary civilian entitlement to weapons remained unchanged. Then quite suddenly, in the spring of 1671, Parliament enacted a game law that altered the hunting restrictions and in so doing deprived the great majority of the community of all legal right to have firearms. It is difficult to wrest from surviving records an explanation for this change of policy. Careful investigation has failed to turn up either personal or official explanations other than the preamble of the act itself. The measure moved swiftly through both houses of Parliament with little dissent. The immediate context, viewed against increasing political tensions, offers some insight. The powers within the new law must provide the rest.

The years immediately preceding that in which the Game Act was passed gave no hint of what was to come. Indeed, there was a strange calm in 1668 and 1669, as if the nation was exhausted after the traumatic years of the Second Dutch War. In February 1669/70 Charles felt sufficiently confident of his popularity to open a new session of Parliament accompanied by his guards, "which," a contemporary remarked, "is the first instance we meet with in history, of the sovereign's entering upon the exercise of his legislative power, under the awe and influence of the sword."[58] A month later Andrew Marvell wrote, "It is . . . my Opinion that the King was never since his coming in, nay, all Things considered, no King since the Conquest, so absolutely powerful at Home, as he is at present."[59] Charles even decided to attend several meetings of the House of Lords, a move which, Marvell commented, was "so disused that at any other, but so bewitched a Time, as this, it would have been looked on as an high Usurpation, and Breach of Privilege."[60] The King's unusual presence at their deliberations had the desired effect on the Lords, for they actually attached a proviso to a bill for suppression of "subversive" religious gatherings, to the effect that nothing in the bill was to infringe upon the King's supremacy in ecclesiastical affairs "or to destroy any of his Majesty's rights, powers, or prerogatives belonging to the imperial crown of this realm, or any time exercised or enjoyed by himself or any of his royal predecessors, Kings or Queens of England since the Conquest."[61] This would have restored all the Crown's civil as well as religious powers. "There was never so compendious a piece of absolute universal Tyranny," Marvell fumed, and an equally astounded Thomas Clifford pointed out, "This Proviso is a giving away all that has ever been given us."[62] The House of Commons sensibly removed the phrase "at any time enjoyed," and the proviso was withdrawn.

The Conventicle Act was passed in March, the last such act against Protestant dissenters. It seemed more concerned with potential insurrection than religious conformity. Its stated aim was to prevent "dangerous practices of seditious sectaries and other disloyal persons who under pretence of tender consciences have or may at their meetings contrive insurrections." There had been bitter debate over its provisions to permit justices of the peace and constables to break open doors of any building where they were informed a conventicle was or would be held, and for trial of offenders by a single justice, "disinheriting the subjects . . . from their birthright as to trials by twelve men their peers, and convicting them of offences for greater penalties, by certificate of one person who may be unskilled and illiterate, and possibly in such an opportunity partial also."[63] One tract argued that, since this provision was "directly against our fundamental laws," the people had an obligation to disobey it "and to give obedience to Magna Charta."[64]

There was widespread resistance to the Conventicle Act. Most militiamen had little wish to arrest and harass those at peaceful Protestant prayer meetings, although at the Crown's urging force was sometimes used. There were ugly incidents in London, however, where the city militia harassed persons at conventicles, "wounded many, and killed some Quakers, especially while they took all patiently."[65] When Protestant offenders were brought before them, jurors refused to convict. In a famous case that autumn, the Quaker William Penn and a colleague were tried for holding an outdoor prayer meeting in London contrary to the law. When the jury stoutly refused to convict them, the enraged judge kept jurors without meat or drink for three days, "til almost starved." When they still refused to alter their verdict, they were fined and imprisoned.[66] The sense that the law was misdirected—that Catholics, not Quakers, were the real menace—grew, and with it impatience at the Court's failure to enforce anti-Catholic statutes.

There would have been far greater anxiety over the King's attitude toward Catholics if Englishmen knew of his brother's conversion or of the secret treaty Charles had signed in May in which he promised the French king he would convert England to Catholicism in return for a pension of £200,000 a year. This income would enable Charles to raise troops without consulting his parliamentary paymasters.[67] In June the King issued a proclamation banishing former soldiers from London and forbidding them to ride with weapons for six months. This was probably intended to perpetuate the notion that the former republicans, not the Catholics, were a danger, and to quiet anxieties about the army.

The inability of the government to enforce the Conventicle Act reflected a significant shift in public opinion and was symptomatic of the tension that existed within the community. Another symptom of this tension, and one of greater significance for the history of the right to bear arms, was an outbreak of rural violence brought on by economic distress and the increased pace of enclosure. Night after night the cattle and horses of wealthy landowners were slaughtered, their trees cut down, and grain stacks, houses, and barns set ablaze. Unfortunately, as with so much else that occurred in rural areas, little is now known about this widespread campaign of violence and mayhem. It first drew the attention of Parliament early in 1670. The assembly dealt with the problem by passing "An Act to prevent the malitious burning of Houses, Stackes of Corne and Hay and killing or maiming of Catle," a statute unique in the nearly three decades from the Restoration to the Revolution of 1688, for it made the commission of these rural crimes a felony.[68]

Despite these signs of discontent public affairs remained calm until an incident in late December 1670 brought all the popular distrust of the monarchy to the surface. The Crown had pressed for more revenues, and in its search for a new source of funds Parliament had appointed a committee to consider taxing patrons of playhouses. The King was very fond of the theater and his courtiers appeared before the committee to argue against the tax on the ground that "the Players were the King's servants, and a part of his pleasure."[69] One member of the committee, Sir John Coventry, replied by asking if "the King's pleasure lay among the men or women Players." Word of this quip promptly reached the Court, and that night, December 21, twenty-five royal guards ambushed

Coventry on his way home and brutally slit his nose. Although Parliament had already recessed for Christmas, news of the attack on Coventry travelled swiftly throughout the kingdom and excited tremendous outrage.

When the MPs returned to London in January, Coventry's colleagues gave vent to their anger. One branded the assault a "horrid un-English act" and "a greater thing than he has ever seen here . . . It concerns the person, justice, and honour of the King, Council, and House of Commons."[70] "This wounds all the Commons of England," Sir Robert Holt argued, and Sir John Monson informed the House that he had never seen a greater concern in the country for such an offence: "They fear we shall come under the government of France, to be governed by an army."[71] The Venetian ambassador in London judged the matter "inflammable, especially as it was a question of defending the liberty of the subject and restraining the king from punishing by his own authority those who use foul language in Parliament."[72]

Members of Parliament refused to consider any other business until they had determined how to deal with Coventry's attackers and prevent such crimes in the future. A bill "to prevent malicious Maiming and Wounding" was drawn up and approved.[73] Coventry's attackers were banished, and the King was explicitly prohibited from pardoning them. The matter seemed settled, but something had snapped. All the resentment over the King's prodigal and immoral court, his continued tolerance of Catholics, his boisterous and numerous guards overflowed. In February, in Charles's presence Lord Lucas uttered his scathing speech against the subsidy bill, decrying the collapse of those high expectations entertained at the time of the King's restoration and deploring the sad state of the kingdom. That same month Parliament drew up a formal complaint about the danger of the growth of "popery." They pointed to the Catholic books and trinkets openly sold in London, the Catholic chapels and schools that operated in all large towns with only a token effort at concealment, Catholics in the royal administration, and the Jesuit college at Combe in Herefordshire. Rumours that the Court was considering proposals for liberty of worship may have made the need to suppress Catholicism seem all the more urgent.[74] In March, as if to corroborate these allegations and fears, the Duchess of York, ailing wife of the heir to the throne, sent on her deathbed for a Catholic priest—public admission of her conversion to her husband's faith. Less than a week later, the Court provoked more public furor and caused a tumult on Fleet Street when it foolishly tried to quarter some soldiers on the people of London, a situation which, a resident protested, "we in the City will not permitt."

It "was timely prevented by the prudence of the Lord Mayor," and the government backed down.[75]

In the midst of this anger at the Crown over the outrageous use of the royal guards, the wanton behaviour of the Court, demands for yet higher taxation, and its unwillingness to stop the growth of Catholicism, a measure was introduced in the House of Commons for the preservation of game and alteration of the qualification needed to hunt. "A Bill to prevent the Destruction of Coneys [rabbits], and other Game" was first read on March 14 and given a second reading the next morning. It was then sent to committee for consideration and amendment. The committee appointed to deal with the bill had 46 named members in addition to all the members from seven counties, for a total of some 184 men. This group acted quickly and a week later brought the bill back before the Commons with several amendments and a clause added for the protection of fish.[76] When questions arose about distress of the goods of offenders and provision for appeal, the bill was returned to committee. On April 4 a final draft was approved by the House of Commons and the measure was sent the same day to the Lords. A fortnight later it returned from the Lords with several amendments, which were read and approved. With the King's assent, the Game Act of 1671, "An Act for the better Preservation of the Game, and for Securing Warrens not Inclosed, and the several Fishings of this Realm," became law.

It had taken slightly longer than a month to pass both houses—certainly an easy passage. In light of the great rush of business on what seem more important bills, the attention bestowed upon this measure is remarkable. When Parliament recessed on May 2, six "considerable bills"—for foreign excise, against conventicles, against papists, for "better observation" of the Lord's Day, to prohibit export of wool, and a general pardon—had not been completed and were lost. Yet precious time had been devoted to the creation of a game act when there were already numerous game acts on the statute books. Although the unanimity of members and the consequent absence of recorded debate make it especially hard to understand their thinking, members obviously regarded the new game act as a vital measure.

A careful reading of the Game Act of 1671 makes it clear that this was not a typical game statute. By way of preamble, it claimed: "Divers Disorderly persons, laying aside their Lawfull Trades and Imployments, do betake themselves to the Stealing, Taking, and Killing of Conies, Hares, Phesants, Partriges, and other Game, intended to be

· 69 ·

Preserved by former Laws, with Guns, Doggs, Tramels, Lowbels, hayes, and other Nets, Snares, hare-pipes, and other Engines, to the great Damage of this Realm, and prejudice of Noblemen, Gentlemen, and Lords of Manors, and others, Owners of Warrens."[77]

This opening was not unusual. A typical game act passed in 1661, "An Act to Prevent the Unlawful Coursing, Hunting, or Killing of deer," had also complained of "many idle, loose, and disorderly persons."[78] A section of the new act extended protection to rabbits in warrens that were not enclosed—often the village common—while another section protected fish in private ponds, pools, and "other several waters."

The act of 1671 then proceeded to create a new structure of law enforcement. All "lords of manors or other royalties not under degree of an esquire" were empowered "by writing under their hands and seals" to appoint one or more gamekeepers to enforce the Game Act on their own estates. Hitherto only the King had created gamekeepers, and it was the responsibility of JPs, constables, and town officials to enforce the game acts on private property. One study of the Stuart game laws has suggested that Charles II was annoyed at the expense of paying gamekeepers and was therefore pleased to see the responsibility shared.[79] But, since local justices, constables, and officials already had responsibility for enforcing the game acts, this duty was already shared. This new class of gentry-appointed officials placed the task of game preservation directly in the hands of the gentry, and could be seen as extending their own power over the sport. It gave them a "kind of private game police."[80]

The act specified the duties of these new gamekeepers. "They may take and seize all such Guns, Bowes, Greyhounds, Setting-doggs, Lurchers, or other Doggs to kill hares . . . ferrets, Tramels . . . Snares, or other Engines, for the taking and killing of Conies . . . or other Game, as within the Precincts of such respective Manors, shall be used by any person or persons, *who by this act are Prohibited to keep or use the same.*"[81] In earlier acts all devices *used* in the act of poaching could be seized, while others designed exclusively for hunting were illegal *per se.* Now all these were illegal *per se.*

The gamekeeper "or any other person or persons, authorized by a warrant from a justice of the peace," could "in the day-time Search the houses, Outhouses, or other places" of any such person or persons the act prohibited from keeping or using these devices. Of course there had to be good ground to suspect that such unqualified persons had or kept in their custody "any Guns, Bowes, Greyhounds," and so forth. Any prohibited equipment discovered during such a search could be kept by the lord of the manor where they were found or "cut in pieces" and destroyed "as things by this Act Prohibited to be kept by persons of their degree."

Prior legislation authorized any constable or "headborough" of a county, city, or town armed with a warrant signed by two justices of the peace to enter and search the premises of suspects. The new act permitted a single gamekeeper or, indeed, "any other person or persons" authorized by a warrant from a single justice of the peace—who might be the property owner himself—to search the home and property of a suspect.

Next came the crucial definition of who qualified to hunt, as well as a list of prohibited weapons and other devices. The entire paragraph was in the negative. According to the new law, "all and every person and persons, not having lands and Tenements or some other Estate of Inheritance, in his own or his Wife's right, of the clear yearly value of One hundred pounds per Annum," or long-term leases of a clear yearly value of £150, other than the heir of an Esquire "or other person of higher degree," were declared "to be persons by the Laws of this Realm, not allowed to have or keep for themselves, or any other person or persons, any Guns, Bowes, Greyhounds, Setting-doggs, ferrets . . . or other Engines aforesaid; But shall be, and are hereby Prohibited to have, keep, or use the same."

This was a break with the past in two respects. The Game Act of 1609, in effect until this act, had required a would-be hunter to have income from land of at least £40 a year, or a life estate of £80, or personal property worth £400. That basic requirement had now increased from £40 to £100 income from land, from £80 to £150 in leases on land, and the category of those who had insufficient income from land but at least £400 in personal property had been abolished. Wealthy merchants, prosperous lawyers, and others who had a goodly amount of personal wealth but insufficient income from land were instantly deprived of their right to hunt and grouped together with those defined in the law as "idle and disorderly." Not only had the category of those qualified to hunt been made narrower than at any time in the past, but, as the great jurist William Blackstone later pointed out, the property qualification needed to hunt was now fifty times the amount needed to permit a man to vote.[82]

It has been argued that sixty years of inflation necessitated this adjustment in order to keep hunting as exclusive as the earlier act had intended. There had certainly been inflation in the course of six decades, and with it, an increase in the number of those permitted to hunt. Now, however, all those whose incomes from land had crept up to the £40 mark were deprived of what they had come to expect as their right; and the new minimum had been lifted to a height they were unlikely to reach. The new act instantly deprived all those with landed income of from £40 to £99 of the right to hunt. These greatly increased minimum incomes must have been especially galling if, as Lord Lucas and others complained, many in the countryside had not prospered in the years prior to the act. The immediate result was that less than 1 percent of those living on the land were entitled to hunt game, even on their own property. Well-to-do yeomen were lumped with their day labourers and wealthy merchants as men unfit to engage in the sport.

The second departure from previous game acts, the list of prohibited "engines," was even more startling and extended the act from the domain of game conservation into that of arms control and public disarmament. The earliest game law to set a property qualification had prohibited laymen who had less than 40s. a year from keeping "any greyhound, hound, nor other dog to hunt" and forbade them from using "ferrets, nets . . . and other engines" for taking game. Only hunting dogs were prohibited *per se*.[83] A similar distinction between things illegal *per se* and those that were legal but were not to be used for hunting was made in game acts passed during the reign of James I.[84] The first of these, passed in 1604, stated that unqualified persons could not keep hunting dogs "or net or nets" to take game birds. This list was expanded the following year to prohibit unqualified persons from keeping "any buck-stalls or engine-hayes, gate-nets, purse-nets, ferrets or coney-dogs." These were devices and animals specifically designed for hunting. Guns, bows, and crossbows as devices having other, legitimate purposes, however, however, were not prohibited *per se*. This basic distinction, in effect when the Game Act of 1671 was drafted, was intended to permit the general population to have and keep guns, bows, pikes, and other weapons necessary for their self-defence, their police duties, and for the militia. The Game Act of 1671 made it no longer necessary to prove that guns and bows had been illegally used; it simply included them in the list of prohibited devices, thus depriving nearly the entire population of a legal right to own them.

There can be no doubt that this change was intentional. The authors of the act repeat the prohibition three times; first empowering the new gamekeepers to "take and seize" all guns, bows, greyhounds, and so on "within the precincts" of their employer's property; second, authorizing gamekeepers to search the houses, barns, "or other places" of any person "by this Act Prohibited to keep or use the same" if they had grounds to suspect that the person in question had or kept "any Guns, Bowes, Greyhounds, etc."; finally, they state unequivocally in the passage cited above that all persons unqualified to hunt are declared persons "not allowed to have or keep, for themselves or any other person or persons, any Guns, Bowes, Greyhounds, etc." None of the earlier statues had language to the effect that unqualified persons may not keep prohibited devices "for themselves or any other person or persons."

Anyone accused of violating the new game act could be tried before a single justice of the peace on the evidence of a single witness. This was not a novelty, but it was less favourable to defendants than most earlier laws. The acts of James I had required "the testimony of two sufficient witnesses upon oath before two or more justices of the peace." This had been the rule until 1651, when the republican regime attempted to stem the slaughter of deer by permitting conviction on the evidence of only one witness before a single justice. The only game act passed in the reign of Charles II prior to 1671, also to halt the slaughter of deer, copied the requirement of 1651 of only a single witness and a single justice to convict. Although both these acts can be viewed as emergency measures, the Game Act of 1671 was far broader in intent and was meant to set up a new and permanent structure. It thus froze the emergency standard and permitted the accused to be convicted on the word of one witness, usually the gamekeeper, before one justice, often the owner of the park in which the poaching or keeping of prohibited devices supposedly oc-curred. The new act afforded those convicted the possibility of an appeal to the justices of the peace at Quarter Sessions.

In contrast to the radical departures the Game Act made in other areas, it is almost casual about the punishment to be meted out to offenders. The "engines," weapons, and dogs belonging to unqualified persons could be confiscated or destroyed, but beyond this punishment the act was relatively lenient. The offender had to "give the party or parties injured such recompence or satisfaction for his or their damages . . . as shall be appointed by the Justice before whom such Offender shall be convicted," and he had to pay the overseers for the poor "such sum of Money, not exceeding Ten shillings, as the said Justice shall think meet." If the offender couldn't or wouldn't pay these fines, he could be com-mitted to a House of Correction for a period not to exceed one month. For the more serious offence of poaching at night, the offender had to pay treble damages to the owner and "suffer imprisonment by the space of three moneths." The game acts passed during the reign of James I had been more severe and required the culprit to pay treble damages for a daytime offence or go to prison for three months. The new act left much to the discretion of the individual justice and put more emphasis on confiscating the weapons of tenants on country estates than on locking up poachers.

On May 2 Parliament recessed and members left for their homes. With all the exciting events of that session, the Game Act attracted little public attention. Yet it set the standard for game regulation for the next 160 years and circumscribed arms ownership more than ever before or since. The absence of contemporary debate is probably one reason it has been frequently overlooked by political historians, although social and constitutional scholars have little doubt of its significance.[85] "Nothing marked more clearly the growing power of the squirarchy in the House of Commons and in the State," Trevelyan judged, "than the Game Laws of the Restoration period."[86] Despite singling out the Game Act's importance to the squirarchy's power, Trevelyan attributed it merely to "the excessive eagerness of the country gentlemen about the preservation of game." Christopher Hill noted ruefully, but without elaboration, that the "iniquitous game laws" of the Restoration "established new privileges and disarmed the lower classes."[87] Numerous other scholars and social critics have addressed themselves to the effects of this act, and with good reason, since it became "an instrument of terrible severity" and helped to advance that "tyranny of the squire over his village" that marked the eighteenth century.[88]

P. B. Munsche, in his important study of the game laws, struggles gamely to determine the motives for the enactment of the act of 1671 and concludes: "There is no direct evidence of the motives behind the Game Act, but it seems likely it was the desire of country gentlemen to redefine and enhance their own social position *vis-a-vis* the urban bourgeoisie, rather than to punish the activities of 'disorderly persons', which lay behind its enactment."[89] This certainly explains the reason for the exclusion from hunting of possessors of non-landed wealth. It does not explain why members of Parliament were so keen at that time on sharing in the King's game prerogative, and it fails to address the sweeping ban on firearms. Yet it was this prohibition alone that was removed by the Declaration of Rights in 1689, precisely because it was a more serious threat to the political, social, and constitutional structure of the realm than stringent hunting regulations.

Why was this game act with its host of unusual articles enacted? Was it, as its authors claimed, simply intended to preserve game and to prevent the idle poor from hunting? Was it merely a means to enhance the prestige of the country aristocracy at the expense of the urban rich? There are several persuasive arguments against the stated claim that the act was meant to protect game from the poor. First, there were already sufficient game statutes to preserve wildlife. If necessary, these might have been more strictly enforced or a new law on the old pattern might have been passed to emphasize the determination of a new generation to enforce the old regulations. If the intention was to narrow the category of persons allowed to hunt, that might have been accomplished without either introducing gamekeepers or prohibiting the ownership of guns. It is the prohibition of guns (bows were no longer commonly employed for hunting or self-defence by the late seventeenth century) and the creation of gamekeepers with rights of search and seizure that need to be accounted for.

Had guns become so common an instrument for poaching and led to such destruction of game that an outright ban on them was justified? It is true, as Trevelyan noted, that anxieties over preservation of game increased with the use of the "shot-gun" in the sixteenth century.[90] But, in fact, guns were seldom used in poaching. They were far too loud. Moreover, seventeenth-century firearms were awkward to carry and difficult to hide if one was discovered tramping through a game preserve. Most poachers preferred snares and nets, which killed quietly and could be left in place to be checked at some convenient time. Although the disarmament of the bulk of the population and the creation of gamekeepers might have been useful for the preservation of game, it was certainly not necessary.

Later criticism of the Game Act has focused on the great power it gave the gentry to disarm their tenants and neighbours; indeed, this seems the most likely intention for all its clauses. In light of the spate of rural violence before its enactment and the determination of the gentry to press ahead with enclosure schemes that would increase resentment against them, an act which permitted them to disarm their tenants must have been appealing. The use of an act for the preservation of game was a customary means to curb lower-class violence.

Gamekeepers gave the gentry the means to police their tenants and neighbours and to search homes and disarm their inhabitants whenever they pleased. Since suspects were tried before a single justice, and that justice did not have to record the incident, the gentry's leverage over these same neighbours increased enormously. Much later criticism of the Game Act viewed it as class legislation.

Since the act gave the gentry direct control over hunting and made them less dependent on the Crown to enforce game laws, some scholars have argued that it made the exercise of the royal game prerogative less necessary, while others contend it was "an act for the Protection and encouragement of the interests of a rising gentry and not directed towards a transference of power from the Crown to subject."[91]

Although all these comments are an indication of the significance of the new law, they miss an extremely important potential of the act. Not only did the new powers give the gentry tighter control over the preservation of game and over their neighbours but they served to assuage their fears about the King's military power and favoritism toward Catholics, by giving them more control over arms.[92] Gentry with Catholic tenants could disarm them when the Crown failed to do so. Indeed, even if the Crown actually released Catholics from the penal acts, as it did a year later with the Declaration of Indulgence, the Game Act offered the means for disarming Catholics on the basis of their income rather than their religion. Moreover, to the extent that the royal militia displeased the gentry and became, in their estimation, a tool for suppression, even members of that force could be disarmed. The act greatly tightened the aristocracy's control over the distribution of weapons in the localities. It also gave them a privilege that wealthy members of the urban aristocracy could not share, however great their income from commerce.

Acting in what they saw as their class interest, the gentlemen sitting in Parliament do not seem to have appreciated the enormity of their actions or the danger that this power to disarm might be used by the Crown. They went home well satisfied with their work. Some, such as Joseph Addison's Tory squire, may have considered this game act the "only good law passed since the revolution." Few acts affected daily life in the countryside as profoundly. It wounded the pride of the more than 90 percent of the population who were forbidden not only to kill a rabbit on their own land but to own a gun for their personal protection. The act effectively transferred nearly exclusive control of the power of the sword to the country gentry.

C H A P T E R   F I V E

Enforcement of Arms
Restrictions

HAD the policy of disarming Englishmen been successful? J. R. Western's examination of the 1680's convinced him that it had. He argues that by 1688 "not only had there been a great increase in the royal standing forces but the physical capacity of the civil population to take up arms, whether for or against the government, was steadily diminishing."[1] Indeed, he detects a "steady decline for a century or more in the number of arms kept and men proficient in their use," a trend halted only temporarily by the Civil War. Yet in 1688, after Charles II's arms restrictions and passage of the Game Act of 1671, the rumour that Catholics were about to massacre them sent Southwark Protestants scurrying for their firearms and kept many of them "in arms all night, shooting guns in all directions."[2]

Poring over early statutes and the powers they gave or took away we are apt to forget that our ancestors were no more likely to be law-abiding than we are. Because the tidy version of life the law prescribes is often at odds with a distinctly untidy reality, it is imperative to examine the enforcement of those statutes that curbed possession and use of firearms to assess not only actual use of weapons but the extent of determination and ability to enforce the game acts and other laws that limited common use of firearms. If the Southwark residents are at all typical, Englishmen were just as prone to reach for their firearms, and firearms were as readily available, at the beginning of the Restoration as at its close. Had the attempt to disarm the public failed? Had there been a serious effort to enforce the Game Act of 1671? Just what was the place of firearms in the daily lives of the people of this period?

In examining firearms restrictions I have focused upon those "suspicious" persons the royal programs were intended to disarm. Unfortunate as such individuals were, they constituted only a minority of the King's subjects, and public sentiment kept them from being as harshly treated as Charles would have liked. In the first months after the King's return, when his regime seemed in genuine peril, so-called suspicious persons were brusquely treated. But measures such as the general canvass for arms after the Venner uprising that sent armed soldiers ransacking hundreds of households in search of weapons provoked such widespread outrage that the government was forced to desist and to issue a public apology. As the people's skepticism grew about the actual danger Quakers posed to the regime, there was even less willingness to approve strong measures against them. The tradition that everyone was entitled to firearms for personal defence ensured that any confiscated weapons, with the exception of excessive stockpiles, were returned.

Despite the exhortations of the Privy Council, therefore, many militia officers in the countryside carried out their duties with moderation and reticence. In April 1661, three months after the Venner rebellion, eighteen barrels of gunpowder were discovered in the home of a prime suspect, a Quaker who had fought against the Crown during the Civil War. The powder was confiscated but three barrels were returned, and other arms and ammunition were left in the suspect's possession "for want of a warrant."[3] Respect for private property and orderly procedure took precedence, in this instance, over the willingness of militiamen to disarm a neighbour.

At the outbreak of the Second Dutch War in 1665 the danger of internal subversion was the pretext for once again disarming dissidents. This policy sent one Mr. Johnes to the door of a Mr. Walmesley, where he "demanded all the armes belonging to him."[4] Since Mr. Walmesley happened to be away at the time, no weapons were actually confiscated, "tho it is said there were found armes and ammunition that would have furnished 100 men." Parliament insisted that Catholics as well as Protestant dissenters be disarmed during the war. The King agreed to remove "all apprehensions from Our good Subiects" by disarming Catholics and suspected Catholics.[5] Nevertheless, in some districts Catholics were merely asked to submit a list of their weapons and required to promise that they would "hold them for the King's service."[6] Two years later the Cheshire grand jury was told that four justices of the peace in their sessions "may by warrant seize all armes and ammunition found in the possession of any Popish Recusant convict, except what they please to allow them for the defence of their persons and houses."[7] In fact, they were generally allowed a quantity of weapons no different from that of their neighbours.

This cautious approach to disarming his subjects did not mean that the King trusted ordinary Englishmen with firearms. Far from it. The royal government did not even trust the purged and reorganized militia, and it increasingly used regular soldiers to maintain internal order.[8] The Earl of Lindsey, lord lieutenant for Lincolnshire, claimed that, although the people of the county were "generally full of duty and affection to the King's service," arms raised for the militia "will not bee safe to leave in their possessions." He conceded, "It wilbee hard to take their armes from them without some satisfaction," and suggested that the government purchase all weapons brought into a public magazine.[9] Lindsey had touched upon the real reason for the government's failure to attempt to disarm substantial sectors of the population: the difficulty of taking the people's weapons from them. Charles's government was never sufficiently popular or secure to launch such a project. Furthermore, disarming people is a blatant sign of distrust, and it is always risky for a government to admit it considers its people unreliable. Thus, the royal program left many Englishmen gun in hand, and even "suspicious persons" with weapons a good deal of the time.

If the twentieth-century researcher, furnished with all the resources a statistically minded society can provide, cannot pin down the numbers of firearms in America today, chances of determining the numbers of guns available to Englishmen in the seventeenth century must be even more problematic. Still, there are means to obtain a fairly good picture of the use, abuse, and availability of firearms in that era. Court records then as now afford information about the sorts of people who owned and misused firearms and the attitudes of law enforcement officials and the public toward this misuse. One can also compare the cost of firearms with the wages of workers to ascertain whether a gun would have been within the average budget. And finally, one can survey the way law-abiding citizens used weapons and their perception of the numbers of guns in circulation. These strategies can supply insight into the place of firearms in that era and the extent to which the program of arms control interfered with the private possession of firearms.

Court cases provide a random sample of the use and abuse of weapons, just the tip of the iceberg to be sure, but a useful tip. Violations involving firearms for which Englishmen were most likely to be hauled before quarter sessions were poaching offences, reckless use of guns, and highway robbery. An amazing array of persons of humble occupation—labourers, wheelwrights, bricklayers, carpenters, weavers, blacksmiths, farmers, and servants of both sexes—appeared before the courts, charged with misusing firearms. Poaching cases constituted the most typical weapons violations, although only a fraction of these cases were recorded and only a small number of poachers used firearms. Of the thirty-four poaching cases that came before the Hertfordshire Quarter Sessions between 1658 and 1683, only three mentioned the use of a gun. Warwickshire's poachers, at least those who were caught, used more firearms; of seventy-one cases between 1631 and 1674, some twenty-six, or better than one in three, involved guns.[10] The culprits in poaching offences were nearly always persons of humble means.

An unusual number of cases of misuse of firearms involved illegal weapons *and* illegal ammunition. Hailshot, forbidden since 1549 to all but a few licenced persons, figured prominently in crimes against persons. Thus a yeoman from Nottinghamshire was charged with shooting a man in the foot with hailshot, and a farmer of that county was brought to court for "shooting hailshot in a gun" and assaulting a justice of the peace.[11] A Middlesex farm wife, accused of shooting one John Haley to death, claimed to have been trying to kill a jay bird when she struck Haley with a badly directed spray of shot.[12] She apparently found nothing unusual in her use of shot. Handguns were common in such cases as well. They had been restricted to persons with incomes of over £100 for more than a century when a poor farmer and his wife and daughter were charged with "riotously assaulting" one William Willson "with handguns and other unlawful weapons."[13]

Typically such offenders succeeded in violating several gun statutes simultaneously by employing illegal weapons, or illegal ammunition, or both, in an illegal manner. In 1664 a Hertfordshire carpenter and a yeoman were both charged with unlawfully shooting hares with handguns, breaking the game acts as well as the law against poorer persons owning handguns. That same year, a Warwickshire labourer violated three laws at once by "shooting in a handgun with hailshot and killing 2 pigeons therewith."[14] Had he killed the pigeons on a Sunday he would have been guilty of still another violation.

Reading between the lines, one notices a certain tolerance in these cases. A willingness to overlook minor peccadilloes is particularly clear in the case of Richard Balard. When he was finally brought to the court's attention, it was asserted that he "doth manie times use to shote in a piece upon doves in the County the which is contrary to Statute. Upon Sunday . . . the 17 December he did kill with his piece six pigines at one shot in a close of Mr. Nistover next to his house at Clerkenleap in the presence of John Hurdman and Roger Hall."[15] Only after Balard had hunted on the sabbath, killing six pigeons in another man's enclosure in the presence of two witnesses, was he at last brought to justice.

Until the Second Dutch War in 1665 there is a striking absence of cases where the sole violation was the mere possession of a handgun or the use of shot. During that war the number of such cases increased, doubtless because of fears that political or religious dissidents might take advantage of the foreign war to launch an insurrection. The great increase in the number of highway robberies at this time must also have prompted stricter enforcement of the law against the handgun, the preferred weapon of highwaymen. Even with this increase in enforcement of handgun statutes the number of such cases was insignificant compared with what appears to have been the substantial number of handguns in the possession of unqualified persons.

The scarcity of indictments for simple possession of handguns and the prevalence of cases in which several gun laws were violated simultaneously raise the suspicion that ownership of an illegal firearm was seldom challenged. Either justices saw little harm in the wide distribution of handguns and the common use of shot, or the restrictions were so generally ignored that enforcement was impossible. Either way the result was the same. During the years 1660 to 1677, when Sir Peter Leicester, a well-known Cheshire judge, reminded county grand juries of the crimes they were to take cognizance of, he included illegal hunting and riding armed "in terrorum Populi," but not once did he mention the illegal possession of a firearm.[16] In Nottinghamshire, complaints about "the great number of persons within the Wapentake of Newarke and Thurgarton Aleigh that keepe and shoote in Gunns contrary to the forme of divers Laws and Statutes" led in 1656 to the constables' being charged with neglecting their duties.[17] As for the act of 1549 banning the use of shot, the statute that repealed it 150 years later explained that "however useful" it may have been "in those days," the said act "hath not for many years last past been put in execution, but became useless and unnecessary."[18] In light of all this information, it would appear that if the ordinary person were moderately discreet, he could keep a handgun or use shot with little fear of arrest or confiscation of his weapon.

Some Englishmen were anything but discreet, however, and broke gun laws and other statutes with verve. The Restoration was the great age of the highwayman, and every member of this tribe carried at least one pistol as part of his regular equipment. The long, lonely roads, sparsely populated countryside, and lack of a professional police force made highway robbery an appealing if dangerous profession: the penalty for those caught was hanging. Robbers tended to lurk behind the hedges and trees that lined well-travelled routes and when a likely victim happened by, they dashed out and ordered him to "stand and deliver!" A pistol "clapped to the breast" usually convinced the traveller to relinquish his valuables. Highwaymen were often ostentatiously polite, leaving their victims their good wishes and a few shillings to finance their journey home. Victims could also take solace in the fact that the parish where the crime occurred was obliged to make good much of their loss.

The highwaymen of this era were drawn from the ranks of unemployed soldiers, sons of impoverished gentry, ne're-do-wells who had squandered their allowance gambling in London, and an assortment of other men and women willing to run the risk of execution for the chance of easy wealth preying on travellers. Oddly, unlike the profession of pickpocket from which some robbers had graduated, highway robbery had a veneer of glamour about it and won at least the sneaking admiration of many law-abiding citizens. Even the "sensible and prosaic" John Verney, in recounting the daring exploits of a pair of highwaymen, remarked at their capture, "T'is great pity such men should he hanged."[19] Victims often hesitated to turn robbers in, in part because they were reimbursed for their losses, and in part because the penalty for robbery was so extreme.[20] When a robber was hanged he was usually accompanied to the place of execution by thousands of persons cheering him and offering encouragement. In 1664 John Evelyn paid a shilling for a good spot from which to view such proceedings, the crowd of some 12,000 to 14,000 making it difficult to see.[21]

Sympathy for robbers wavered, however, when their numbers reached epidemic proportions during the Commonwealth period and into the 1660's. Legend has it that Thomas Fairfax's proclamation that his officers should apprehend robbers and the offer of rewards for their capture were taken as a challenge by the rogues. To demonstrate the highwaymen's scorn, a well-known robber, Captain Hind, and his men, who preyed upon the region near Barnet, supposedly committed some forty robberies in that area within two hours.[22]

The administration of Charles II had no greater success curbing robbers than had its predecessor, and Parliament's efforts to deal with the problem had little effect.[23] A Buckinghamshire proverb of the time claimed, "Here if you beat a bush, its odds you'd start a Thief."[24] Criminals became so brazen that in 1677 a thief actually stole the Chancellor's mace and would have stolen the Great Seal of England as well "had it not been under the chancellor's pillow."[25] In 1683, so the story goes, Judge Holt went to visit a friend in prison whom he had just sentenced. When the judge asked after their old college friends, he was informed: "Ah my lord they are all hanged now but myself and your Lordship."[26]

Legends about various highwaymen and women illustrate not only the invariable use of pistols but how easy it apparently was to acquire these weapons. Those who had been soldiers often deserted with their weapons, and others robbed while still in the army. *The Newgate Calendar* reports that Sawny Douglas, an unemployed Scottish soldier, decided to enter England after the Restoration and try his hand at robbery. Because he needed both "horse and accoutrements" he waited by the road until a servant came near, "well mounted, with pistols before him," and at the first opportunity gave him "an effectual knock on the pate, which, followed with four or five more, left him insensible on the ground, while our young adventurer rode off with the horse" and, of course, the pistols.[27] According to popular information, however, it was not necessary to steal handguns. Thomas Gray, nephew of the Exeter hangman, wrote that when he and a friend found themselves broke in London they decided to take up robbery. "We had not been in London above a week," he purportedly reminisced, "before we lost all our money, and almost all our senses; but recalling some of the latter we (by pawning part of our clothes) got each of us a brace of pistols, and took an airing toward Barnet."[28] Whatever the truth of the particular tale, apparently inexpensive pistols were believed to be available in the capital without regard to the legal qualifications of the buyer. It is possible, however, that law-abiding citizens found weapons more difficult to obtain.

The cost of firearms is of paramount importance in determining whether the public was actually able to afford them. Of course, had commoners not been able to afford firearms the government would not have been concerned about the widespread ownership of such weapons. And, in fact, the evidence indicates that the cost of firearms, particularly simple muskets and birding guns, was within the reach of all but the poorest members of the community. The gunmakers' rates set by a royal committee in 1631 listed a new musket at 15s.6d. and a pair of pistols at £2.0d. By 1658, when the republican government arranged to purchase weapons, the price had decreased to 11s.0d a musket.[29]

Had the government gotten a bargain? Since the Ordnance Office bought in bulk, it ought to have been able to purchase arms more cheaply than the average citizen, but governments seldom get bargains. When Samuel Pepys began buying for the navy during the reign of Charles II, he was appalled at the inflated prices and outright cheating that were commonplace among manufacturers dealing with the Crown. "It is impossible," he concluded, "for the King to have things done as cheap as other men."[30] The 11s. price for a musket seems reasonable, for in 1664, when the government considered reimbursing citizens who turned in serviceable muskets, a rate of 10s. was to be paid for each weapon.[31]

Was 11s. within the range of a typical income? In 1664, the year the government was offering 10s. per musket, a foot soldier was paid 18d. a day while on duty, a figure which would have permitted him to amass funds for a new musket in little more than a week. Although he could not be expected to devote his entire wage to such a purchase, he could certainly afford a firearm at this rate of pay. The wage for standing watch was 8d. a night, a sum that would require little more than a fortnight to accumulate funds for a musket. Descending the economic ladder, an agricultural day labourer earned 6d. a day during harvest and 3d. a day at other times. At the former rate it would take three weeks of work, at the lower rate six weeks, to afford a gun, probably making such a purchase unrealistic. We have, however, been referring to the purchase of a new firearm. Used weapons would have been much cheaper. For instance, a handgun stolen in 1628, at a time when a new pair of pistols cost about £2.0d., was valued at only 3s.[32] Outside the capital, weapons may have been priced more modestly. Local blacksmiths were able to manufacture gun and rifle barrels and stocks with their ordinary equipment and fit them with locks from gunshops.[33] Of course firearms did not always have to be bought since they were handed down in families, and during the Civil War they could be found among the debris of the battlefield. Legally or illegally, firearms were available to a large portion of the population.

It was fortunate that firearms were affordable, for seventeenth-century Englishmen lived in an age when these weapons were needed. The extensive operations of highwaymen made arms mandatory for a traveller. A study of travel in this period found that "to travel well-armed was an ordinary precaution. Weapons gave the traveller heart to set out on his journey, though when the test came . . . the sword might never be unsheathed and the pistol never cocked."[34] Although watchmen tried to protect the highways, a former highwayman explained why the traveller could expect little help from that quarter:

> When any one has lost his purse to thieves, there a Watch is placed at the country's cost. Thereupon travellers, thinking it impossible, being thus guarded, that they should lose their money, grow careless, and the thief can "doe his list, and freely passe, the watchmen nere the wiser; for they stand Setled at one place", and know nothing of what is passing beyond their station. Or, if they do happen to be present at an encounter, being "poore, silly, old, decrepped men, that are Fitting for nought else", they stand "Amaz'd affrighted", not daring to make a sound, until the robbing done and the birds flown, they set to crying "Thieves, thieves."[35]

To be fair the task of the local watch had become far more difficult because of the greater numbers of robbers and their use of firearms.

Wealthy travellers not only carried their own weapons but were accompanied by servants equipped with muskets and pistols. The Verneys wrote of a visit from a mysterious, but obviously important, gentleman "and 3 more servants in livery; all extreamly well Horsed, and armed with Pistolls, and Carbines."[36] Other travellers hired guards to protect them. Pepys noted in his diary that when he set out on a fine moonlit night to walk from Woolwich to Redriffe, he had "three or four armed [men] to guard me . . . I hear this walk is dangerous to walk alone by night, and much robbery committed here."[37] Pepys regarded it as a mark of his importance, "a joy to my heart," that "people should of themselfs provide this [guard] for me, unspoke to." Guns were also used to protect the Englishman in his home, and it was not uncommon to place a blunderbuss in a window to warn thieves to keep away.[38]

During periods of tension firearms played a central role. When the plague was at its height in the autumn of 1665, for instance, guns were used to keep persons exposed to plague from roaming about and spreading the contagion. Several people from a plague-infested village "stole into our town," Elizabeth Sherard wrote to the Verneys, "and brought in ther Goodes in the night. My husband hearing of it armd himselfe with his pistoles and went about 9 at night and saw them all shut up with thos as resived them."[39] According to Mrs. Sherard, those under quarantine "would run about did not sum stand with guns redy to shoot them if they stur."

The panic created in the autumn of 1678 by allegations of a "popish plot" to murder the King and massacre Protestants increased the resort to arms. "The credulous all over the kingdom were terrified and affrighted," the Earl of Ailesbury wrote, and "the Countess of Shaftesbury had always in her muff little pocket pistols, loaden to defend her from the papists, being instructed by her lord, and most timorous ladies followed her fashion."[40] The panic led to a rigorous attempt to disarm Catholics throughout the country. Militia officers ransacked Catholic homes in search of arms and ordered their men "to inquire what Armes and Ammunition of papists are either hidden and concealed, or otherwise conveyed and put into the hands of other persons to be kept for their use."[41] Anyone found guilty of holding arms for Catholics on the pretence that they were his own was to be "proceeded against as parties and confederates with papists, unlesse they deliver the said armes to be seized on and secured for his Majestie's use." If Sir Richard Astley's case is typical, for once Catholics seem to have been thoroughly disarmed. Astley had to swear allegiance to the King and go right up to the Privy Council "to retrieve his duelling pistols."[42] John Kenyon in *The Popish Plot,* however, stated that the number of arms actually confiscated was "pitiful."[43] He found many depositions citing great caches of arms in Catholic hands all over the country, but "though every such deposition was followed up, and some more than once, not a single one was ever substantiated." It is not, at present, possible to ascertain whether the Catholic arms caches had been wildly exaggerated or the meager result of searches was due to prudent removal of weapons beforehand.

The use of firearms by Protestants, however, does not seem to have diminished in the period leading up to 1671. Both robbers and travellers were equipped with firearms, homes were guarded with them, and their cost made them accessible to much of the population. In the aftermath of the attack on Sir John Coventry in 1671, a member of Parliament mused sadly on the trend toward carrying firearms, even in the precincts of Parliament. "Times and manners are altered, and men are," he complained. "Time was, when none should go armed in Parliament-time."[44]

The Game Act of 1671 placed in the hands of the kingdom's aristocracy the perfect tool with which to remove firearms from both Protestants and Catholics. In commenting on the change brought about by this act, William Blackstone wrote: "The forest laws established only one mighty hunter throughout the land, the game laws have raised a little Nimrod in every manor."[45] Since the squires themselves were directly responsible for the act's enforcement, it was indeed a tool of a very personal sort. Did they use it?

Unfortunately, the private manner of enforcement and the fact that the justices did not have to record convictions have deprived us of any public record for the majority of cases. Usually only those cases that were appealed to quarter sessions were recorded, and they appear with approximately the same frequency and, in fact, the same charges before and after passage of the new act. Cases of men charged merely with ownership of a firearm are still negligible. Between 1658 and 1700 there is not a single case in Hertfordshire's Quarter Session records of anyone charged with illegal possession of a full-length firearm. Nor during this period was there a single case for the mere possession of a gun in Lincolnshire, Middlesex, or Nottinghamshire.[46] However, Warwickshire, with a large number of poaching cases, did show a decline in the use of guns in poaching. Of some seventy-one poaching cases between 1631 and 1674 nearly one-third involved firearms, whereas of some twenty-two cases recorded between 1674 and 1682, only three, or one in seven, involved guns.[47] Only one case is recorded for simple possession of a firearm. Several cases came before the Buckingham Quarter Sessions in which the accused was charged with wrongfully keeping guns along with other devices for hunting, but the only instance of a defendant's being charged solely with "keeping guns" cited the statute of Henry VIII against handguns for its authority.[48] Apparently this was not an isolated instance of reliance upon that act after 1671. P. B. Munsche, in *Gentlemen and Poachers*, found that after passage of the Game Act of 1671 the statute of 33 Henry VIII continued to be used in preference to the new act against those charged with unlawful possession of a gun.[49]

It is difficult to know what to make of the failure to use the Game Act of 1671 in these instances. Munsche attributes this to the fact that it did not prescribe a penalty for illegal possession, and relegates the entire issue to a footnote.[50] The penalty for illegal possession was confiscation of the weapon, the same penalty prescribed for owning other illegal hunting equipment. In any case, Munsche's hypothesis is incorrect because the statute of Henry VIII merely prohibited ownership of handguns, and the act of Edward VI, which he also cites, outlawed shot. These measures were in no way comparable to the total ban prescribed in the act of 1671. Munsche's conclusions about enforcement of the act of 1671 are significant:

> An examination of quarter session records for four counties, supplemented by information from three others, suggests that there was a common pattern to game law enforcement during this period. To judge by this evidence, passage of the Game Act was not followed by an immediate increase in the number of game cases heard at quarter sessions. Only in the late 1670's and early 1680's did prosecutions begin to increase . . . In none of these counties, however, was it a sustained increase. On the contrary, after a few years the number of prosecutions declined to a level equal to, or even below, that of the 1670's.[51]

Everything, of course, turned on the local squire's determination to enforce the act and become "a little Nimrod." The very small group that benefited from the act, as opposed to the great numbers hurt, made enforcement difficult. In eighteenth-century Wiltshire less than 0.5 percent of the population is estimated to have been qualified to hunt, and in all of Staffordshire only some 800 persons were so qualified.[52] Comparable studies have yet to be undertaken for the seventeenth century.

Even the most resolute gamekeepers and their employers were isolated on scattered estates, marooned in a sea of people unqualified to hunt or to be armed, people who were generally disposed to sabotage the Game Act. Not surprisingly gamekeepers hesitated to make enemies of their friends and neighbours, and some are accused of having connived "at freeholders, tradesmen and unqualified persons poaching in their lord's manors for a half-crown at Christmas, and a jug of ale when they call upon them." Sometimes they sold the game themselves, "by which un-justifiable practice [they] may make near as much per annum as their wages."[53]

No evidence has come to light that any squire attempted to disarm his tenants and neighbours. Instead we find the occasional squire prepared to spend whatever sums were required and to employ whatever means were necessary to prevent poaching. His gamekeepers kept all-night vigils to guard game preserves and watch the cottages of suspects. Poachers were rigorously prosecuted and their hunting gear and guns confiscated. The greatest weapon in the keeper's arsenal was the right to search. Search warrants were required before a home could be entered, but in practice, magistrates often granted general warrants that keepers carried with them, filling in the name of a suspect whenever they chose. Justices of the peace required no grounds for issuing warrants and keepers re-ceived them for the asking.[54] Any evidence obtained could be brought before a local justice, often the landlord, for immediate action.

Although public records on enforcement are inadequate, the journal of an individual justice of the peace is a valuable aid in demonstrating just how thoroughly the act was enforced. William Holcroft, a justice of the peace for Essex and an officer of the Forest of Waltham, kept such a journal of the cases brought before him between 1661 and 1688.[55] Holcroft's jottings enable us to examine the type and frequency of those cases brought as a result of the new act. The first case occurred in October 1671, when a keeper brought in one William Sparkes of Wood-ford, a tailor, whom he had apprehended the previous day "not far from the Green Man," an inn. Sparkes was carrying "a gunn which was into 3 peeces by which meanes he raised it under a coate," the gun being charged with powder "ready to put a bullet into." Sparkes confessed that he intended to shoot rabbits with this ingenious weapon. "Upon this confession," Holcroft wrote, "Sir William Herick and I committed him to the prison at Stratford." After a gap of ten years, during which Holcroft had little to do with game enforcement, a few other cases are noted. In 1682 Sir William Maynard searched the house of one Gilliard Holdep and found "one long gun charged with 7 bullets and one sluge and a birding pair charged with shot." Several days later a carpenter was bound over to appear in court upon a complaint that he had been shooting a gun in the forest. After an interval of two years, Holcroft noted in an entry that Sir William Maynard had once again delivered a culprit to justice. This time one Ralfe Tyle was charged with being in the forest with a gun about 1:00 A.M. and in the company of several other men at a house where blood and the remains of a deer were discovered. This case was followed three months later by one involving a husbandman in whose home "bullets and bullet molds" and the remains of a deer had been found. Again there is a gap of two years before the next poaching case involving a firearm. This time a labourer, a bricklayer, and an unidentified man were brought in by a gamekeeper because they had been seen on a Sunday in the woods, at which time "a gun was heard to go off." In another case a man described only as a lodger was brought before Holcroft. He had been apprehended in the forest with a "short bullet gun" and was unable to give a good account of what he had been doing.

If any conclusion can be safely drawn from this patchy record it is that there was no vigorous attempt to completely disarm the parish population. With one exception, all those accused of possessing firearms had been, or were suspected of, illegal hunting. The exception, Holdep, whose house was searched for weapons, may well have been suspected of this too but only firearms were discovered.

John Paulet, Marquis of Winchester, was one large landowner determined to sweep the homes of his tenants for hunting equipment. In July 1675 he sent his agents to the Somerset Quarter Sessions to complain "that divers idle persons in the hundreds of Crew Kern, Houndsborowe, Coker Southpetherton and Kingsbury East keep dogs, nets, and engines to destroy gentlemen's game, having no estates to justify their doing so."[56] The Court ordered that Winchester, "or any servant or agent appointed by him, do forthwith seize and destroy all such dogs, nets and engines, and that all constables, tithingmen and other royal officers do aid and assist him and them therein." Although the Court readily acceded to Paulet's wishes, there is a note of frustration in this plea for a crackdown on violators of the Game Act. Winchester must have had problems getting constables and other officials to take action and felt a court order would compel them to enforce the law. Such an expedient appears to have been unusual, as this is the only complaint of its kind uncovered.

Because the King was the preeminent landowner in the realm, his response to the new game act is of some interest. Charles had ordered general sweeps of the households of forest residents several times before the Game Act was passed, but of course residents of royal forests suffered from a variety of liabilities unknown to the average Englishman. One of these sweeps was ordered for the forests of Ayles Holt and Woolmer just prior to the new act's passage. The King wrote to the chief keeper, George Legge, of information "that great spoyles are made upon our Game in and about our said Forest . . . by divers persons with setting doggs, greyhounds, gunes nets and other engines contrary to the statutes of this our Realm," and that "for the better Preservation of our Royall game both within and adjacent to our sayed forest" Legge and his deputies were "to seize and take away all such setting dogs, greyhounds, guns, netts, etc. which you shall find within the sayed forrest or within tenn miles compass thereof."[57] The aim here seems merely to protect game, not disarm people. Local officials were instructed to assist in this effort, but there is no indication to what extent they actually did.

Kings often had difficulty enforcing game acts in their forests. Most residents of forest areas were happy to see poachers keep down the number of deer and rabbits, and local justices were reluctant to convict offenders whose imprisonment might leave their families a charge upon the parish. From 1604, when James I passed his first game act, there were repeated complaints that the acts were not properly enforced. This was still the problem a century later when, in 1717, yet another game statute was enacted. The Treasury Solicitor reported of the new act, "The keepers can scarce prevail with the Justices to take their affidavits, and when they do they will not levy the penalties."[58]

When local gentry refused to convict those who broke the law, the King was helpless. Such an incident took place in 1679. Some royal deer had lain upon ripening grain and the enraged farmers slaughtered the animals. When the Crown tried to arrest six or seven of those accused of killing the deer "dangerous riots" erupted. Several men were apprehended, but they were rescued by forty of their friends "who cried out that they would all suffer alike" and refused to hand over their guns.[59] Judge Jeffreys, sent by the King with a special commission to try the culprits, was utterly foiled when the gentlemen of the Grand Jury refused to cooperate.

Charles could and did act on his own to make an example of especially impudent poachers. This he did in the same manner and with the same frequency both before and after the act of 1671. The poachers so chosen were hauled before the Privy Council, made aware of the enormity of their crimes, then treated with leniency. In February 1672, for instance, two Middlesex men, one of them "having a gun on his shoulder," were spotted with three greyhounds and a spaniel hunting hares on royal land. A witness claimed that when they were scolded for "their shamefull poaching," one of the men replied that "he would keepe greyhounds and hunt where he listed." The two were brought before the Council but dismissed when they promised not to offend thereafter.[60] A second case, also in February 1672, concerned one William Wagland of Great Wishford, Wiltshire, a tailor who was accused of being "a common disturber of the Game in and about the Forest or Chase of Groveley." A gamekeeper had found Wagland walking with a gun, "ready primed," which he seized from him. Soon thereafter, Wagland's gun "was rescued" by some of his friends and Wagland was alleged to have threatened the keeper. The Council ordered Wagland taken into custody, but when he appeared before them a month later he was discharged upon payment of the usual fines.[61] In these instances the illegal firearms were only confiscated because they had been used in the course of illegal hunting. No example was made of any royal tenant for simply owning a firearm.

Despite the admittedly fragmentary nature of the evidence it seems apparent that there was no systematic search and seizure of firearms as a result of the Game Act of 1671. Munsche in his investigations found little evidence "that Englishmen as a whole were disarmed by the game laws" and much evidence to the contrary.[62] His evidence includes poaching cases involving firearms, the popularity of shooting matches among unqualified gunowners, and the openness with which unqualified men acknowledged their possession of firearms. As an example of the last type he cites the case of Ralph Willis of Oxford, a labourer, "very poore havinge a wife and six small children to maintaine," who applied to quarter session in 1687 for relief. On his own testimony his distress had been caused when "in discharging of a gunne your Petitioner hath lost his thumbe."

Instead of mass disarmament the old battle between squires and poachers seems to have continued unabated. Squires now had gamekeepers and search warrants but the poachers were wonderfully inventive, elusive, and protected by the rural community. They intimidated gamekeepers by poaching in large groups. If any were caught they provided alibis for one another and even, as the preamble of the Game Act of 1691 explained, paid one another's fines.[63] When a case came to trial, local jurors refused to convict. A particularly egregious case of this sort involved George Sole of Flitwick in Bedfordshire. Sole had been charged in 1679 with consorting with highwaymen, and in 1683 he was brought before the assizes on charges of poaching in rabbit warrens, "riotously assembling with swords and sticks at night," breaking into Woburn Park with another man, and unlawfully keeping a greyhound. A servant of the Earl of Bedford spotted Sole and four other men coming out of a lane near the park at 3:00 A.M. with a greyhound and a bundle of staves of the sort commonly used for "pitching a net to catch deer."[64] Sole's companions escaped. He confessed to catching rabbits but denied stealing deer. The jury, however, found him innocent of all charges, even those to which he had confessed.

Although the new act does not seem to have been used to disarm the community, it did provide gentlemen with the opportunity to selectively disarm, or at least harass, individuals or groups. Munsche has found some indication of this in Lincolnshire in 1683 when eight people, including three women, were indicted for offences against the game laws.[65] After examining the history of the defendants, however, Munsche came to the conclusion that the "real crime" was non-attendance at church on Sundays. He concluded, "The indictments may have been a form of harassment against Catholics or dissenters, rather than retaliation against poachers."

Two political events were to affect the availability and use of firearms toward the end of Charles II's reign. The first was the panic known as the Popish Plot, which began in the autumn of 1678. In an attempt to reassure his subjects that they were safe from the Catholics in their midst, the King issued a proclamation asking all constables to list Catholics and suspected Catholics in their parish. Those so listed were to have the oaths of allegiance and supremacy administered to them. If they refused, and thereby acknowledged themselves to be Roman Catholics, they were to be disarmed. The many accusations of great caches of arms in Catholic homes were followed up, but, Kenyon points out, no great stock was ever found.[66] The House of Lords drafted a bill banning Catholics from the trades of "gunsmiths, Armourers, Sword-cutlers, Booksellers and Printers," but the measure was dropped by the House of Commons.[67] Fear for their safety, however, drove Protestant men and women to their local gunsmith for additional weapons. Once the panic abated, weapons belonging to Catholics were returned.

The second event, the so-called Rye House Plot in 1683, enabled the Crown to disarm prominent leaders of the Protestant opposition. The facts surrounding the plot are still a mystery. An obscure individual revealed to Lord Dartmouth of the navy department details of a scheme to murder the King and the Duke of York and to set the Duke's Protestant daughter, Anne, upon the throne. One plan for murdering Charles was purported to have involved an attack upon the King as the royal coach passed the moat of the Rye House on its way from Newmarket. Various persons were implicated in the scheme on little more evidence than their opposition to royal policy, among them William Lord Russell and Algernon Sidney. Both men were executed and many supposed sympathizers disarmed. The Crown used this cloudy conspiracy to disarm all its leading opponents. One of these, Sir Robert Atkyns, a former judge, not only was outraged at the indignity but "felt himself defenceless against the enemies which his judicial career had brought him and was afraid to leave his house."[68] What was especially ominous was not merely the indignity the government inflicted upon its opponents, but the fact that for the first time the weapons seized were not restored.

Instead they were handed over to the militia or the Ordnance. An ominous sign, but as yet only a sign.[69]

On February 6, 1685, less than two years after escaping from the alleged attempt on his life, Charles II died. Eveyln judged him "a Prince of many virtues, and many greate imperfections" who "would doubtlesse have ben an excellent Prince, had he ben less adicted to women" and not so liable to be "manag'd by crafty men, and some abandon'd and profane wretches."[70] He left a large number of natural children, of whom James Scott, Duke of Monmouth, was the most famous, but no legitimate heir. Charles was succeeded, therefore, by his brother, James, Duke of York, a Catholic. Apparently Charles would not have been upset by a Catholic succession, since he is reported to have refused the Protestant sacrament on his deathbed and to have sent for a Catholic priest.

Evelyn was present in the palace at the time of Charles's death and reported that the new king went immediately to the Council, where he declared his sorrow with great passion. More important, he promised the councillors that "however he had ben misrepresented as affecting arbitrary power, they should find the contrary, for that the laws of England had made the King as greate a monarch as he could desire"; that he would "maintain the Government both in Church and State, as by Law establish'd"; and "would never depart from the just rights and prerogatives of the Crown . . . and preserve (the nation) in all its lawful rights and liberties."[71] The Council ordered James's protestations published immediately "as containing matter of greate satisfaction to a jealous people upon this change."

Then, as custom demanded, the Lords of the Council proceeded in their coaches to various points throughout the capital, at each of which they descended to stand, bareheaded, while heralds proclaimed the new king. The following Sunday, "to the greate griefe of his subjects," the new monarch "did now for the first time go to masse publickly in the little Oratorie at the Duke's lodgings, the doors being set wide open."[72] It remained to be seen whether James would preserve the rights and liberties of his people as he had promised, or whether all their fears of the link between tyranny and Catholicism, between Catholic kings and standing armies, would prove justified.

James II and Control
of Firearms

WHEN James Stuart succeeded to the throne that bleak February morning in 1685, he found himself in a position his Stuart forbears would have envied, for he had within his grasp the opportunity to establish a truly absolute monarchy. This was due in no small part to his ability to concentrate in his hands the power of the sword and employ it to limit his subjects' liberties. He was indebted to his predecessor for this promising situation. During the final years of his reign, Charles II shook off his lethargy sufficiently to launch a concerted attack upon the independence of England's cities, Parliament, and militia. He revised city charters to increase royal control over the selection of local officials and to remove the franchise from their freeholders and bestow it upon the mayor and council.[1] The possibilities this afforded for royal interference in the day-to-day life of municipalities and for stacking parliaments with members submissive to the Crown were staggering.

More important, James also inherited a promising military establishment, with a militia and commission of the peace that had been purged of the Crown's opponents and a permanent peacetime army of unusual size. Ironically, much of the tension Charles had capitalized upon to achieve this result—notably the anxiety over a Catholic uprising and a Catholic succession—was to prove the basis for James's own undoing. If the majority of Englishmen agreed on anything it was their fear of Catholicism and hatred of standing armies. To appreciate both the promise and the peril James faced one must examine the circumstances that enabled Charles to leave his brother in such an advantageous position.

What triggered opposition to the Crown and provoked Charles II's own determination to enhance his control was James's conversion to Catholicism. James became a Roman Catholic in 1669, but his conversion only became general knowledge in June 1673, when anxiety over the evasion of anti-Catholic legislation and "a wonderful spirit of zeal against the papists" induced Parliament to pass the Test Act.[2] This was designed to ferret out Catholics by requiring all public officials to swear to the oaths of allegiance and supremacy, as well as a declaration against transubstantiation, and then to take the Anglican sacrament. Rather than do this James resigned his post as Lord High Admiral. While Englishmen were reeling from the news, he proceeded to marry a Catholic princess.

In the years that followed, the "wonderful spirit of zeale" against Catholics continued to grow. In 1678 the Popish Plot whipped tensions still higher. Subsequent revelations that much of the plot had been invented never shook public certainty that "there was at that time a Popish Plot, and that there has been one since the Reformation, to support, if not restore the Romish Religion in England."[3] In the wake of the plot, Charles had dissolved the long Cavalier Parliament, but the parliaments of 1679, 1680, and 1681 that succeeded it proved even less to his liking, and he dissolved each as it became obsessed with the need to exclude his brother from the throne. According to a participant in the exclusion debates, the argument for exclusion was "that we should, in case of a Popish Successor, have a Popish Army."[4]

Although an exclusion bill never became law, Charles's fury at the exclusion movement provoked him to purge all those who had aided or sympathized with its proponents from the militia, the commission of the peace, and town governments. In 1683 the Rye House Plot enabled the Crown to implicate and prosecute those who had argued for and supported exclusion. Victims of these purges ranged from some of the most distinguished peers of the realm to scores of ordinary justices of the peace.[5] Many of those ousted suffered the additional humiliation of having their homes ransacked for weapons and of being presented at quarter sessions on various pretexts, an object lesson in the costs of undutiful behaviour.[6] As a result, doubts about a Catholic heir were driven underground, but, as Robin Clifton reminds us, religion was "the one issue which could at the time unite Englishmen of all social conditions and political persuasions, to create a truly popular rebellion."[7]

In addition to a purged militia and commission of the peace, Charles bequeathed to his brother a standing army of some 9215 men and 24 independent companies, an impressive force for a time of peace.[8] With Tory support, however, Charles managed to quash his opponents and guarantee his brother's succession without resort to his military establishment.

At first many of James's subjects tried hard to look at the bright side, and we are assured that the new monarch was received "by some with a real, by all with a pretended satisfaction att least."[9] John Evelyn remarked that the new king's prosaic personal life had excited "greate expectations, and hopes of much reformation as to the late vices and prophanenesse both of Court and Country."[10] There was even grudging admiration of James's candour about his faith. But candour and private virtue were inadequate to calm James's subjects.

They had reason to be suspicious. Notwithstanding his published promise to preserve the faith and liberties of his subjects, James hoped to return England to the Roman Catholic fold, and he was ready, if necessary, to stretch his prerogative powers to achieve this. Although John Miller argues that James "had no intention of imposing his religion by force," he concedes that the actions he took to return the realm to Catholicism "were alarming" and "seemed to threaten to destroy both the laws and the independence of Parliament, the very foundations of the traditional constitution."[11] So things stood on that February morning when James ascended the throne, full of promises to preserve English liberties and religion and determined to alter both.[12]

There are those who argue that it was the uprisings against him that diverted James from the path of moderation. In England, rebellion afforded the excuse to embark upon an expansion of royal power through a redistribution of firearms, but no such pretext was available or necessary in Ireland. James's Irish program was inaugurated before either Argyll or Monmouth had launched their invasions and is significant for the tactics used and the fears it aroused about his intentions toward England.

The recall of James, Duke of Ormonde, the distinguished lord lieutenant of Ireland, just prior to James's accession removed a potential obstacle to his plans. Ormonde had insisted that only members of the Church of England be permitted to serve in the Irish army.[13] Until Ormonde's successor was chosen Ireland was officially governed by a body of commissioners but actually run by the King's confidante, Richard Talbot, Earl of Tyrconnel. Tyrconnel was an old enemy of Ormonde's, an abrasive and vigorous champion of the Irish Catholics and commander of the Irish army.

James's formal instructions to his Irish commissioners, dated March 27, 1685, ordered them to reverse the preponderance of firepower within that kingdom "forthwith."[14] Before this could be accomplished, however, it was necessary to disarm the Protestant militia.[15] The Irish Protestant militia had been fully armed since the Popish Plot scare of 1678. In Instruction 28 of his orders James pointed out that because "a great part" of those arms were "in the hands of persons very ill affected to the Government," they were to order them returned to the magazines.[16] While Protestants who were potential opponents were to be disarmed, Instruction 29 required "that the arms taken from our Roman Catholic subjects upon Otes's pretended discovery should be restored to them; and that they should also be put in the same capacity with our other subjects of being Sheriffs, JPs, etc."

To ensure a redistribution of weapons, firearms needed to be strictly monitored. In May, James informed the Irish commissioners of the need "for regulating the importation, sale and use of gunpowder."[17] Sheriffs throughout Ireland were ordered to turn in complete lists of all weapons in private hands in their jurisdiction, along with the names of their owners.

The disarming of those suspected of disaffection proceeded swiftly. By early July the militia of northern Ireland had been disarmed, reportedly with "no noise."[18] Later that same month the obstacles to Catholics serving in the Irish army were removed when the Lords Justices were ordered not to administer the usual oaths of supremacy to garrison governors, officers, and soldiers in Ireland. All that was now necessary for new military personnel was an oath of fidelity to James.[19] As Childs points out in his study of James's army, with this change "the gates were wide open."[20] By November, when the eldest son of the old lord chancellor, the Earl of Clarendon, arrived in Ireland to assume the duties of lord lieutenant, the Irish Protestants were seriously alarmed. Clarendon shared their anxiety and asked that any weapons taken from them be returned. He also sought permission from the Privy Council "to dispense with the execution of the 29th article of my instructions [for rearming Catholic Irishmen] in such particular cases as I shall think fit."[21] "It is a thing of great consequence," he reminded the president of the Council, "what persons should be intrusted with arms, and ought to be very well considered before any are delivered out."

James scarcely needed to be reminded of that fact. Nor did his man Tyrconnel, who, with his approval, had been at work for months replacing Protestant officers and rank-and-file soldiers of the Irish army with Catholics. By the end of September 1686, out of a sanctioned strength of some 7485 privates in the Irish army, 5043 were Catholics—by October some two-thirds of the entire Irish army were Catholics.[22] As Catholics were added Protestant officers were being discharged, albeit at a slower rate; by the same date, 166 of the 406 officers were Catholic. The purge of officers was nearly complete by the autumn of 1687, with only 2 Protestant colonels, for example, still holding their commands beyond March 1688.[23] But before that, in February 1687, James had removed the reluctant Clarendon from his post and placed the Irish government in the hands of the man who had really been managing it all along, the Catholic Earl of Tyrconnel.

James was more cautious about the redistribution of firepower in England, but just as intent upon the establishment of greater royal control. Control began with a submissive parliament. His administration made use of every possible means of exerting royal pressure, reviving shady practices from earlier times to ensure that the reign's first and only parliamentary election produced such a body.[24] Towns were much easier to manipulate since their new charters reduced the number of electors, often to the town officials themselves, and these men were removable by the Crown. Narcissus Luttrell, a contemporary diarist, described some of the methods employed to influence election results:

> At some places, as Bedford . . . they chose at night, giveing no notice of it; in other boroughs, as St. Albans, they have new regulated the electyors by new charters, in putting the election into a selected number, when it was before by prescription in the inhabitants at large: in counties they adjourned the poll from one place to another, to weary the freeholders, refuseing also to take the votes of excommunicated persons and other dissenters . . . king commanding some to stand, and forbidding others . . . foul returns made in many places; and where gentlemen stood that they called whiggs, they offered them all the tricks and affronts imaginable.[25]

Lords lieutenant played an active role in the selection and promotion of candidates. They were asked to attend county elections and as many borough elections as possible, and occasionally used the militia to intimidate opposition candidates.[26] Similar tactics had been used during the last years of Charles's reign, but never to the same extent or with such blatant orchestration by the Crown.

The result was a parliament that has been labelled "the most compliant Commons of the century," and of which James remarked: "There were not above forty members, but such as he himself wished for."[27] It was a parliament of new men, with only 135 of the 505 members having had prior parliamentary experience. In greeting the members on May 19, the King warned them not to try to force him to call frequent parliaments by granting niggling financial support, which he characterized as "feeding me from time to time by such proportions as they shall think convenient."[28] Members obliged and voted him the revenues for life his predecessor had enjoyed, apparently unaware that the proceeds from those revenues were now much greater.[29] Their one flicker of spirit at the time was consideration of resolutions reiterating their devotion to the Church of England and urging execution of the laws against Catholics, but these were abandoned when it was made clear that their passage would give offence. This ought to have reminded James, however, that even the most loyal Tories were anti-Catholic.

The spectre of rebellion had enabled Charles II to tighten his grip on his kingdoms, and two uprisings early in James's reign did the same for his brother. In contrast to the Venner fiasco, however, the rebellions launched by the Earl of Argyll and the Duke of Monmouth to place a Protestant on the throne posed a genuine threat, if only because of a general sympathy for their aims.

The two rebellions enabled James to immediately boost his regular income and enlarge his army. In response to Argyll's rebellion, Parliament agreed on May 30 to the request for revenues to pay off Charles II's debts and to purchase military supplies. James was also granted the proceeds of duties on wine and vinegar, tobacco, and sugar for eight years, an amount worth some £400,000 annually.[30] When only days later news of Monmouth's rebellion reached Parliament, it voted the King an additional £400,000 for five years and was considering a further grant of £700,000 when it was prorogued. In addition, the Scots Parliament voted James £260,000 a year for life. As a result, the new king had a yearly revenue of more than £2,000,000, an enviable financial situation that afforded him an unusual degree of executive independence.[31]

The emergencies gave the King the excuse, the money, and the wherewithal to more than double his standing army from 9215 men in 1684 to 18,984 in 1686. As the French ambassador wrote to Louis XIV on June 25, 1685, "The king of England is very glad to have the pretence of raising troops and he believes that the Duke of Monmouth's enterprise will serve only to make him still more master of his country."[32] The army would more than double again by October 1688 to 40,117, but for most of James's reign it was twice as large as Charles II's army.[33]

As it turned out, the two rebellions were quickly suppressed. Argyll was the son of the Scottish leader who had led an army against Charles I and was executed in 1661 for aiding Cromwell. Argyll inherited the family's fierce Presbyterianism and inclination to meddle in politics, and had escaped a death sentence only by fleeing to Holland. On May 6, 1685, he returned to Scotland with three small ships and some 300 men to rally his clansmen and the Presbyterians of southwest Scotland. His plot was exposed prematurely and he encountered stiff military resistance. Unable to capture his capital, Inverary, Argyll fled to the island of Bute, only to return to the mainland to begin a desperate march on Glasgow. By June 18, little more than a month after his daring uprising began, he was captured. Two weeks later he was executed.

Argyll's rising was intended to draw royal troops north and pave the way for a successful rebellion in the south on behalf of James, Duke of Monmouth, Charles II's illegitimate Protestant son. This vain, brash young man was highly popular and has been described as "the only Stuart who understood the common man."[34] He landed with a small force at Lyme Regis on June 11 and promptly published a declaration charging James with a series of crimes, including setting the Great Fire of London and poisoning the late king. The declaration also affirmed the Duke's support for the basic Whig planks of annual parliaments, toleration for all Protestants, and opposition to standing armies. Monmouth brought only a small corps of soldiers and 1500 of the very latest European foot arms—he counted heavily upon the support of local people, desertions from the militia and royal army, and risings in London. His expectation of support from local people was not disappointed. He wisely chose to begin his campaign in the West Country, a region strong in its Protestantism and roughly treated by Charles II on that account. Within a week Monmouth's army had swollen to 7000 men, mainly from the poorer and middling sections of the community—miners, artisans, farmers, and clothworkers. The gentry of the region remained aloof.

Monmouth's men were notoriously ill-armed. The very reason the area was so favourable to his cause—its history of dissent and staunch support for Parliament during the Civil War—had made it a target of Charles II's disarmament efforts. City walls had been levelled, corporations purged, and the initial Restoration militia disarmed. After the Rye House Plot only two years earlier, the Crown had disarmed prominent Whig leaders. Macaulay writes that the Duke's army "might easily have been increased to double the number, but for the want of arms"; and he notes that "great numbers who were desirous to enlist were sent away."[35]

With many militia officers in London for the meeting of Parliament, the militia bands of the West either refused to fight or deserted to Monmouth's army. An astute observer judged that it was not the wild charges against James or even "love to Monmouth" that won the pretender so much support. "The true reason was, Monmouth had declared to mainteine the Protestant relligion, and that the Kinge would sett up Poperie; and this was the true cause the militia would not fight; not a love to Monmouth, but a hatred to Poperie."[36]

The rebellion was doomed by the disarming of potential supporters in other parts of the kingdom and by Monmouth's own indecisive leadership, which kept his army marching in circles until it was, in fact, encircled. The final battle came at Sedgemoor on July 6. When his cause appeared hopeless, Monmouth abandoned his wretched followers but, like them, was captured. He was beheaded on July 15; his followers suffered later when George Jeffreys earned his reputation for brutality by prosecuting rebels in what have ever since been known as "the Bloody Assizes."

Except for the West Country regiments, the militia had performed relatively well. That exception, however, was sufficient to provide James with an excuse to attack the entire institution. Within a fortnight after the rebellion he had sent orders to all lords lieutenant to estimate the monies needed to support their militia regiments, with the intention of diverting these funds to his army. His order immediately aroused suspicions, which the Court made no effort to allay. John Bramston was warned that he must not underestimate the expense of his militia regiment. He countered that it must not be overvalued, "for the design is visible," whereupon the King's lieutenant general conceded that "the king was displeased with the militia in generall, and that the behaviour of those in the West give him just cause; wherefore it was conceaved he would make noe more use of them, but have the money that expence came to, and manteine forces in every countie proportionable."[37]

James's assault on the militia became public on November 6, when he opened the new parliamentary session by remarking "how happy his forces had been in reducing a dangerous rebellion in which it had appeared how weak and insignificant the militia was."[38] He argued that the poor showing of the militia demonstrated that "there is nothing but a good force of well-disciplined troops in constant pay that can defend us from such as, either at home or abroad, are disposed to disturb us." That being the case, he explained that "for all their security" he would maintain his army, which, thanks to the rebellion, now stood at 20,000 men. This news was the more disturbing because nearly 100 Catholic officers had been commissioned to command the enlarged force. Charles II had some Catholic officers in his army but prudently kept them stationed abroad except during hostilities; as soon as these were over they were disbanded or sent abroad again.[39] When it was pointed out to James that these commissions to Catholics violated the Test Act, he replied that "it was up to his law officers to find expedients acceptable to the laws."[40] James advised Parliament that good officers were scarce and he intended to keep his new Catholic officers.[41] After the King's speech, John Bramston noted, "There was observed a great dejection of countinance in very manie consideringe men in the House."[42] Bishop

Burnet judged that James had fallen "upon the two most unacceptable points that he could have found out; which were, a standing army, and a violation of the act of the test."[43]

The spectre of subjection to a "papist" army proved too much for many of the King's hand-picked MPs, and angry debate followed James's announcement. Many members attacked the maintenance of a large army and defended the usefulness of the militia, for, as John Childs points out, however ineffective the militia was, "it was their force and not the king's."[44] To those who questioned the need for any army, James replied that "the venom and seeds of that rebellion was not removed out of the harts and minds of a very great part of the nation, who were apt still, if opportunitie served, to rise, and that the militia as it is formed cannot be usefull on such occasions."[45] Members objected that the militia had been useful, "even in that rebellion," and could be made more so. And while they were prepared to provide funds to this end, the King's request for revenues for his army was defeated. Bramston judged that members of Parliament "were not willinge to establish an armie officered by Papists." Since the King had dispensed with the Test Act in the case of his new Catholic officers, "all or as many as the King pleased" might be added in the future.[46] A bill "to make the militia usefull" was passed but failed to become law because James prorogued Parliament the very next day. The entire session had lasted less than a fortnight. John Miller in his biography of James finds this prorogation of Parliament "as significant as it was unexpected. . . . It marked, after just nine months of James's reign, a break with the Tories who had supported him since 1680. James's conduct had reminded them that church and constitution could be threatened from above as well as from below, by Popery and arbitrary government as well as by Dissent and republicanism. Loyal the Tories might be, but their sense of self-preservation made them reluctant to provide the money to pay a standing army, still less one which contained Catholic officers."[47]

James was intent upon placing those he considered his friends in positions of power and authority throughout the realm while, quite literally, disarming his enemies. Who did the King regard as friends? George Jeffreys explained to the new chief justice of King's Bench at his induction that James's test was a simple one: "They that are not for us are against us."[48] Those "against us" opposed James's religious policies. As the King's intentions became plain—and justified the worst fears of his subjects—the number of those reckoned friends shrank, making the task of redistributing the kingdom's firepower more and more difficult.

As commander of the militia James could mobilize it as he pleased. What he pleased was to permit it to fall into disuse. Militia regiments were occasionally called upon to disarm suspicious persons, but no musters were ordered. Nor, as lords lieutenant were to learn, could they muster their militia on their own initiative. This royal policy was made explicit on May 25, 1687, when lords lieutenant were commanded that the "militia within your lieutenancies . . . be not mustered" until the King so ordered.[49]

Despite the policy of permitting the militia to lapse, James embarked upon another, yet more thorough, purge of its officer corps and of the commission of the peace. Hundreds of individuals, men whose families had been prominent in local and county affairs for generations, found themselves sacked. By 1688 at least half the lords lieutenant in the realm and some 800 justices of the peace had been ousted.[50] Their places were filled by Catholics or Protestant dissenters.

The King was anxious from the outset to reduce the arsenal of private arms kept in great houses and little cottages throughout England. The campaign began before Argyll's invasion and continued after Monmouth's rebellion. The obvious tactic was to strictly enforce all firearms restrictions. The much-maligned militia was called upon to assist. Militia officers were notified that James wanted rigorous disarming of suspicious persons. On the day after Monmouth's execution, the Earl of Burlington wrote to assure the Earl of Rochester of the great care he meant to take "in this present conjuncture" to disarm potential troublemakers:

> [I] do now assure your Lordship, that the power which the law gives us, shall not only be extended to its utmost limits, in the point of searching and disarming, but we will take the liberty to use the exercise of our discretion, in . . . interpreting the sense of it to the advantage of his Majesty's service. The Deputy Lieutenants have been all the last week, and are still very busy in their several divisions, about disarming, an account of which I very suddenly expect from them, which I shall transmit to Mr. Secretary; and if upon the view thereof, I shall judge an additional search shall be requisite, I will have one.[51]

Burlington may not have been as diligent as he pretended, but he certainly knew what response would please the King.

James also insisted upon strict compliance with the game acts. He ordered his forest officers to enforce the traditional game acts vigorously and broadly. Warrants enjoined them to take care to preserve the royal game not only within the protected areas but for ten, twelve, and up to twenty miles around them.[52] Officials such as the Earl of Chesterfield and Sir William Stanhope, who were jointly responsible for Thorny

Woods Chace, were instructed to "search the houses of all such as you shall suspect to be maelfactors and disturbers of our game and to take from them all such nets, buckstalls, guns, cross-bows or other engines as you shall have cause to suspect are kept for the destruction and disquiet of the deer."

But James needed a statute that would enable him to disarm those citizens beyond the range of royal forests and those it might be difficult to disarm as suspicious persons. He thought he had found such a device in the ancient law of Edward III restricting the carriage of arms. This statute, passed in 1328, a period of growing anarchy, forbade men "great or small" from coming before the royal judges and ministers with force and arms, from riding armed "in affray of the peace," and from going armed "by Night nor by Day, in Fairs, Markets, nor in the Presence of the Justices or other Ministers, nor in no Part elsewhere, upon Pain to forfeit their Armour to the King, and their Bodies to Prison at the King's Pleasure." Although men were occasionally indicted for carrying arms to terrorize their neighbours, the strict prohibition against going armed "by Night nor by Day . . . in Fairs, Markets . . . nor in no part elsewhere" had never been enforced.

The idea of resorting to the law of 1328 emerged in the course of Crown attempts to curtail the activities of Sir John Knight, a Bristol merchant and militant Anglican. Knight, former sheriff of Bristol, had won his knighthood in 1682 for his avid persecution of Protestant dissenters. Being a man of principle, he was just as avid a persecutor of Catholics. In the spring of 1686 the mayor and magistrates of Bristol received word of the King's "resentment of their late proceedings [against Catholics] and of Sir John Knight's behavior."[53] Undeterred, they continued to enforce the laws against Catholic worship. On May 1 the president of the Privy Council wrote to the local lieutenant that the King had been informed that the Bristol magistrates had "lately seized upon a priest, who was going to officiate privately in a house there, committing him and those present, who exceeded not seven or eight persons, to prison." He added that "Sir John Knight was not only the informer but a busy actor in the matter by going himself to search." The Bristol city fathers were warned "to have a care not to be drawn into inconveniences by the pretended zeal of Sir John Knight."[54]

The case became something of a cause célèbre as the London newsletters monitored the Crown's efforts to curtail the legal activities of this militant Anglican. In June James hit upon the idea of charging Knight with wrongful use of a firearm, "creating and encouraging fears in the hearts of his Majesty's subjects."[55] Knight was brought to trial before King's Bench in November on the charge that he "did walk about the streets armed with guns and that he went into the Church of St. Michael in Bristol in the time of Divine Service with a Gun to terrifie the King's Subjects."[56] After due deliberation the jury acquitted him, while the Court specifically recognized a "general Connivance to Gentlemen to ride armed for their security." King's Bench was not prepared to approve the use of this statute to disarm law-abiding citizens.

It was very likely the unwillingness of the Court of King's Bench to apply the statute of 1328 in Knight's case that drove home to the King the need for a more general statute to disarm subjects. James believed he had found that more general statute in the Game Act of 1671. On December 6, 1686, just two weeks after Knight's embarrassing acquittal, the president of the Council informed the lords lieutenant of the northern and western counties that the King had information "that a great many persons not qualified by law under pretence of shooting matches keep muskets and other guns in their houses."[57] They were to instruct their deputies "to cause strict search to be made for such muskets or guns and to seize and safely keep them till further order." This was the first and only attempt by a monarch to order a general disarmament using the Game Act of 1671. Since only the letters sent to certain counties are extant, it is uncertain whether other lords lieutenant were sent similar orders; it is also unclear whether the order was strictly legal, since the statute was intended to be enforced by landlords on their own estates. Still, the Game Act did specify who was and who was not entitled to have firearms, and it was well known that large numbers of unqualified persons did, in fact, own these weapons.

The records are silent about whether the King's orders were actually carried out. There is no evidence of mass disarming or of further instructions to lords lieutenant on this matter. On the whole it seems highly unlikely that James's orders were obeyed. General disarming was an awesome task and most deputies and their militia would not have wanted to alienate the majority of their neighbours and friends by confiscating their firearms. It was one thing to disarm particular individuals, quite another to disarm entire villages. Moreover, by this time James had already begun to denigrate and weaken the militia, failing to authorize musters and appointing Catholics to posts as lords lieutenant.[58] Of the six lords lieutenant whose orders to execute the Game Act survive, four were displaced within the year for their unwillingness to remove the Test Act. In fact, five months after this attempt at disarmament James seems to have given up on the militia and instructed lieutenants not to muster their regiments again unless specifically ordered to do so. Furthermore, there is evidence that unqualified persons continued to have firearms after the royal order for their removal. Not only did game cases involving the use of firearms continue to arise but unqualified persons openly admitted to owning guns.[59]

James's attempt to impose the Game Act of 1671 made it crystal clear that he felt it within his jurisdiction, and in his interest, to order a general disarming. This was a frightening reminder of royal pretensions. The militia had failed to carry out its orders, but there was no assurance that a militia dominated by Catholics or a standing army would prove as reluctant.

In letters so large as to detract from their appearance, the cannon of James's troops in Scotland bore on their muzzles the short, sharp philosophy of their commander-in-chief: "Haec est Vox Regia" and "Non Sine Fulmine Regnat."[60] Although modern historians may doubt James's sinister intentions, his contemporaries were sure he meant to create an absolute kingship patterned after that of his hero, Louis XIV, and to return England to the Catholic fold through the offices of a large standing army.[61] If this was his aim, he came perilously close to succeeding.

Although James's army was a source of severe anxiety during his reign, many modern historians regard these fears as unfounded. They readily acknowledge that, blessed as he was with ample revenues, James was able to create this large, independent military institution without recourse to parliaments. But admittedly, a force of some 20,000 men is not impressive by modern standards. In a recent study of James's army, however, John Childs argues persuasively that contemporaries were right to regard the size of the army as ominous. The ratio of James's soldiers to the English population was comparable to that of Louis XIV's soldiers to the French population during the 1680's.[62] Childs finds James's army not only of sufficient size to coerce the country but "very different from that of his brother . . . and well advanced along the road to being an absolutist force by the time of William's intervention."[63] This was due, he argues, not merely to its size, or even to its inclusion of Catholics, but to its changed relationship to society. James's army was more professional, more detached from the community, reliant solely upon the Crown. James increased the number of professionals from foreign regiments. He purged his officer corps of malcontents and replaced them with men "dependent on him for their livelihood and prospects."[64] He also gave the army a new legal independence. All its judicial business, both civil and military, was referred to a weekly court-martial, rather than being heard in the common law courts. In the opinion of James's judge advocate-general, George Clarke, this "effectively removed the military from the competence of the civil power and made it an independent force reliant solely upon the orders of the king."[65]

This separation of the army from the civilian courts resulted in the soldiers' disrespectful attitude toward civilians. The impunity of the military from the normal courses of the law apparently reached the point that men seeking to escape the law "had only to be mustered into the army to avoid its clutches."[66] James, unlike Charles, posted his army throughout the country. This led to problems in billeting. Although the Disbanding Act of 1679 made it illegal to compel private householders to receive soldiers into their homes against their will, billeting of soldiers in private homes continued. Their hosts were paid, but serious abuses occurred.[67] In the opinion of a contemporary, their privileged status permitted James's soldiers "to outrage and injure whom they pleased almost without restraint."[68]

According to J. R. Western, the remarkable revival of both the army and the navy under James "really meant that it was no longer possible to start a great rebellion against the King."[69]

The pace of James's institutional and religious transformation of the realm quickened during the summer of 1686. In June 1686, 13,000 of the King's troops assembled on Hounslow Heath for their summer encampment, where their numbers intimidated residents of the capital. The following month James created a body reminiscent of the Court of High Commission. These ecclesiastical commissioners were to exercise jurisdiction over all spiritual and ecclesiastical matters including oversight of the universities and all other schools. Two days later four Catholics were sworn to the Privy Council. Attempts to intimidate opponents and place Catholics in posts of all sorts culminated in April 1687 in a royal Declaration of Indulgence to suspend the Test Act and oaths of allegiance for officeholders and to introduce toleration for Catholics and Protestant dissenters. The declaration contained the King's wish "that all the people of our dominions were members of the Catholic church" and expressed his hope that when Parliament met the following December it would approve the measure. To ensure that it would, James undertook yet another campaign to purge the militia, the municipalities, and all government administration of everyone opposed to the suspension of the Test Act and the Declaration of Indulgence.

To ferret out possible dissidents, James tried something new. During the summer, lords lieutenant throughout the kingdom were ordered to put three questions to their deputies, the sheriffs, and justices in their counties and report their answers: (1) Will you, if returned to Parliament, vote for the repeal of the penal laws and the Test?; (2) Will you support candidates who are in favour of such a measure?; and (3) Will you live neighbourly and friendly with those of a contrary religion? Anyone who refused to present these questions or who answered them in an unsatisfactory manner was summarily ejected from his post.

A majority of respondents tried to avoid this fate with answers that were carefully devised to appear strictly correct, if unenthusiastic. Very few answers were to the King's liking, however, and the entire exercise, according to a contemporary, merely "created an assurance in manie, that were otherways wavering, to be of that number [of opposers]."[70] Indeed, he continued, many "who approved the thing, were yett of the number of those that denied compliance, that they might not dissent from their friends. And 'tis most certain, that a great manie chose to loos their places which were beneficiall, rather than submitt themselves to the censure of their countries, by whom they had been trusted in former parliaments." Hundreds of Englishmen of every rank and shade of political opinion, from peers of the realm to humble revenue clerks, were ejected. Fully half of the lords lieutenant and some 800 justices of the peace were sacked or forced to resign. "Not since the Norman Conquest," J. H. Plumb claims, "had the Crown developed so sustained an attack on the established political power of the aristocracy and major gentry."[71]

Sir John Bramston reported that under the town of Maldon's new charter, the King was able to remove the mayor, five aldermen, several "capital" burgesses, the recorder, and "myselfe from the office of High Steward of the burrough, an office I had held ever since the returne of King Charles the Second."[72] Bramston was also "put out of the commission of the peace, and from beinge a Deputy Lieutenant. With myselfe were about 30 gentlemen put out of the commission of the peace, few of the old Justices left in commission." Under London's new charter the Crown was authorized to remove not only city councillors but masters, wardens, and assistants of all the guilds. In September more than 800 Londoners were turned out of their offices for their opposition to the removal of the Test Act, and several months later others were added to the numbers of those purged.[73]

At the same time James began a campaign to revise, yet again, municipal corporations. But this time municipalities simply refused to surrender their charters. To force them into compliance the royal army was billeted on them, although this practice had been proclaimed illegal in the Petition of Right some sixty years earlier. James even went so far as to consult the Chief Justice of King's Bench on the feasibility of a royal declaration that the Petition of Right could not control his prerogative.

It became exceedingly difficult to find anyone ready to comply with the King's wishes. After twenty-four Reading aldermen were ousted, twenty-three of their replacements had to be dismissed in their turn when they declared against the Indulgence. For the same reason, the borough of Yarmouth had three different sets of magistrates within a matter of days. Few Anglicans were willing to accept the vacated posts, which James then filled with Catholics and Protestant dissenters. Many of the latter, however, were just as opposed to the toleration of Catholics as were Anglicans. The new appointees were usually men of lesser standing in the community or of no standing at all. For lack of suitable candidates for lord lieutenant of the militia, James had to assign two shires to Jeffreys, and even the Jesuit Father Petre was made a lord lieutenant.

Protestants continued to hope that all this would be reversed if James died without a male heir and the monarchy passed to his eldest daughter, Mary. Mary's husband, William of Orange, was deeply involved in fighting for the Protestant cause in Europe. In December 1687, however, James announced that the Queen was with child. It was the unlikelihood of this ever happening that had induced Englishmen to be patient with James. Mary of Modena had not conceived since 1681, and her record in childbirth has been summed up as "abysmal."[74] If she now had a daughter, the child would be third in line for the throne behind Mary and Anne, James's Protestant daughters; if a son, he might yet be raised a Protestant if James died while he was a youth. Nevertheless, the possibility of a Catholic male heir was worrisome.

James was aware of these fears and of the possibility that William might invade England to protect Mary's interests. He forbade any of his subjects entering into the service of a foreign prince and demanded the return of the men serving in six British regiments in the army of the United Provinces. These regiments had been raised in Holland, where the men had been exposed to the views of opposition leaders such as their former commander Henry Sidney, living in exile there.[75] When the States-General refused James's order, he issued a stern proclamation commanding his subjects to return home upon pain of being considered outlaws. His timing was poor. The proclamation was published before, rather than after the regular regimental payday. Nor was any assurance given to returning soldiers that they would be employed in the royal army. Few soldiers obeyed, and these Dutch regiments played an important role in William's invasion.

In the meantime James pressed ahead with his efforts to enhance the position of English Catholics. On April 4 he reprinted his Declaration of Indulgence and ordered it read in every parish church during divine service. The Archbishop of Canterbury and six bishops drew up a petition to protest this order on the ground that the King's suspension of legislation on such a scale was illegal. The vast majority of clergymen agreed, and the royal declaration was "only read in some few places."[76] James was incensed and committed the "seven bishops" to the Tower "for Contriving, Making, and Publishing a Seditious Libel against his Majesty and his Government."

On June 10, to the King's great joy, the Queen was delivered of a son. Twenty days later, to the inexpressible joy of English Protestants, a jury found the seven bishops not guilty. When the verdict was announced, a great cheer like "a train of gunpowder sett on fire" went up and down the river and along the streets, "to the astonishment even of those that contributed to it," in honour of "a joyfull deliverance to the church of England."[77] Bonfires were lit and guns discharged, "tho forbid," in noisy celebration. That same day seven prominent Englishmen quietly sent an invitation to William of Orange urging him to come to England to save the realm and assuring him of the support of nineteen-twentieths of its people.

James was about to reap the whirlwind. At first he did not appreciate the seriousness of the situation and went about his usual business. He ordered lists drawn up of clergymen who had refused to read his Declaration of Indulgence. Not until late in September did he realize his danger. In a panic he called upon his subjects "to lay aside all jealousies and animosities, and to prepare to defend their countrye."[78] He hurriedly began to reverse the policies that had caused offence and disrupted his realm. Lords lieutenant were ordered to recall deputy lieutenants who had been dismissed and the Ecclesiastical Commission was dissolved. Then, on October 17, "having received several Complaints of great Abuses and Irregularities committed in the late Regulations of the Corporations," James abruptly restored to the cities and towns of the realm their "Ancient Charters, Liberties, Rights and Franchises." But the very issue of the *London Gazette* that announced this proclamation contained a notice of the baptism of the new Prince of Wales, with the Pope himself and the Queen Dowager officially listed as godfather and godmother to the infant.[79]

No wonder a mood of cynicism prevailed. Among Protestants recently ejected from their posts the King's reversal of policy was regarded as no more than "plums for children."[80] Men such as Sir John Bramston, when suddenly invited by a Catholic lord lieutenant (in his case the Jesuit Father Petre) to resume their offices as deputies or justices of the peace, excused themselves on one pretext or another. "The gentlemen in all counties almost where the Lieutenants were removed, and Papists put in," Bramston wrote, "refused to take commissions under them."[81] Only now did James realize that his subjects were not prepared to serve under Catholic or sectarian officers. In desperation he tried to restore the former lieutenants. But when the Earl of Oxford took over from Father Petre in Essex, Bramston informed him that "he would find gentlemen not forward to take commands; some would thinck one kick of the breech enough for a gentleman."[82] This proved too true. All over the realm the men and officers of the militia refused to serve.

On November 5, after a stormy voyage, William of Orange and his Dutch fleet docked at Torbay. William had intended to land in the north of England but had diverted to the West to avoid the English fleet. The Prince's ship flew the English colours emblazoned with the motto "the Protestant Religion and the Liberties of England." William made no claim for himself but called for a free parliament and an inquiry into the birth of the Prince of Wales, who, some claimed, was not the King's child but had been smuggled into the birth room in a warming pan.

Residents of the West Country were still a bit gun-shy after Monmouth's rebellion but began to join William in increasing numbers, while, despite much urging, the neglected and abused militia regiments refused to fight against him. Lord Bath wrote to the King from the West: "The common people are so prejudiced with the late regulations and so much corrupted that there can be no dependence at present on the militia but only upon his majesty's standing forces."[83] Lord Bath was correct in his estimate of the militia, but quite wrong about the royal army. James's attempt in September to introduce Irish Catholic recruits into his English regiments had led to a vigorous protest by regimental officers. Some were cashiered as a result, and in response others laid down their commissions. Many probably feared that James meant to make the English army as Catholic as its Irish counterpart, eventually ousting all Protestant soldiers. Beyond this, James's men were not only soldiers but Englishmen and Protestants. Visitors to their camp on Hounslow Heath noted that the soldiers engaged in endless political discussion, taking sides "as if they were in the House of Commons."[84]

As William marched toward London James's army suffered some serious defections. Lord Cornbury, Clarendon's eldest son, defected with his regiment; soon after, Lord Churchill, a personal friend of the King's, slipped off from the army, taking with him the colonels of his Tangier regiment. James tried to stop the desertions by issuing a pardon on November 22 for those who had been "seduced to take up Arms . . . to joyn themselves with Foreigners and Strangers, in a most Unnatural Invasion upon Us."[85] The desertions continued. In growing panic James left his troops and returned to London. He offered to negotiate with William but on December 10 received a list of conditions from the Prince which he regarded as unacceptable. To stall for time he promised to return an answer the following day, but instead hustled the Queen and the Prince of Wales off to France, ordered the disbandment of his army, and in the early morning hours of December 11 set off for Sheerness and France, tossing the Great Seal of State into the Thames as he left London.

Across the kingdom wild crowds stormed Catholic chapels. In the name of the Prince of Orange the Lord Mayor of London ordered the disarming of all Roman Catholics gathered there. He also ordered searches begun for weapons, "which," one commentator held, "did the Prince of Orange no little service here in this town tho I am well informed it was really none of his."[86] A "glorious revolution" was about to occur.

Western, as noted above, argued that the revival of the army and the navy under James "meant that it was no longer possible to start a great rebellion against the King."[87] But the impossible happened and produced what Bishop Burnet described as "one of the strangest catastrophes that is in any history." "A great king with strong armies, and mighty fleets, a vast treasure, and powerful allies, fell all at once: and his whole strength, like a spider's web, was so irrecoverably broken with a touch, that he was never able to retrieve what for want both of judgement and heart, he threw up in a day."[88]

It was the stubborn attachment of Englishmen to their faith and their liberty that had caused their king's strength, "like a spider's web," to be "broken with a touch."

CHAPTER SEVEN

Arms for Their Defence:
The Making of a "True, Ancient,
and Indubitable Right"

O N THAT cold January day in 1689 the crowded chamber crack-led with passion and excitement. The day before the Convention Parliament had voted that the throne was "vacant." The House of Commons was now asked to fill it by declaring James II's daughter Mary and her husband, William of Orange, king and queen of England. Anthony Cary, Lord Falkland, rose to object: "It concerns us to take such care, that, as the Prince of Orange has secured us from Popery, we may secure ourselves from Arbitrary Government. The Prince's Declaration is for a lasting foundation of the Government. I would know what our foundation is . . . Therefore, before you fill the Throne, I would have you resolve, what Power you will give the King, and what not."[1] Falkland clearly meant to "not only change hands, but things," a goal vigorously seconded by others present. "We have had such Violation of our Liberties in the last reigns," Mr. Garroway exclaimed, "that the Prince of Orange cannot take it ill, if we make conditions, to secure ourselves for the future; and in it we shall but do justice to those who sent us hither, and not deliver them up without very good reason." "When we have considered the preservation of the Laws of England for the future," Sir William Williams agreed, "then it will be time to consider the persons to fill the Throne." "Redeem us from Slavery," another member implored, "What you omit now is lost for ever."[2] Sir Richard Temple, among others, promptly began to rehearse recent encroachments on their rights, including the use of the Militia Act "to disarm all England" and the need "to provide against a Standing Army" in peacetime.

Other parliaments—in particular the Convention of 1660—had heard similar pleas to protect the subject's rights against future trespass and had remained unmoved. Even at this juncture there were sound reasons to ignore the appeal again. After all, was it not courting disaster to debate liberties while the kingdom remained leaderless? And there was sense in the old argument: "That all our Privileges cannot be set down in this short Time . . . Besides setting down our Privileges in Writing, much more dangerous than to keep them by Use. This were to exclude all those Things which are not set down."[3] Some members of the Convention voiced reservations on just these scores. Mr. Pollexfen was appalled that his colleagues meant "to stand talking, and making Laws, and in the mean time have no Government at all." But his doubts, and Serjeant Maynard's misgivings that "we may sit five years, and never come to an end of what has been moved," were countered by Edward Seymour's challenge, "Will you do nothing, because you cannot do all? . . . Will you establish the Crown, and not secure yourselves?" The dangers of delay were very real, but as members knew at firsthand, so too were the dangers of failing to shore up their liberties. Indeed, they specifically faulted the Convention of 1660 "for taking no better care" and charged it with responsibility for "many hard laws made grievous to the people."[4] Hence, the House agreed "to assert" the "Rights and Liberties of the Nation," and appointed a committee "to bring in general Heads of such things as are absolutely necessary for securing the Laws and Liberties of the Nation." The Convention had taken upon itself the formidable task of drafting a document meant to be no less than "a new magna charta."[5] The new magna carta, unlike the old, was to include a *right* for Englishmen to possess arms.

In accordance with his promise to call a freely elected parliament and to abide by its decision, William had followed the precedent of 1660 and summoned a "convention." Only a king, of course, could summon a parliament. Convention members worked with deliberate dispatch, mindful that the kingdom remained in jeopardy until the throne was filled and the government settled.

According to the minutes of the Commons journals, the terse notes of John Lord Somers, chairman of the committee that drafted the Declaration of Rights, and the jottings of an anonymous Convention participant, the assembly opened with a wide-ranging debate on the grievances endured at James's hands and the need to devise a workable succession. Two committees were formed. The first, chaired by Sir George Treby, a distinguished judge and former recorder of London, was instructed to organize those complaints raised during the discussions into "heads of things absolutely necessary to be considered, for the better Securing of our Religion, Laws, and Liberties." The second committee, led by John Lord Somers, was charged with amending a motion proposed by the Lords for the succession of William and Mary.

Members of the Convention who held so-called Whig opinions, that is, those who had been most outspoken against standing armies and for the exclusion of James from the throne, held a majority of not quite twenty members in the House of Commons. However, they had sizeable majorities on each of these crucial committees, with an edge of twenty-eight to twelve on the Treby committee and sixteen to six on the Somers committee.[6] (It was the Whigs who had suffered most from forcible disarmament during the reigns of Charles and James.) The two committees were eventually combined under the chairmanship of Somers and brought in a single bill that listed grievances against James, restated rights he had violated, and recognized William and Mary as king and queen. A series of conferences was held between the Commons committee and its counterpart from the House of Lords, and various amendments were proposed and voted upon. A final version was approved on February 12 and presented to William and Mary on February 13.

Within the month the Convention had presented William and Mary with a Declaration of Rights that enumerated the ways in which James II had subverted the constitution of the realm; listed thirteen rights and liberties of the people of England it characterized as "true, ancient, and indubitable" that were to be recognized unequivocally; and elevated William and Mary to the throne as king and queen of England. While the right of subjects to have arms had been singled out as one of the "true, ancient, and indubitable" rights to be included in the Declaration of Rights, it was neither true, ancient, nor indubitable. The Convention members themselves were its authors. Their motive for transforming this customary duty into a right is of critical importance. The clues lie in the preceding history already examined, the sketchy information remaining to us of the Convention's proceedings, and the successive drafts that shaped that article.

Regrettably, the sparse records of the Convention yield only an outline of the discussions which took place and no account of what occurred either within the committees that drafted the Declaration of Rights or at conferences between the committees for the two Houses. Yet this patchy evidence reveals the anxieties of Convention members and the compromises they made to protect and strengthen the ability of Englishmen to have weapons.

In their debates Convention members expressed their outrage at the disarmament of law-abiding subjects during the reigns of Charles and James. The Militia Act of 1662, which permitted militia officers to disarm subjects at their discretion, was singled out as the means by which this had been accomplished. It was particularly galling that the militia, their citizen-army, had been used to disarm and degrade critics of the Crown, and had done so just as the might of the royal army was increasing. It was this political use of disarmament to enhance the Crown and its standing army, not the stringent qualifications of the Game Act, that they objected to. Forcible disarmament was personally humiliating—some members had been disarmed—and politically dangerous, with its spectre of arbitrary rule. Sir John Maynard, at the age of eighty-six the "father of the House," was incensed that "an Act of Parliament was made to disarm all Englishmen, whom the Lieutenant should suspect, by day or night, by force or otherwise—This done in Ireland for the sake of putting arms into Irish Hands."[7] He branded it "an abominable thing to disarm a nation, to set up a standing army." Sir Richard Temple, a spokesman for the antiarmy faction, agreed that the Militia Act had given the Crown "power to disarm all England" and pointed again to the use of that tactic in Ireland. Mr. Boscawen complained that the militia, "under pretence of persons disturbing the Government, disarmed and imprisoned men without any cause," adding, "I myself was so dealt with."

James had demonstrated the political uses of disarmament, providing a preview of how dangerous to the maintenance of English liberties a disarmed citizenry might be. William Sacheverell, a Whig leader, angrily denounced the practice. The need for the private possession of weapons to restrain the Crown was pressed by Mr. Finch, who explained that there was "no safety but the consent of the nation—The constitution being limited, there is a good foundation for defensive arms—It has given us right to demand full and ample security." Finch's point was well taken, for, since the monarchy was a limited one, there was both a personal and a national interest in the ability of citizens to have "defensive arms." Citizens had the "right to demand full and ample security."

In addition to a precis of this debate on the ownership of firearms, a manuscript copy of a speech by Thomas Erle, veteran of several parliaments, a militia officer and Whig, has survived.[8] There is no proof that Erle's speech was actually delivered, but since he had gone to the trouble of writing it he probably presented it in one of the early debates. In any case, the speech affords important clues to the thinking of many members, especially the Whigs. Erle saw no justification for a standing army in England or for the monarch to have "any greater gards" than Elizabeth I or James I had maintained. He had several complaints against the militia and various suggestions for its reform. He asked that "the mallitia Acts" be "made mor certaine soe that those that complaine of Arbitrarynesse in others may not be arbitrary themselves." He wanted only men with at least a moderate income, not the poor, to serve in the trained bands on the usual ground that "they that have something to loose will be careful to preserve it." Of more interest, Erle recommended that "besides the mallitah armes every man that hath £10 and every subtantiall householder in any towne or Citty should be provided of a good muskett in case of an invasion." In anticipation of the objection that these armed men "will destroy the game," he maintained that "there is a law made against it soe that tis not the gun or muskett that offends but the man that makes an ill use of his Armes and he may be punished for it by the law." It was this suggestion, or something very like it, that members must have had in mind, for it dovetails with the language of the first version of the arms article, which declared that Protestants "should provide and keep arms for their common defence."

Treby's committee paraphrased and arranged these and other grievances and reported to the full House on February 2 with a list of twenty-three articles, to which the Commons added another five—a mixture of complaints, suggested reforms, and assertions of rights, all "absolutely necessary to be considered, for the better Securing of our Religion, Laws, and Liberties." The opinions members had expressed about the power of the sword were reflected in articles 5, 6, and 7.

5. The Acts concerning the Militia are grievous to the Subject.

6. The raising or keeping a Standing Army within this Kingdom in time of Peace, unless it be with the consent of Parliament, is against Law.

7. It is necessary for the publick Safety, that the Subjects, which are Protestants, should provide and keep Arms for their common Defence:
   And that the Arms which have been seized, and taken from them, be re-stored.

All three articles were approved by the full House.

Two days later, after vigorous debate, members conceded that for the sake of orderliness and efficiency those ancient rights among the twenty-eight "heads of grievances" ought to be separated from articles that required new legislation, with only the former "to be declared as the rights of the Subject."[9] This was a wise decision. It would have taken weeks to draft legislation to correct the lengthening list of desirable reforms and in the process divisions would have been provoked, whereas all could presumably agree on the rights that were the undeniable inheritance of the people. Moreover, there is real doubt whether the Convention, not having the status of a parliament, could legislate. The Treby committee was instructed "to distinguish such of the . . . heads as are introductory of new laws, from those that are declaratory of ancient rights."

Five days later Treby's committee returned with its revised report. This time it began by enumerating areas in which James II had trespassed upon his subjects' liberties or had attempted to subvert their laws and religion. Complaints 5 and 6 read:

> 5. By raising and keeping a Standing Army within this Kingdome in time of Peace without Consent of Parlyament.
>
> 6. By causing several good Subjects, being Protestants, to be disarmed.[10]

There were thirteen complaints and they were balanced by a reaffirmation of the thirteen rights the King had endangered. Rights 5 and 6 read:

> 5. That the Raising or Keeping of a Standing Army within the Kingdom in time of Peace, unless it be with Consent of Parliament, is against Law.
>
> 6. That the Subjects, which are Protestants, may provide and keep Arms, for their common Defence.

Two significant alterations had been made in the articles dealing with the power of the sword. First, although a right for Protestant subjects to have weapons is declared, the complaint about the Militia Act had been weeded out from the list of articles because reform would require new legislation.[11] Second, article 6, dealing with the right of individuals to have arms, had been altered. The insistence that public safety required subjects to have arms had been dropped, and the assertion that Protestants "should provide and keep arms" had been changed to "may provide and keep arms." While superficially identical, this change was substantial. The original version implied that there was a positive duty to acquire arms for the public good, whereas the amended version made having arms a legal right. The article still referred to the use of private arms for "their common Defence," but the rephrasing shifted the emphasis away from the public duty to be armed and toward the keeping of arms solely as an individual right.

Is it fair to attribute shifts of emphasis to slight alterations in language? Fully half the members of the committee that drafted the Declaration of Rights were lawyers. Lois Schwoerer reminds us that "lawyers were sensitive to nuances in the meanings of words, rather more so than persons not trained in the law. It is legitimate to assume that those of them who assisted in framing the Declaration of Rights considered carefully what they were saying and what political impression they wished to convey."[12]

On February 6 the House committee reported amendments suggested by the Lords, but items 5 and 6 were unaffected. On February 11 another conference with the Lords' committee produced an amendment to article 6 of James's misdeeds. After the statement that James had caused "several good Subjects, being Protestants, to be disarmed," they added, "at the same time when Papists were both armed and imployed, contrary to Law." The record explains that this was "a further Aggravation fit to be added to this Clause."[13] The following day, after what proved to be the last conference between the Commons and Lords committees, amendments of a more serious nature were added. The Commons Journal records without explanation a new version of the article on the right of individuals to have arms. It now read: "That the Subjects which are Protestants may have Arms for their Defence suitable to their Conditions and as allowed by Law." The phrase "may provide and keep arms for their common defence" had been altered to read "may have arms for their defence," and two new restrictions had been added at the end, "suitable to their Conditions and as allowed by Law."[14] These changes had been pressed by the Lords and approved by the Commons without recorded dissent during their final debate on the bill. The very next day the Declaration of Rights was presented to William and Mary.

What effect did these last-minute amendments have on the meaning of article 7? They seem to have marked a final shift away from the private ownership of arms as a political duty and toward a right to have arms for individual defence. Very likely the phrase "may have Arms" was substituted for "may provide and Keep Arms" because "provide" smacked too much of preparation for popular rebellion to be swallowed by the more cautious Lords or, for that matter, by William. Even more indicative of the new emphasis, Protestants were guaranteed the right to have arms "for their defence" rather than for "their common defence." Western insists that the amendments in the House of Lords had "emasculated" this article: "The original wording implied that everyone had a duty to be ready to appear in arms whenever the state was threatened. The revised wording suggested only that it was lawful to keep a blunderbuss to repel Burglars."[15] On the other hand, although downplaying the role of the armed citizenry in maintaining liberty, the article claimed for the individual a right to be armed. In light of this shift, it is particularly ironic that some modern American lawyers have misread the English right to have arms as merely a "collective" right inextricably tied to the need for a militia.[16] In actual fact, the Convention retreated steadily from such a position and finally came down squarely, and exclusively, in favour of an individual right to have arms for self-defence. Not only was the militia left out of the Declaration of Rights, but even the notion that private arms were necessary for common, as opposed to individual, defence was excluded.

It is more difficult to decide what to make of the new clauses tacked to the end of the article—"suitable to their conditions and as allowed by law." For generations citizens had been required to contribute arms to the militia according to their condition, that is, according to their rank and income. And for just as long it had been regarded as proper for wealthy landowners to amass quite large arsenals, although a man of modest means who did so was considered a potential revolutionary. Certain laws, notably the act of Henry VIII on handguns and the Game Act of 1671, regulated possession of firearms in accordance with one's condition. The statute of Henry VIII did not interfere with ownership of full-length firearms, but the Game Act deprived nearly the entire population of its right to have weapons. If the Game Act was still in force despite the Declaration of Rights, the right to have firearms would be a right merely for the wealthy. Furthermore, despite their outrage at the powers in the 1662 Militia Act that act still remained in force. With both the Game Act and the Militia Act unchanged, the assertion of a guaranteed right for Protestants to have arms seems empty rhetoric, the ringing declaration that followed the list of rights that "noe Declarations Judgements Doeings or Proceedings to the Prejudice of the People ought in any wise to be drawne hereafter into Consequence or Example" just so much fine-sounding verbiage.

Practical politics was to blame for the final form of the arms article. The entire Declaration was very much a compromise measure composed of general statements that the majority of Englishmen could support. The legislative reforms proposed by the Convention, such as a modification of the Militia Act, had been left to future parliaments. This meant the arms article declared a right that current law negated, with the understanding that future legislation would eliminate the discrepancy. The pressure for haste and for compromise was not the only factor affecting the enactment of the Declaration. A recent essay has made a convincing case for the conservative influence exerted by William of Orange upon the final version of the Declaration of Rights.[17] William was dependent upon the support of Convention members but, of course, they needed him just as much. And while he felt obliged to accept a reaffirmation of existing rights, he was openly hostile to any extension of popular liberties at the expense of the royal prerogative. The original call for all Protestants to provide themselves with arms "for their common defence" was not, strictly speaking, an infringement of royal rights, but its clear intent was to keep royal power in check. The last-minute amendments that changed that article from a guarantee of popular power into an individual right to have arms was a compromise forced upon the Whigs. The vague clauses about arms "suitable to their conditions and as allowed by law" left the way open for legislative clarification and for perpetuation of restrictions such as that on ownership of handguns. But though the right could be circumscribed, it had been affirmed. The proof of how comprehensive the article was meant to be would emerge from future actions of Parliament and the courts.

Before considering the way the new right to have arms was applied, it might be helpful to consider why its novelty has hitherto escaped detection. The revolution settlement and its centerpiece, the Declaration of Rights, has, on the occasion of its anniversary, been subjected to much close scrutiny. The Declaration of Rights, which Edmund Burke described as that "immortal bill," has been at the center of the controversy. The Convention itself was to blame for at least part of this criticism, for, although it resolved to "not only change hands, but things," it was at pains not to leave that impression. The new magna carta claimed it contained none but "true, ancient, and indubitable rights." That claim has been, on the whole, accepted uncritically. To Macaulay the so-called glorious revolution was still more glorious because "not a single flower of the crown was touched. Not a single new right was given to the people. The whole English law, substantive and adjective, was, in the judgment of all the greatest lawyers . . . exactly the same after the Revolution as before it."[18]

But was it? Hume was closer to the mark when he wrote that in the Declaration of Rights "all the points which had of late years been disputed between the king and people were finally determined," leaving the royal prerogative "more narrowly circumscribed and more exactly defined."[19] Modern critics of the Declaration of Rights find the rights it includes disappointing in their lack of novelty or specificity, and point to the absence of legislation to correct inconsistencies or reform abuses. Lois Schwoerer roundly upbraids such skeptics and charges that "historians who regard the revolutionary settlement as nothing more than a restatement of acknowledged rights have misread, or not read at all, the legal and constitutional background of the thirteen rights claimed in the Declaration of Rights and the Bill of Rights."[20]

The present study can claim to add significant evidence to the dispute over the originality of the rights proclaimed and the criticism about the subsequent lack of legislation to enforce a right contradicted by contemporary law. For the Declaration of Rights contained, among its thirteen specific liberties, the right of Protestant subjects to have arms for their defence, a right never included in earlier lists and one subjects did not have in existing law. It is also a right Schowerer fails to include among the eight rights in the Declaration that she found were "*not* justly described as 'undoubted' and 'ancient'."[21]

Modern American critics have argued that the right to have arms in the English Bill of Rights was so circumscribed and uncertain that it was "more nominal than real."[22] If this appeared the case when the Bill of Rights was passed, by the early eighteenth century legislation and court interpretation had made it clear that an individual right to bear arms belonged to all Protestants. The Whigs continued to claim that the right not only ensured individual self-defence, but served as a restraint on government. This second justification gradually came to be accepted in the eighteenth century. Ironically, of the three aspects of control of the sword debated by the Convention Parliament—an individual right to weapons, reform of the militia, and parliamentary control of standing armies in peacetime—the individual right to have weapons proved the least difficult to ensure. In the months following passage of the Declaration of Rights, however, there was great confusion about the interpretation of the arms article in light of restrictive laws still on the books.

Arms possession was one of the issues Parliament had to address immediately. Their debates over disarmament of Catholics, reform of the militia, and a new game act reveal both the thinking of MPs on this issue and the strenuous efforts of the Whigs to strengthen and clarify the right to have arms as a guarantee of popular power.

Prevention of a Catholic counter-revolution was of paramount concern. Upon his arrival in London, William had proposed that "all Papists, and such Persons as are not qualified by Law, be Disarmed, Disbanded, and Removed from all Employments, Civil and Military."[23] About a month after Parliament passed the Declaration of Rights, it took up the problem of disarming Catholics. Significantly, there was no mention of disarming other "persons as are not qualified by Law," even as a means of disarming Catholics. John Maynard suggested that "all Papists should resort to their own dwellings, and not depart without licences from the next justices; and . . . that all those of that religion bring all their fire-arms in, unless for the necessary defence of their Houses, to officers appointed."[24] There was general agreement that for the time being Catholics should be deprived of all arms except those needed for personal defence.

The discussion then focused on how a subject's Catholicism was to be determined, because, as Mr. Wogan pointed out, "If you find not a way to convict them you cannot disarm them." This statement implies that the House clearly meant the new right to have arms to include all Protestants, whatever their condition. The Speaker agreed that the bill should include a method for conviction, convinced that the new law would be ineffective "unless they are convicted, and being not convicted they will say they are not concerned . . . and not one man will go out of town, nor deliver their arms."

A bill was duly passed "for the better securing the Government by disarming Papists and reputed Papists." It decreed that no one of the Catholic faith "shall or may have or keep in his House, or elsewhere, or in the Possession of any other Person to his Use, or at his Disposition, any arms, Weapons, Gunpowder, or Ammunition (other than such necessary Weapons as shall be allowed to him by Order of the Justices of the Peace, at their general Quarter sessions, for the Defence of his House or Person)." This measure is particularly interesting for the assumptions members made in the course of the debate. They assumed that everyone had a right to own firearms unless he could be conclusively convicted of Catholicism. Even in this time of danger, Catholics were considered to have a right to own arms for their personal defence and the defence of their households.

Parliament's efforts to revise the Militia Act of 1662, despite the nearly universal outrage at its dangerous powers, were a failure. This was not for want of trying. A majority of the Commons passed a measure in July 1689 designed to make the militia more efficient, strengthen local, as opposed to royal, control over it, and eliminate its powers to search for and seize the weapons of so-called suspects. But the act "for the ordering the Forces in the several Counties of this kingdom" ran into resistance in the House of Lords and was lost when Parliament was adjourned. Possibly this disappointing result was due to the fact that many of the lords believed a crisis was no time for militia reform. As Sir William Williams, a militia officer, put it: "Tis no time to form a law for the militia; let us make use of it as it is; you ought to execute the laws as they are, and let them for the Militia as well as they can."[25] The new king was undoubtedly anxious to keep the militia unreformed, since the proposed changes would have reduced his powers and deprived him of the possibility of disarming political foes. As it turned out, the Militia Act of 1662 was to remain in force with only insignificant changes for many years to come.

The Whigs made two further attempts to reform the militia. When a new parliament convened in the autumn of 1690, the Commons appointed a committee to prepare a bill "for the better regulating and making the Militia of the Kingdom more useful." The committee was ready to present the bill on November 29, but the presentation was postponed and the matter later dropped. More than a year later, William himself pressed for an amendment to the Militia Act that would permit him to mobilize men without repaying money forwarded for their previous service. The Commons dutifully prepared a bill along these lines, but when it was returned to committee for final revision they ordered committee members to "prepare and bring in a Bill for the better settling the Militia, for the Service of their Majesties and the Kingdom," a title encompassing more general reform.[26] This surprise tactic failed. When the measure came up for a final vote it was again the original, narrow bill the King had requested. Either William and his supporters felt this was the wrong time for extensive change in the militia, or they believed alterations would deprive the Crown of useful powers.

On the other hand, Parliament did not rest content with those articles in the Bill of Rights that were meant to limit the threat of royal armies in peacetime. It hastened to bolster its arsenal of protective measures with the Mutiny Act of 1689.[27] Englishmen had long opposed the introduction of martial, or military, law in England for fear it would be extended from professional soldiers to members of the militia and would encroach upon the common law and civil liberty. Still, military discipline was essential and certain crimes such as mutiny and desertion were peculiarly military offences. After considerable hesitation Parliament agreed to an act that sanctioned capital punishment for soldiers found guilty of mutiny, sedition, or desertion, but otherwise left military culprits subject to the regular processes of the common law. The Mutiny Act preserved the preeminence of common law while permitting needed military discipline. But it did more. Parliament agreed only to a six-month duration for the Mutiny Act and thereafter renewed it for only one year at a time. This tactic was designed to ensure annual parliamentary oversight of the royal military establishment.

It is one thing to have a structure for control, it is another to exercise it. Parliament's claim to control the Crown's peacetime armies was put to its first real test between late 1697 and the spring of 1699, when it became clear that the King hoped to maintain a large standing army even after the Treaty of Ryswick.[28] The issue provoked a passionate debate in Parliament and the press over parliamentary control of standing armies. Dire warnings were sounded of the danger armies posed to law and liberty and the contrasting safety of militias. Yet there was uncertainty whether the King would accept Parliament's decision in the matter. Whig writers were particularly prominent among those opposed to William's maintenance of a sizeable peacetime army. They drew upon the theories of Machiavelli and Harrington, staunch defenders of an armed citizenry. Harrington placed a premium upon the landowner's independence, which, to his mind, was "in the last analysis measured by his ability to bear arms and use them in his own quarrels."[29]

One of the most influential of these antiarmy writers was John Trenchard, whose tracts were widely read in both England and her American colonies. His best-selling pamphlet, "An Argument Shewing that a Standing Army Is Inconsistent with a Free Government, and Absolutely Destructive to the Constitution of the English Monarchy," singled out reliance upon a citizen militia as *the* reason Englishmen had managed to preserve their liberty while other peoples had succumbed to repression. "And if we enquire how these unhappy nations have lost that precious jewel *Liberty*, and we as yet preserved it, we shall find their miseries and our happiness proceed from this, that their necessities or indiscretion have permitted a standing army to be kept amongst them, and our situation rather than our prudence, hath as yet defended us from it."[30] In language reminiscent of Harrington's, Trenchard insisted that a citizen militia was necessary since "no nation ever preserved its liberty that maintained an army otherwise constituted."[31] As he saw it, "Whereever the militia is, there is or will be the government in a short time," and he quoted with approval Harrington's observation. "Whatever nation suffers their servants to carry their arms, their servants will make them hold their trenchers."[32] Despite general agreement that a militia was preferable, thoughtful men conceded that it could be misused. There were dangers in a militia of propertyless men and in a "select militia" whose members were chosen for their political or religious affiliations. Trenchard recommended that the militia "consist of the same persons as have the property."

Ultimately, Parliament's objections to maintenance of a large army prevailed. William agreed to reduce the size of his army. But he did not agree to disband it. Parliament had been persuaded to approve a small permanent force.

Ironically, despite the Convention's outrage at the Militia Act and its broad claim for parliamentary control of standing armies, reformers had far better success in relaxing the stringent prohibition against popular ownership of firearms imposed by the Game Act of 1671.[33] Insistence on the principle of a right to be armed must have seemed adequate protection against forcible disarmament by the militia. With William's approval, a stiffer law against deer poachers was passed in 1691. The following year Parliament settled down to consider the entire array of game legislation and to draft a bill "for the more easie Discovery and Conviction of such as shall Destroy the Game of this Kingdom." This first reconsideration of game law since 1671 afforded an opportunity to bring game law into line with the right of Protestants to have firearms. The new act's preamble voiced the usual complaint that existing game acts were not being enforced and ordered the execution of "every article and thing in them contained, and not herein and hereby altered or repealed." This would have meant stricter enforcement of the prohibition against firearms had it not been "altered or repealed."

In the Game Act of 1671 guns led the list of prohibited devices. In the act of 1692 guns were not listed at all. True, they might arguably be included under the final catchall prohibition against "other Instruments for destruction of Fish, Fowl, or other Game," but if this was the case it is hard to see why guns were removed from the list of devices expressly named. According to the seventeenth-century rule of law for such omissions, "a later statute, contrary to a former statute, takes away the force of the first statute, without express negative words."[34] Indeed, a later case followed this rule in deciding whether a person was qualified to hunt under the new law. The Court found that "the qualifications being distinctly and severally mentioned, the omission of one is fatal."[35] When the issue of gun ownership arose in the eighteenth century, the courts agreed that guns were definitely not prohibited. In the meantime the law was softened but vague.

The Whigs wanted positive approval, not grudging tolerance, for ownership of firearms and fought to add such a clause to the new game act. Their tactic, the same they used that winter to try to broaden the militia bill, involved introducing some change late in the bill's progress through the House. In this instance, on February 23 when the new game bill was given its final reading, the committee introduced a clause as a rider to the act: "That any Protestant may keep a Musquet in his House, not withstanding this or any other Act."[36] A heated debate ensued, with the clause opposed by the majority Tory party and urged by the Whigs. Sir Christopher Musgrave and Sir Joseph Tredenham argued that it was "irregular to bring in a clause to repeal a law without leave first had," and that this clause would override any laws that limited the keeping of muskets. They also argued that it was inappropriate for a game act: "It is a clause that quite destroys your bill and the intent of it." In its defence, the rider's promoters insisted that it was "for the security of the government that all Protestants should be armed sufficiently to defend themselves." This was too much for Sir John Lowther, a member of the committee that drafted the 1671 act. Lowther protested that the rider was "not proper for this bill, which is for preservation of the game," and worse, that it "savours of the politics to arm the mob, which I think is not very safe for any government." The question of whether the clause should be given a second reading caused a rare division in the House. It was defeated by a vote of 169 to 65. The conservatives who controlled Parliament were willing to proclaim a right to have weapons and to eliminate the prohibition against firearms from the new game act, but they were not prepared to endorse ownership of firearms as a political check on the government, or even to encourage such ownership.

Although subsequent legislation brought statute law into conformity with the right to have arms enshrined in the Bill of Rights, there was still confusion in the counties. Even at the best of times there was bound to be a lag between statutory change and change in the provinces. Difficult questions would ultimately be resolved in the courts, but in the meantime there was disarray. In 1690, for example, a petition by residents of the parish of St. James in Westminster complained that militia captains were summoning "several hundreds of poor inhabitants of the liberty who are not qualified by law to bear arms," and when the poor failed to turn out they were fined.[37] In 1691 a case before King's Bench questioned whether the act of Edward VI against use of gun shot was still in force and decided that it was.[38] As late as 1701 a case was brought by a Shropshire man for trespass after his home had been searched and his gun seized under the 1671 Game Act.[39] In this case the Court failed to deal with the issue of whether a gun could be so seized, but confined itself to matters of jurisdiction. Yet three years later, the Devonshire Quarter Sessions was explicit about the illegality of disarming Englishmen for the protection of game. The Court had been informed that "diverse mean and disorderly persons" were "taking and killing" game with "dogs, nets, guns, harepipes, and other Engines" and were catching fish. The Court authorized constables and tithingmen to search houses and other buildings of persons suspected of keeping "doggs, netts, or other Engins"; and if any were discovered they were to "breake such guns, hang such dogs, burne such netts, and destroy such Engines." But they cautioned "*none of her Majestie's Protestant subjects* were to be 'by virtue hereof disturbed in keeping arms for their own preservation.'"[40]

After passage of the Bill of Rights as before it, most justices of the peace seem to have shied away from using the Game Act of 1671 to disarm poachers and relied instead on the earlier acts against handguns and shot. It is difficult to find a case in which anyone was fined for possession of a gun of any sort unless it was connected with a poaching incident or with possession of other hunting equipment.

Stuart magistrates relied upon legal manuals for guidance. Unfortunately, the most popular legal guidebook of the period, Michael Dalton's *The Country Justice: Containing the Practice of the Justices of the Peace out of Their Sessions,* was no help in this instance.[41] It had been written in 1618 and was revised in 1661 and again in 1697 after Dalton's death. The 1661 edition was obviously dated by the end of the century, and the 1697 edition, which ought to have clarified changes in law resulting from the Glorious Revolution, bears all the marks of a rushed and patchy update. The chapter on guns listed the acts of Henry VIII and Edward VI even though the latter had been repealed two years before. The section on hunting lists the 1671 Game Act and relegates the more recent game acts of 1691 and 1692 to an addenda where portions, including the revised list of prohibited devices, are presented without comment. With the turn of the century, however, the law became clearer and both legal and public opinion left no doubt about the general right to have firearms.

It was during the eighteenth century—a period of boastful satisfaction with the nice balances within the English constitution—that Englishmen came to accept the Whig view of the utility of an armed citizenry. The armed citizen was not only affirmed to be protecting himself but, together with his fellows, provided the ultimate check on tyranny. First, however, came repeated pronouncements of the right for Protestant subjects of all ranks to have firearms.

The century began with a change of monarch. James II's younger daughter, Anne, came to the throne in 1702 upon the death of King William. It was a period of growing Whig power in Parliament. In 1706 Parliament passed yet another game act, which, like the Game Act of 1692, omitted guns from the list of devices forbidden to unqualified persons.[42] This time, however, we have not only the testimony of a member of Parliament who argued for the continued omission of guns from that list but a series of court cases explicitly removing all doubt about the meaning of that change.

Joseph Chitty, an expert on game law, wrote of the omission of guns from the 1706 act: "We find that guns which were expressly mentioned in the former acts were purposely omitted in this because it might be attended with great inconvenience to render the mere possession of a gun *prima facie* evidence of its being kept for an unlawful purpose."[43] Evidence of this intentional omission comes from Lord Macclesfield, who apparently told the solicitor-general that he was not only present in the House of Commons when this act was drafted but had himself objected to the insertion of the word "gun" in it "because it might be attended with great inconvenience."[44]

Several court cases specifically dealt with the question of whether guns were meant to be included under prohibited devices. The most important of these, *Rex versus Gardner,* came before King's Bench in 1739. The defendant had been convicted by a justice of the peace of keeping a gun contrary to the 1706 act.[45] There was no evidence that the gun in question had been wrongfully used, but it was argued that a gun is mentioned in the Game Act of 1671 and considered there an engine, and the act of 1706, having the general words "other engines," should be taken to include a gun. The defence objected "that a gun is not mentioned in the statute [of 1706], and though there may be many things for the bare keeping of which a man may be convicted, yet they are only such as can only be used for destruction of the game, whereas a gun is necessary for defence of a house, or for a farmer to shoot crows." The Court agreed with the defence and concluded: "We are of the opinion, that a gun differs from nets and dogs, which can only be kept for an ill purpose, and therefore this conviction must be quashed."

Thirteen years later a similar case came before King's Bench. In *Wingfield versus Stratford and Osman,* the plaintiff had appealed his conviction and the confiscation of a gun and dog, the dog being a "setting dog," the gun "an engine" for killing game. By this time the Court was not only adamant that guns were not illegal *per se,* but amazed that anyone should think they were. The conviction was overturned because it amounted to a general issue, but the Court made a point of explaining that it would have been bad in any case because it was not alleged that the gun had been used for killing game:

> It is not to be imagined, that it was the Intention of the Legislature, in making the 5 Ann. c.14 to disarm all the People of England. As Greyhounds, Setting Dogs . . . are expressly mentioned in that Statute, it is never necessary to alledge, that any of these have been used for killing or destroying the Game; and the rather, as they can scarcely be kept for any other Purpose than to kill or destroy the Game. But as Guns are not expressly mentioned in that Statute, and as a Gun may be kept for the Defence of a Man's House, and for divers other lawful Purposes, it was necessary to alledge, in order to its being comprehended within the Meaning of the Words "any other Engines to kill the Game," that the Gun had been used for killing the Game.[46]

It is interesting to note that these defences of the legitimate need for firearms did not rest upon, or even mention, the need to keep weapons for the militia.

As the century progressed the general right of Protestants to have weapons became increasingly explicit, and the Whig view that armed citizens were a necessary check on tyranny became orthodox opinion. It was William Blackstone in his classic work *Commentaries on the Laws of England* who set the stamp of approval upon the need for citizens to be armed to guarantee freedom. After listing the rights of Englishmen in his first chapter, Blackstone wrote: "But in vain would these rights be declared, ascertained, and protected by the dead letter of the laws, if the constitution had provided no other method to secure their actual enjoyment. It has therefore established certain other auxiliary rights of the subject, which serve principally as outworks or barriers, to protect and maintain inviolate the three great and primary rights, of personal security, personal liberty, and private property."[47] He identified five "auxiliary" rights, the last being the right of the people to have arms. "The fifth and last auxiliary right of the subject, that I shall at present mention, is that of having arms for their defence, suitable to their condition and degree, and such as are allowed by law . . . and is, indeed, a publick allowance under due restrictions, of the natural right of resistance and self preservation, when the sanctions of society and laws are found insufficient to restrain the violence of oppression."[48] Blackstone's comments on this subject are of the utmost importance since his work immediately became *the* great authority on English common law in both England and America. Blackstone emphatically endorsed the view that keeping arms was necessary both for self defence, "the natural right of resistance and self preservation," and "to restrain the violence of oppression."

These tenets were soon to be severely tested, for in June 1780, while revolution raged in America, England suffered the most violent riots of the century at the very center of government, in London. The immediate provocation was Parliament's passage of an act to relieve Catholics of civil liabilities, but the deeper cause was the discontents of working-class Englishmen. Nearly 120,000 Protestants signed a petition to protest the statute and Lord George Gordon, accompanied by some 60,000 persons, marched to Parliament to deliver it.[49] This peaceful protest turned violent and for several days Londoners were at the mercy of the mob. Crowds demolished Catholic chapels and ransacked Catholic homes. Still more alarming, they broke open the prisons, set Newgate, the largest, ablaze and attacked the Bank of England and other public buildings. The army, with help from the militia and voluntary military associations, eventually restored order, but not before some 450 persons had been killed.

With the mobs quieted the government faced a storm of more civil, if no less vehement, complaint. Members of Parliament faulted it for its inaction, which left them and the city vulnerable, and for some of the actions it eventually took. In the last category the Duke of Richmond cautioned ministers that illegal measures adopted during the emergency were "defensible only upon the ground of necessity" and ought be cured by an act of indemnity.[50] He was especially incensed by a letter in which Jeffrey Lord Amherst, the senior army officer, authorized one Twisleton, the lieutenant colonel on duty in London, to disarm city residents. Instead of endorsing the Lord Mayor's plan "to arm all the inhabitants or housekeepers of every ward," Amherst had ordered Twisleton to confiscate any firearms found in the hands of persons "except they are of the city militia, or are persons authorised by the King to be armed." Amherst replied that in his view it was "both improper and unsafe to trust arms in the hands of the people indiscriminately, or into (sic) the hands of a rabble, or a mob."[51] Two days later two of Amherst's letters on the subject, the Lord Mayor's plan, and the Declaration of Rights were read to the House of Lords, after which Richmond rose to demand a formal inquiry.[52] He assured the Lords that if Amherst's instructions "had been any thing short of a direct violation of one of the leading articles in the sacred and inviolable statute he had just alluded to" he would not be censuring it: "But when he read, and considered the clause in the above Bill of William, which says, 'that every Protestant subject shall be permitted to arm himself for his personal security, or for the defence of his property,' and compared it with the general tenor of the letter . . . particularly the passage in it, which directs the inhabitants of the city of London to be disarmed, the militia only excepted, or those who were authorised by the King . . . it was impossible for him so far to forget the duty he bore his country as a citizen and a senator, as not to demand some species of punishment for the blow directed against her dearest privileges, and for the prevention of similar violations in future."[53] Richmond moved that Amherst's letter be branded "an unwarrantable command to deprive the Protestant subjects of their legal property, and a dangerous attempt to violate their sacred right, 'to have arms for their defence, suitable to their conditions, and as allowed by law.'"

In the ensuing debate Amherst was defended on an assortment of somewhat contradictory grounds.[54] His supporters argued that no violation had been intended, but legal or not, the order made sense under the circumstances. During a crisis there was no time for attention to "verbal *minutiae*," nor was it to be conceived that "a man educated in the field should be acquainted with all the privileges of the Bill of Rights." They claimed that the Lord Mayor had sent similar orders to some quarters of the city, also with "an eye to the lower or disorderly, and to them only." Twistleton had not entered the home of any "sober" citizen and "deprived him of his legal means of defence." Even if he had, with Londoners sending their rusty weapons to be cleaned and a violent conspiracy under way, "how could an intelligible discrimination have been made?" Necessity "demanded extensive and certain relief." The Lord Chancellor, in a long, rambling defence of the government, seemed to leave no argument untried. The head of the armed forces, he submitted, shouldn't be expected to be a "complete lawyer," but in any case, the spirit of Amherst's letter was not against the constitution. The accusation that the letter contained a dangerous doctrine was wrong because it contained "no doctrine whatever." Moreover, how could the King, whose powers derived from the law and the constitution, delegate to others powers he did not have? "It would be a construction violently strained indeed, were the particular sentence of lord Amherst's letter . . . to be construed to be interpreted otherwise, than as describing men authorized by law to bear arms." Richmond had misconstrued the letter. Even had the letter "accidentally militated against the Bill of Rights in point of obvious construction of the wording," Twistleton had done nothing illegal as a result, and there had been no evil intent. Richmond's resolution was defeated.

If it is true that difficult cases make bad law, the Gordon riots assuredly qualify as a difficult case. Richmond and his supporters insisted that a constitutional right for all Protestants to have weapons be maintained, even in the midst of ferocious riots. A majority in the House of Lords was unprepared to go that far. No one denied that all Protestants had a right to have weapons, but during the crisis the government took extraordinary actions, among them disarming some poorer Londoners. Spokesmen denied any intent to violate the constitution, but argued that, under the circumstances, disarming suspicious persons was not illegal.

The Gordon riots left a host of issues demanding clarification, high among them the right of the individual to have and use firearms and the roles of the army, militia, and voluntary military associations in maintaining domestic order. Immediately after the riots, therefore, we find a variety of queries about the extent of the individual's right to have weapons. The response came in statements from a variety of sources reconfirming that right. In a polemical tract written in defence of the armed citizen and the militia, Granville Sharp insisted that the phrase in the Bill of Rights "suitable to their conditions and as allowed by law" referred only to the act of Henry VIII "restraining use of some particular sort of arms, meaning only such arms as were liable to be concealed, or otherwise favour the designs of murderers," but proper arms for defence "are so far from being forbidden by this statute, that they are clearly authorized, and the exercise thereof expressly recommended by it."[55] He claimed that "the laws of England always required the people to be armed, and not only to be armed, but to be expert in arms." No Englishman, he argued, "can be truly loyal" who opposes these essential principles of English law whereby the people are required to have "arms of defence and peace" for "mutual as well as private defence."

Sharp's passionate defence of the militia raises the question of whether the right of Englishmen to have arms as a political, as opposed to an individual, safeguard was inextricably bound to the institution of the militia. Certainly the most outspoken proponents of the right to have arms were usually opponents of standing armies and supporters of the militia. But support for the militia as a concept, the appeals of previous activists, and the efforts of concerned statesmen all failed to halt the militia's irretrievable decline during the eighteenth century. Attempts to devise a more suitable arrangement for militia service failed to make service popular or the militia effective, and from 1740 on, its role in suppressing riots and keeping the peace had been largely taken over by the army.[56] By the end of the century, some 20,000 troops had been stationed throughout the country for that purpose.[57]

The main reason for reluctance to use the militia was the government's view that in many instances its members would side with the lawbreakers. Western, in his fine study of the English militia in the eighteenth century, notes that in 1738 ministerial spokesmen in Parliament made law enforcement, normally a duty of the militia, one of the main reasons for maintenance of a standing army: "Walpole was sure that if called on to suppress smuggling, protect the turnpikes or enforce the gin act, the militia would take the wrong side. Lord Hinton said in the Lords that the militia was composed of the low sort of people who would side with their like."[58] Parliament had hoped to change this with its restructuring of the militia in 1757, but the better-off still could, and did, escape "compulsory" service by hiring a substitute.

In place of the militia, the government permitted formation of voluntary armed clubs such as the London Military Foot Association, composed of middle- and upper-class men "acting in their own self-interest." We are told "they could be highly effective against rioters—even, if necessary, against the militia."[59] The militia was declining, its role transferred to the army and private armed groups, but the right of all Protestant Englishmen to have arms was quite independent of the militia and explicitly safeguarded in statutes and the law courts and affirmed in legal and polemical literature.

In the immediate wake of the Gordon riots, in which the London Military Foot Association had played a prominent role, concern arose about whether armed groups, as well as armed individuals, were protected by the law. The recorder of London, the city's legal advisor, was called upon to give his opinion of the legitimacy of these organizations and did so in July 1780. His elaborate response provides perhaps the clearest summation of the right of Englishmen to have arms at the time of the American Revolution and after the Gordon riots:

> The right of his majesty's Protestant subjects, to have arms for their own defence, and to use them for lawful purposes, is most clear and undeniable. It seems, indeed, to be considered, by the ancient laws of this kingdom, not only as a *right,* but as a *duty;* for all the subjects of the realm, who are able to bear arms, are bound to be ready, at all times, to assist the sheriff, and other civil magistrates, in the execution of the laws and the preservation of the public peace. And that right, which every Protestant most unquestionably possesses, *individually,* may, and in many cases *must,* be exercised collectively, is likewise a point which I conceive to be most clearly established by the authority of judicial decisions and ancient acts of parliament, as well as by reason and common sense.[60]

Blackstone's *Commentaries,* with its insistence upon the necessity for the Englishman's right to be armed, continued to dominate legal thought. Indeed, in an edition of the *Commentaries* that appeared in the 1790's, the editor, Edward Christian, went out of his way to clear up any confusion about that right. After reprinting Blackstone's rationale for game acts, which included disarming the people, Christian added: "Ever since the modern practice of killing game with a gun had prevailed, everyone is at liberty to keep or carry a gun, if he does not use it for the destruction of game."[61]

By the late eighteenth and early nineteenth century, Parliament, the courts, and legal opinion were in agreement on the right of Protestant Englishmen to be armed and the place of this right in their nation's delicately balanced constitution. And if, during the ferocious Gordon riots, extraordinary measures had been taken to disarm some Londoners, care was taken that this not be drawn into precedent or detract from the constitutional right. The right of individuals to be armed had become, as the Bill of Rights had claimed it was, an ancient and indubitable right. It was this heritage that Englishmen took with them to the American colonies and this heritage which Americans fought to protect in 1775.

The Second Amendment and the English Legacy

Born in a country shaken for centuries by the struggles of parties, a country in which each faction in turn had been forced to put itself under the protection of the laws, they learned their political lessons in that rough school; and they had more acquaintance with notions of right and principles of true liberty than most of the European nations at that time.

ALEXIS DE TOCQUEVILLE

The language of the Constitution cannot be interpreted safely except by reference to the common law and to British institutions as they were when the instrument was framed and adopted.

EX PARTE GROSSMAN, 267, US.87, 108–109

ACCORDING to an American Bar Association report of 1975, there is less agreement, more misinformation, and less understanding of the right of citizens to keep and bear arms than on any other current controversial constitutional issue.[1] "The crux of the controversy," the report points out, "is the construction of the Second Amendment to the Constitution." Yet its authors find little point in dwelling on that construction since they conclude, "It is doubtful that the Founding Fathers had any intent in mind with regard to the meaning of this Amendment."[2]

This chapter takes a different tack. It starts from the premise that James Madison and his associates took seriously the task of selecting and defining the liberties that constitute the American Bill of Rights; that they had a specific intention in each instance; and that in this particular instance their views were profoundly, albeit not exclusively, shaped by the British model. If this is correct, then the attitudes embodied in the English right to have arms and the intent behind it can offer some badly needed insight into the meaning of the Second Amendment.

Whatever the merits of the Bar Association report, the authors did not exaggerate the wholesale confusion about the intent of the Second Amendment. The amendment reads: "A well-regulated militia being necessary to the security of a free State, the right of the people to keep and bear arms shall not be infringed." Although the amendment's drafters presumably believed it quite clear, the shared understandings upon which it was based have vanished and this single sentence has proven capable of an amazing range of interpretations. Its most troublesome aspect is the purpose of its pronouncement "a well-regulated Militia being necessary to the security of a free state." Two hundred years after its passage there is no agreement why it is there or what it means. Was it meant to restrict the right to have arms to militia members; to indicate *the* most pressing reason for an armed citizenry; or simply to proclaim the need for a free people to have a conscript, rather than a professional, army? And what sort of militia did the framers have in mind—a select group of citizen-soldiers, every able-bodied male citizen, or didn't it matter? Emphasis on the militia clause has been proffered as evidence that the right to have arms was only a "collective right" to defend the state, not an individual right to defend oneself. Emphasis on the main clause with its assertion of the inviolability of the people's right to have weapons has been cited as proof of an individual right to have arms.

Since 1975, the Bar report notwithstanding, there has been an increasingly impressive debate over interpretation.[3] In an effort to understand the amendment's meaning, authors have stressed the philosophical impact on the founders of classical and enlightenment views of armed citizens and citizen-armies and the practical effect of the wilderness, egalitarianism, and individuality on American thought and practice. The significance of English common law and English liberties has received less attention. When Americans have turned to the English tradition for guidance their efforts have been hampered by the absence of studies of the Englishman's right to have weapons or of the place of firearms in English society. Little wonder that American legal scholars have often misunderstood the English right, English practice, and sometimes English history as well.[4]

There are legitimate reasons to approach the English legacy warily. More than a century elapsed between passage of the English and American bills of rights with important repercussions for both nations. Moreover, there are obvious differences of setting and political philosophy. And while American drafters adopted some English rights verbatim, the language of the two pronouncements on arms differs markedly and importantly. The English drafters claimed for Protestants a right to "have arms for their defence," provided that these were "suitable to their condition and as allowed by law." These restrictions have led some

American scholars to conclude that any traditional right of Englishmen to own weapons was "more nominal than real."[5] By contrast, the American right claims for "the people"—presumably regardless of their religion, state, or condition—a right to keep and carry weapons that the government, or at least the federal government, must not breach. The American language is much broader, unless one restricts the entire right to members of a well-regulated militia. Yet if colonial Americans regarded their right to be armed as one of their rights as Englishmen, they are unlikely to have narrowed it.

In a second departure the militia, so prominent a focus of the American right, isn't mentioned in the English right or in later justifications of it. Yet such is the zeal of some American scholars seeking to confine a right to bear arms to members of the militia that they have attempted to graft a nonexistent militia clause onto the English right. Roy Weatherup, for instance, insists the English guarantee that "the Subjects which are Protestants may have arms for their defence" actually meant: "Protestant members of the militia might keep and bear arms in accordance with their militia duties for the defense of the realm."[6] Notwithstanding the fact that the Convention which drafted the English Declaration of Rights explicitly rejected the phrase "their common defence" in favor of "their defence," Weatherup found "no recognition of any personal right to bear arms."[7]

In this chapter I do not intend to retell the story of colonial constitutional history or to dwell upon the intellectual origins of that history, both of which have been covered by others.[8] Rather, I track the transmission of the English duty and right to be armed to colonial America to discover how both were adapted to the American context. I assess the impact of English strategies to control the sword upon Americans when they came to design their own constitutions. Lastly, the language of the Second Amendment is interpreted as the Court in *Ex parte Grossman* suggested, "by reference to the common law and to British institutions as they were when the instrument was framed and adopted."

When Alexis de Tocqueville visited the young American republic he was struck by the pervasive English influence. To his mind there was "not an opinion, custom, or law . . . which the point of departure will not easily explain."[9] De Tocqueville's otherwise sharp eyes picked out the broad pattern but obviously missed importance differences; yet his impression is an important reminder that the colonists were men and women steeped in English laws, English customs, English prejudices, and English habits of mind. Indeed, the transplantation of an English legal framework was official policy. The entire body of the common law was to be applied in the new setting except where circumstances made it impracticable. "Let an Englishman go where he will," Richard West, counsel to the Board of Trade, explained in 1720, "he carries as much of law and liberty with him as the nature of things will bear."[10] To this English base colonists speedily added their own laws and regulations. While Kermit Hall sees this as an active process by which "informed persons made choices that were always important under often novel, and invariably difficult circumstances," he finds that "English law remained the source of authority" and that "this transatlantic connection persisted even after the colonies achieved independence."[11]

This continuity, especially of rights, was significant. The English government's great success in luring Englishmen to America's wild shores was due in part to pledges that the emigrants and their children would continue to possess "all the rights of natural subjects, as if born and abiding in England."[12] A guarantee of these rights, for example, was incorporated into the charters of Virginia, Connecticut, and Massachusetts, and fundamental principles of English jurisprudence, with their protection of personal liberty and private property, were specifically incorporated into the laws of the Maryland General Assembly in 1639, the Massachusetts Body of Liberties in 1641, the West New Jersey Charter of Fundamental Laws in 1676, and the New York "Charter of Libertyes and Privilidges" in 1683.[13]

As English imperial policy evolved and the rights of Englishmen were refined and expanded in the wake of the Glorious Revolution, shrewd observers wondered how fully Americans would or could enjoy these rights. In his study of the effects of the Glorious Revolution on the colonies, David Lovejoy contends that "despite significant changes won by Englishmen in England, the lesson the Revolution taught colonies was that they were dominions of the Crown to be dealt with as the King wished, with no assurance of Englishmen's rights on permanent bases."[14] If Americans did learn this lesson before the eighteenth century, they nevertheless continued to believe that they were entitled to the rights of native-born Englishmen, as their charters and their laws proclaimed. Since 1689 these rights included the right of Protestants to keep and use weapons. Unlike the thorny problem of colonial representation in Parliament, nothing stood in the way of the transmission of this right to the New World. In fact, circumstances in the colonies ensured that both the right and the duty to be armed were broader than the English original.

Despite a diversity of colonial settings, each with its "richly textured pattern of legal institutions and activity," the approach to private arms ownership and the employment of an armed citizenry was remarkably uniform from colony to colony.[15] The perils of frontier life did have an impact on the colonists' retention of an armed citizenry, but the effect was to modify an old tradition rather than to create a new one.[16] Every colony passed legislation to establish the familiar institutions of the militia and watch and ward.[17] Like the English militia, the colonial militia played a primarily defencive role, with armies of volunteers organized whenever an offensive campaign was planned.[18] All men between the ages of sixteen and sixty were liable for militia service, with some exceptions for clergy, religious objectors, and Negroes.

The dangers all the colonies faced, however, were so great that not only militia members but all householders were ordered to be armed. A 1623 law of Plymouth colony, for example, stipulated that "in regard of our dispersion so far asunder and the inconvenience that may befall, it is further ordered that every freeman or other inhabitant of this colony provide for himselfe and each under him able to beare armes a sufficient musket and other serviceable peece for war . . . with what speede may be."[19] A similar Virginia statute of 1640 required "all masters of families" to furnish themselves and "all those of their families which shall be capable of arms (excepting negroes) with arms both offensive and defensive."[20]

Colonial law went another step beyond English law and required colonists to carry weapons. A Newport law of 1639 provided that "noe man shall go two miles from the Towne unarmed, eyther with Gunn or Sword; and that none shall come to any public Meeting without his weapon."[21] Early Virginia laws required "that no man go or send abroad without a sufficient partie well armed," and "that men go not to worke in the ground without their arms (and a centinell upon them)." They even specified that "all men that are fittinge to beare armes, shall bring their pieces to the church uppon payne of every offence, if the mayster allow not thereof to pay 2 lb of tobacco."[22]

It is scarcely surprising that settlers living in the wilderness would enact measures for their individual and mutual protection; a century later, however, Connecticut's revised militia act still ordered *all* citizens, both "listed" soldiers of the militia and every other householder, to "always be provided with and have in continual readiness, a well-fixed firelock . . . or other good fire-arms . . . a good sword, or cutlass . . . one pound of good powder, four pounds of bullets fit for his gun, and twelve flints."[23] And in 1770, not long before the Revolution, the colony of Georgia felt it necessary "for the better security of the inhabitants" to require every white male resident "to carry firearms to places of public worship."[24] In this instance the purpose was to defend colonists "from internal dangers and insurrections." But whether the threat came from foreigners, Indians, or slaves the means of defence was the same—the arming of the citizenry.

The emphasis of the colonial governments was on ensuring that the populace was well armed, not on restricting individual stocks of weapons. They had neither the incentive nor the ability to replicate common law restrictions on the type or quantity of arms a citizen owned based upon his condition or religion. Nor was the protection of game a consideration in America. Game was plentiful and prospective emigrants were guaranteed the "liberty of fishing and fowling."[25] The usual restrictions on the use of firearms in crowded areas or with intention to terrify were put in place, but the emphasis was on the duty to be armed and a freer use of private firearms than existed in England. This was true even in the aftermath of insurrection. An act passed in 1676 after Bacon's Rebellion against the colonial administration in Virginia forbade five or more armed persons to assemble without authorization, but was careful to affirm that "liberty is granted to all persons to carry their arms wheresoever they go."[26]

This liberality did not extend to all New World residents. Just as the English regarded Catholics as potential subversives who were permitted the use of firearms only on sufferance, Indians and black slaves were the suspect populations of the New World. With certain exceptions both groups were barred from owning firearms. The authors of a recent study of the right of blacks to have firearms argue that the need for racial control was instrumental in the transformation of the English right to have arms into a broader right for white Americans.[27]

Efforts were made to prevent Indians from acquiring firearms. The Massachusetts general laws of 1648, the Commonwealth's first legal code, made it a crime for anyone to "directly or indirectly amend, repair . . . any gun, small or great, belonging to any Indian . . . Nor shall [he] sell or give to any Indian, directly or indirectly, any such gun, or any gun-powder . . . upon payn of ten pounds fine."[28] Yet in 1675–1676, during the great Indian uprising in New England known as King Philip's War, the Indians were "well supplied with muskets, bullets, and powder" and described as "dead shots."[29] No wonder a Virginia statute that same year made selling arms or ammunition to Indians a crime for which the culprit was to die "without benefit of clergy" and to forfeit his estate.[30] As non-citizens Indians were neither expected, nor usually allowed, to participate in the militia.[31]

The second group forbidden to possess weapons were black slaves, with restrictions sometimes extended to free blacks. These restrictions varied with the particular colony's degree of reliance upon slave labour and the state of its internal and external security. Northern colonies were ambivalent about blacks possessing firearms. The policy they adopted was similar to that applied to Catholics in England. Blacks in Massachusetts and Connecticut were permitted to keep private firearms but did not serve in the militia. New Jersey excluded blacks from militia service but permitted free Negroes to have firearms.[32] A Virginia statute of 1639 that required white men to be armed at public expense did not require, but did not specifically prohibit, black men from having arms.[33] The following year, however, Virginia passed "An Act Preventing Negroes from Bearing Arms" directed against slaves, and in 1680 a further statute forbade all Negroes, slave and free, from carrying weapons.[34] Free Negroes in Virginia could keep one gun in their home, however, and blacks living on frontier plantations, whether slave or free, were permitted to have firearms. South Carolina at first permitted free blacks to be armed and serve in the militia, but during the eighteenth century reversed the policy.[35] Georgia insisted upon a license for even temporary use of a gun by a slave.[36]

Neither the Indian nor the slave was a citizen, therefore neither was entitled to the rights of English subjects. Both were, like English Catholics, also regarded as a threat to the established order, and even free blacks were treated with caution. Their inability to legally own weapons merely confirmed their status as outsiders and inferiors.

If the development of an armed citizenry in the American colonies was influenced by English law, liberty, and custom and enhanced by the perils of the wilderness and racial tensions, it was undergirded by an antigovernment and antiarmy legacy from seventeenth- and eighteenth-century England. English theory on the respective merits and hazards of armies and militia remained unshaken during the late seventeenth and eighteenth centuries, even when English practice diverged from English professions and when the much-eulogized English militia failed to live up to its billing and become an effective or reliable substitute for the army.[37] The issue of the incompatibility of freedom and standing armies was kept in the public eye by domestic alarms, such as King William's plan to maintain a large peacetime army, and continental events, and remained a favourite theme of pamphleteers. The dilemma of how to ensure the security of the realm while preserving the liberty of its people was made more formidable by the so-called military revolution on the Continent.[38] But as an island nation England could more easily afford to cling to principle for the sake of individual liberties. An ocean and vast wilderness offered a similar luxury to its American colonies. In addition there were legal protections. When large armies were necessary during wartime, or when the army began to take over the militia's domestic peacekeeping duties, Englishmen counted upon the stipulations in the Bill of Rights that no standing army could be maintained in time of peace without consent of Parliament, that Protestant subjects had the right to have arms, and the annual Mutiny Act to protect their civil liberties.[39] Even as the role and size of the English army increased, therefore, Englishmen on both sides of the Atlantic remained highly skeptical of that institution and looked to their legal protections up to the eve of the American Revolution.

The American colonists followed the lively English debates over the retention of a standing army and pored over the works of the radical Whigs and authors such as John Trenchard. Indeed, Bernard Bailyn finds that "to say simply that this tradition of opposition thought was quickly transmitted to America and widely appreciated there is to understate the fact. Opposition thought in the form it acquired at the turn of the seventeenth century and the early eighteenth century, was devoured by the colonists."[40] These works constituted a rich mine for American opponents of British colonial policy and afforded a ready source of material when colonists found a British army stationed in their midst in peacetime. Although armies were particularly feared, the colonists were also alert to the dangers of a "select militia," which Trenchard and others pointed out.[41] The American minister Simeon Howard, for example, cited Francis Bacon's warning "that wise men have thought a people might be in danger from their own militia unless great caution was used in the direction of it."[42] The militia was essential but it needed to be composed of the right sort of men and used sensibly.

The influence of the radical Whigs on Americans of the founding era is generally acknowledged, but the profound impact of a more moderate English author has usually been underestimated. The first volume of William Blackstone's *Commentaries on the Laws of England* did not appear in Britain until 1765, and the fourth and last volume until 1769, yet nearly 2500 copies had been sold in America by the start of the American Revolution in 1775.[43] Blackstone's work not only sold well but was regarded immediately as authoritative. The author of a study of the influence of English and European writers on eighteenth-century American political thought tabulated the frequency with which some thirty-six authors were mentioned by major American political writers between 1760 and 1805. Blackstone was the most cited English writer, second only to Montesquieu overall.[44] Blackstone's views on the right of individuals to be armed are of importance, therefore, for penetrating the minds of the American founders.

Blackstone was firmly convinced that subjects needed to be armed to defend themselves and to avoid dependence on professional armies, but he also expanded the role of an armed citizenry beyond the individual's own preservation to the preservation of the entire constitutional structure. He dubbed the right of the people to be armed an "auxiliary" right of the subject that served "to protect and maintain inviolate the three great and primary rights, of personal security, personal liberty, and private property."[45] "To vindicate these rights, when actually violated or attacked," Blackstone insisted that English subjects were entitled "in the first place, to the regular administration and free course of justice in the courts of law; next to the right of petitioning the king and parliament for redress of grievances; and lastly to the right of having and using arms for self-preservation and defence."[46]

As for standing armies, Blackstone recommended they be treated with utmost caution. "In a land of liberty," he wrote, "it is extremely dangerous to make a distinct order of the profession of arms."[47] He advised Englishmen to look upon their professional soldiers "as temporary excrescences bred out of the distemper of the State, and not as any part of the permanent and perpetual laws of the Kingdom."[48]

Pinning down intellectual influence is always difficult, yet when the reliance upon Blackstone is added to other evidence it seems clear that English attitudes and practices toward the use of weapons shaped American attitudes and practices. Americans were more consistent, however. Practice and profession did not diverge in America as they did in England. Professional armies had no "permanent and perpetual" role in America until 1763. Rather, the settlers' jealousy of their personal right to have weapons was magnified by what one historian characterized as their "almost panic fear" of a standing army, a legacy handed down from generation to generation by forbears "who, if they were Southern Cavaliers recalled Cromwell and his major-generals, and if they were New Englanders the attempts of the Stuarts to raise regular armies and govern through their sanction."[49] Americans' belief in the virtues of the militia for military defence and their distrust of standing armies mirrored English opinion. Any attempt to impose a professional army upon the colonies was bound to be seen as the preface to tyranny.

George III had not been long upon the British throne before the colonists' worst fears about government by an army appeared about to be realized. The new king and his ministers were determined to enforce existing trade regulations and to see that colonists shouldered some of the costs Britain incurred on their behalf. The story is a familiar one, but has tended to stress the provocative impact of Parliament's direct taxation of imports in 1764 and internal articles in 1765. Yet concern over taxation by a parliament in which they were not represented was preceded by, and coupled with, another fear—the fear of government by an army. The militia acts of 1757 through 1763, the last passed a year before the Sugar Act, authorized British lords lieutenant or their deputies "to seize and remove the Arms, Clothes and Accoutrements" of the militia whenever the officer "shall adjudge it necessary to the Peace of the Kingdom."[50] They also permitted the Crown to mobilize the militia "in case of actual invasion . . . or in case of rebellion" and place it under the general officers of the regular army. Thus General Thomas Gage, commander of all British forces in North America, was entitled to vast powers over the colonial militia, including the power to disarm it at his discretion. Such power in the hands of a military man raised the spectre that Britain meant to govern by means of a standing army, a scenario that became more credible when Britain failed to remove its army in 1763 after the French and Indian War. Military protection may have been needed along the frontiers, but this army was stationed in the cities. Simeon Howard, an outspoken clergyman, conceded that "the keeping up troops sufficient to guard exposed frontier posts may be proper," but echoed Blackstone and the radical Whigs when he opined, "To have an army continually stationed in the midst of a people, in time of peace, is a precarious and dangerous method of security."[51]

Insult was then added to injury in 1764–1765, when the proceeds from the new, direct tax on sugar and other imports and the infamous Stamp Act were earmarked for the support of this peacetime British army. The Massachusetts House of Representatives did not mince words: "A military force if posted among the People, without their express Consent, is itself, one of the greatest Grievances, and threatens the total subversion of a free Constitution."[52]

An American boycott of British goods led to repeal of the Stamp Act in 1766, but the troops remained. A year later Parliament enacted the General Revenue Act, again taxing goods at American ports, again to support the standing army in America. The sharp denunciation of this measure by the Massachusetts legislature and its letter on the subject to other colonial assemblies led to the dispatch of some 4000 troops to Boston, 1 soldier for every 4 inhabitants.

Colonists began to look to their own defences. By 1769 citizens of Boston were "calling upon one another to (be) provided with arms." Charges that this was seditious behaviour provoked the *Boston Evening Post,* a newspaper widely printed throughout the colonies, to reply: "For it is certainly beyond human art and sophistry to prove the British subjects, to whom the *priviledge* of possessing arms is expressly recognized by the Bill of Rights, and, who live in a province where the law requires them to be equip'd with *arms,* etc. are guilty of an *illegal act,* in calling upon one another to be provided with them, as the *law directs.*"[53] A subsequent article cited the English Bill of Rights, natural law, and William Blackstone as proof of the individual's right to have firearms. "It is a natural right which the people have reserved to themselves, confirmed by the Bill of Rights, to keep arms for their defence; and as Mr. Blackstone observes, it is to be made use of when the sanctions of society and law are found insufficient to restrain the violence of oppression."[54] American recourse to the guarantee in the English Bill of Rights against standing armies in peacetime required some logical contortions. The English Bill of Rights specified that there be no standing army in time of peace without the consent of Parliament, but Parliament *had* consented. In 1774, therefore, the Continental Congress paraphrased the Bill of Rights article to read: "A standing army in these colonies, in time of peace, without the consent of the legislature of that colony, in which such army is kept, is against law."[55] All arguments from the Bill of Rights became still less credible when colonial charters were revoked.[56] Without charter guarantees it was questionable whether colonists still possessed all the rights of native-born Englishmen.[57] Americans fell back on the thesis that these rights, once granted, were irrevocable or, as in the case of Blackstone's defence of the right to be armed, were natural rights that common law might propound but did not create and could not revoke.

By 1775 any spark could have ignited a general conflagration. As in the English Civil War the militia provided the fuel. The American militia found itself in an ambivalent position as tensions between the Crown and the colonists mounted. Composed of colonials, the militia was regarded as unreliable by the Crown. Subject to government orders, it was regarded as an uncertain protector by the colonists. Both sides raided militia arsenals lest its weapons fall into the wrong hands. By late 1774 and early 1775 "patriots" in many colonies began to organize an alternative "select" militia, comprising right-thinking individuals and officers, the famous minute men. Preparations were also begun to amass weapons at Concord, Massachusetts, for a volunteer army of some 15,000 men. The attempt to confiscate these weapons led to bloodshed.

On the evening of April 18, 1775, General Gage ordered some of his regulars to march from Boston to Lexington and Concord to confiscate military supplies stored there for the planned army and to arrest radical leaders staying in Lexington. The colonists were alerted in time to warn John Hancock and Samuel Adams to flee, but the minute men did not flee and by the time Gage's men returned to Boston, war had begun. It is the final irony that the creed that recognized the rightness of resistance in extreme circumstances, along with the liberties Americans prized and the constitutional theories they professed, were a legacy of that mother country from which they now sought freedom.

The colonists' concern about civilian control of the military and the individual's right to be armed resonated through the constitutional documents and declarations that accompanied the American Revolution. The Declaration of Independence, for instance, charged that George III had "kept among us in times of peace Standing Armies (and ships of war) without the consent of our legislatures. He has affected to render the military independent of and superior to the Civil power. He has combined with others to subject us to a jurisdiction foreign to our constitution, and unacknowledged by our laws;—For quartering large bodies of armed troops among us:—For protecting them, by a mock trial, from punishment for any murders which they should commit on the inhabitants of these States."

During the course of the Revolutionary War Americans were obliged to craft constitutions of their own. The Articles of Confederation of 1777, predecessor of the American constitution, enabled the thirteen colonies to act in concert. Although it was drafted during a desperate war, its authors were nevertheless at pains to limit standing armies. They specifically forbade any colony from maintaining a standing army in peacetime "except such number only, as shall be deemed necessary by the United States in Congress assembled, for the defence of such state . . . nor shall any body of forces be kept up by any state in time of peace, except such number only, as in the judgment of the United States in Congress assembled, shall be deemed requisite to garrison the forts necessary for the defence of such state."[58] However, in keeping with English tradition and their own practice, the Articles decreed that every colony "shall always keep up a well-regulated and disciplined militia." Most political authority was left in the hands of individual states, and it was their constitutions that dealt with political life in detail and touched more nearly the lives of the citizenry.

Individual colonies were forced into constitution-making because their charters were no longer valid. Most devised new governments patterned on the system of representative government in effect before the crisis. Since it was unclear whether traditional English liberties were still legally protected, many constitutions contained their own bills of rights. Those that took this precaution were careful to indicate their preference for a militia over a standing army and either specifically stated that the people had a right to be armed, or made it necessary by insisting upon a citizen militia that was a general, not a select, militia.[59]

Typically several statements about the use of weapons were lumped together in one or two successive articles. The Virginia Bill of Rights of 1776, for example, stated in paragraph thirteen: "That a well regulated militia, composed of the body of people, trained to arms, is the proper, natural, and safe defence of a free state: that standing armies in time of peace, should be avoided, as dangerous to liberty; and that in all cases the military should be under strict subordination to, and governed by, the civil power."[60]

The Delaware Declaration of Rights had two separate articles on the subject:

18. That a well regulated militia is the proper, natural and safe defence of a free government.

19. That standing armies are dangerous to liberty, and ought not to be raised or kept up without the consent of the legislature.[61]

The assertion that it was illegal to raise or keep a standing army in time of peace without the consent of the legislature, repeated in one new constitution after another, was a straight borrowing from the English Bill of Rights.[62] The New Hampshire Bill of Rights contained the following articles:

2. All men have certain natural, effectual, and inherent rights; among which are—the enjoying and defending life and liberty—acquiring, possessing and protecting property—and, in a word, of seeking and obtaining happiness.

24. A well regulated militia is the proper, natural, and sure defence of a state.

25. Standing armies are dangerous to liberty, and ought not to be raised or kept up without consent of the legislature.[63]

The Massachusetts constitution of 1780 began with a declaration of rights that asserted:

1. All men are born free and equal and have certain natural rights; among which may be reckoned the right of enjoying and defending their lives and liberties, that of acquiring, possessing, and protecting property; in fine, that of seeking and obtaining their safety and happiness.

17. The people have a right to keep and to bear arms for the common defence. And as, in time of peace, armies are dangerous to liberty, they ought not to be maintained without the consent of the legislature; and the military power shall always be held in an exact sub-ordination to the civil authority, and be governed by it.[64]

The right of a citizen to bear arms for personal defence as well as civic duty was specifically stated in the "Declaration of the Rights of the Inhabitants of the State of Pennsylvania": "That the people have a right to bear arms for the defence of themselves and the state; and as standing armies in time of peace, are dangerous to liberty, they ought not to be kept up. And that the military should be kept under strict subordination to, and governed by, the civil power."[65] On the other hand the North Carolina and Massachusetts declarations merely asserted "That the people have a right to bear arms for the defence of the state" and contained the usual strictures against standing armies. A specific right to have arms for personal use was not directly mentioned.

Other colonies failed to include any bill of rights. In instances where a right to have arms for individual defence is not specifically stated or where there is no bill of rights at all, two questions must be resolved if one is to determine whether an individual right to arms was intended. First, is it certain that states which failed to mention a right to have arms for individual defence intended a general, rather than a select militia? A general militia would have included all, or nearly all, adult men, and presumed that the male population would be armed and trained in arms. Second, what rights were intended in states that decided not to include any bill of rights?

In answer to the first question, the famous Virginia Bill of Rights of June 1776 expressly stated that "a well-regulated Militia, *composed of the body of the people,* trained to arms, is the proper, natural, and safe defence of a free State."[66] The New York State constitution proclaimed it "the duty of every man, who enjoys the protection of society, to be prepared and willing to defend it" and laid down the rule that the state's militia was to be constantly armed "as well in peace as in war," disciplined "in readiness for service," and "a magazine of warlike stores, proportionate to the number of inhabitants, be forever hereafter . . . established, maintained, and continued in every county of this state."[67] Because of their long-standing prejudice against a select militia as constituting a form of standing army liable to be skewed politically and dangerous to liberty, every state had created a general militia.

In addition, the individual's right to be armed, where not specifically mentioned, is unmistakably assumed. For example, state constitutions generally began with a preamble patterned after that of the Declaration of Independence. But after stating the right of the people to life, liberty, and property—the traditional English triumvirate—they added the people's right to defend themselves and their property. Both Pennsylvania, which specifically listed a right to bear arms for self-defence, and Delaware, which did not, have initial articles in their constitutions which read: "That all men are born equally free and independent, and have certain natural, inherent, and unalienable rights, amongst which are, the enjoying and defending life and liberty, acquiring, possessing, and protecting property, and pursuing and obtaining happiness and safety."[68] The Massachusetts constitution in its list of rights merely declared that the people had "a right to keep and to bear arms for the common defence," yet its first article claimed for all men natural rights, "among which may be reckoned the right of enjoying and defending life and liberty."[69] It is difficult to see how the right to defend one's life could be fully exercised if citizens were deprived of the right to be armed.

This leaves the question of states such as New Jersey, New York, South Carolina, and Georgia, which had no bill of rights at all. In these instances was the individual's right to be armed denied or regarded as unimportant? If so, then other unlisted rights were also in jeopardy. All the reasons given for failure to incorporate a bill of rights assumed that basic freedoms were sufficiently well protected without such a listing, just as Americans often had to claim prior to the revolution. In an essay printed in 1772 entitled "The Rights of the Colonists," Samuel Adams listed "Natural Rights of the Colonists as Men," and in this category he put their right to life, liberty, and property "together with the right to support and defend these in the best manner they can."[70] These were, he argued, "deductions from the duty of self-preservation, commonly called the first law of nature."[71] According to this theory, Americans retained all their rights without having to list or specify them. George Nicholas later argued this same point in regard to the absence of a bill of rights in the original federal constitution: "A bill of rights is only an acknowledgment of the preexisting claim to rights in the people. They belong to us as much as if they had been inserted in the Constitution."[72]

Theorists also pointed out that since the new states were republics the people had never relinquished their personal liberties and a list of protected rights was therefore superfluous. Indeed, a list might imply that state governments had some control over such rights.[73] Others believed the checks within their constitution and its incorporation of English common law afforded all the protection necessary. New Jersey's constitution, which had no bill of rights, explicitly incorporated "the common law of England, as well as so much of the statute law as has been heretofore practised in this colony . . . such parts only excepted as are repugnant to the rights and privileges contained in this charter."[74] Even that firebrand in the cause of individual liberty, Patrick Henry, argued that the absence of bills of rights from state constitutions did not imperil freedom because "they had the substance of a bill of rights contained in their constitutions, which is the same thing. I believe that Connecticut has preserved it, by her Constitution, her royal charter, which clearly defines and secures the great rights of mankind—secures to us the great important rights of humanity; and I care not in what form it is done."[75]

Finally, all the states approved of the principle laid down in the Declaration of Independence that whenever government becomes destructive of the ends for which it is intended it is the right of the people to alter or abolish it. The New Hampshire constitution stated this rule in particularly feisty terms: "Whenever the ends of government are perverted, and public liberty manifestly endangered, and all other means of redress are ineffectual, the people may, and of right ought, to reform the old, or establish a new government. The doctrine of non-resistance against arbitrary power and oppression, is absurd, slavish, and destructive of the good and happiness of mankind."[76] This was, after all, what Blackstone himself declared every Englishman's right. It is noteworthy that the people, not the militia, are to preserve their liberties by the overthrow of an oppressive government. The militia could be "select" and unrepresentative and was, after all, always under government command. It was safer to entrust the people themselves with the protection of their liberty.

These first constitutions reflected traditional attitudes toward professional armies, militia, and the right of individuals to be armed. They denounced standing armies and endorsed a militia, provided that it was a general and not a select militia. Such a militia required general ownership of firearms, and general skill in their use. Some states also included a specific right for an individual to have firearms for his own defence. But even states that failed to include a list of rights affirmed a citizen's right to defend himself and his property and incorporated English statute and common law with the English Bill of Rights provision for individuals to have arms.

The English model was constantly before the framers of the American Constitution. They saw themselves continuing the English precedent of special conventions that began with the barons who imposed Magna Carta on King John and included the Convention Parliament that recalled Charles II from exile and the convention of 1689 that drafted the English Bill of Rights and declared William and Mary king and queen.[77] One of the delegates' urgent tasks was to strengthen the military power of the central government. Individual states were vulnerable to invasion and powerless to suppress insurrection. The long American frontier required constant protection, yet under the Articles Congress had no authority over state militia and could not compel states to contribute to an army. Delegates needed to protect the community without jeopardizing liberty. Happily, English strategies for prudent control of the sword were ready to hand. When delegates copied English policies the public was reassured. When they departed from them there was grave concern, which was not allayed until passage of the Second Amendment brought the American system more into line with English practice. Here, then, is the key to the meaning and intent of the much-misunderstood Second Amendment.

Delegates to the Constitutional Convention understandably approached the subject of military arrangements with caution, but in the end the need for a permanent military establishment took precedence over traditional distaste for standing armies. Gouverneur Morris, a Pennsylvania delegate, recalled the disillusionment of many delegates with the militia and their acceptance of the need for a standing army. "The danger we meant chiefly to provide against was, the hazarding of the national safety by reliance on that . . . force [the militia]. An overweening vanity leads the fond many, each man against the conviction of his own heart, to believe or affect to believe, that militia can beat veteran troops in the open field and even play of battle. This idle notion, fed by vaunting demagogues, alarmed us for our country, when in the course of that time and chance, which happen to all, she should be at war with a great power."[78] Morris concluded, "To rely on undisciplined, ill-officered men, though each were individually as brave as Caesar, to resist the well-directed impulse of veterans, is to act in defiance of reason and experience."[79] Like Morris, Charles Pinckney of South Carolina had "but a scanty faith in Militia" and believed that "there must also be a real military force. The United States had been making an experiment without it, and . . . [would] see the consequence in their rapid approaches toward anarchy."[80]

Although delegates appreciated the need for a professional army, Governor Edmund Randolph of Virginia believed "there was not a member in the federal convention who did not feel indignation at such an institution."[81] They took great care to create checks and balances that could prevent misuse of military power. The president, like the English king, was to be commander-in-chief of the armed forces, but Congress was given the power "to raise and support armies." To ensure that these armies remained subject to civilian control, delegates proposed that "no appropriation of Money to that Use shall be for a longer Term than two Years." And whereas in English practice it was the King's prerogative to declare war, the proposed constitution gave this power to Congress.

These seemed inadequate precautions to delegates such as Elbridge Gerry of Massachusetts, who objected to the appropriation of the military budget for a two- rather than a one-year period as was the case in England, a departure "for which he could not conceive a reason—that it implied there was to be a standing army which he inveighed against as dangerous to liberty, as unnecessary even for so great an extent of Country as this, and if necessary some restriction on the number and duration ought to be provided. Nor was this a proper time for innovation. The people would not bear it."[82] Roger Sherman of Connecticut defended the biennial appropriation as necessary since "the Legislature is to be biennially elected," but said that he "should himself like a reasonable restriction on the number and continuance of an army in time of peace."[83]

The absence of any statement about the undesirability of standing armies in time of peace, a second American departure, also caused consternation. Some members were merely uneasy and, like George Mason, "hoped there would be no standing army in time of peace, unless it might be for a few garrisons."[84] Others, such as Elbridge Gerry, warned that "there was no check here against standing armies in time of peace . . . The people were jealous on this head, and great opposition to the plan would spring from such an omission."[85] He and Alexander Martin of North Carolina moved to add to the clause "to raise and support armies" the words "provided that in time of peace the army shall not consist of more than ———— thousand men."[86] Madison noted, "His idea was that the blank should be filled with two or three thousand."[87] The motion failed.

Fault was even found with the third departure from English precedent: the decision to give Congress the power to declare war. It was pointed out that in England a declaration of war was the King's prerogative, while approval of funds was left to Parliament. The American modification gave Congress control of both the purse and the war-making power.[88]

During the Constitutional Convention the militia was no less a concern than a standing army. The Articles of Confederation had left the states broad control over their own militia, merely requiring that a militia be maintained and be "well regulated and disciplined" and "sufficiently armed."[89] Only when "land-forces" were raised for "the common defence" was Congress empowered to appoint higher ranking militia officers. By 1787 each state's virtual autonomy over its militia had resulted in considerable diversity and even serious neglect.

The majority of delegates opted to follow English practice and to grant the central government a far greater measure of control over the militia. Those who approved the change were swayed by various considerations. A few, such as Gouverneur Morris and Charles Pinckney, had no faith in the militia and felt it might as well be subject to greater federal control. But most delegates agreed that central oversight was required to ensure uniformity and effectiveness.[90] James Madison favored greater federal control in the belief that only if there was an effective militia could they avoid reliance upon a standing army. Madison argued, "As the greatest danger is that of disunion of the States it is necessary to guard against it by sufficient powers to the Common Government and as the greatest danger to liberty is from large standing armies, it is best to prevent them by an effectual provision for a good Militia."[91] George Mason agreed that if the standing army was to be kept small, the militia "ought therefore to be the more effectually prepared for public defence. Thirteen States will never concur in any one system, if the disciplining of the Militia be left in their hands."[92] Congress was given the power to impose standard drill and equipment.

To enable the federal government to use the militia instead of an army, Congress was authorized to summon state militia "to put the laws of the union in execution." Madison and Randolph defended this congressional power with the same argument used to justify greater federal oversight of state militia—that the alternative was to use "regular forces."[93]

The federal government's power to appoint militia officers caused further dissention. Under the Articles of Confederation, unless "land-forces" were being raised for common defence state legislatures appointed all militia officers.[94] The delegates considered limiting state appointment to officers "under the rank of General officers," an idea that Roger Sherman found "absolutely inadmissible" and Gerry believed would make the States mere "drill-sergeants." Gerry told his colleagues he "had leif let the Citizens of Massachusetts be disarmed, as to take the command from the States, and subject them to the General Legislature."[95] He believed it would spell the end of state governments: "Let us at once destroy the State Governments have an Executive for life or hereditary, and a proper Senate, and then there would be some consistency in giving full powers to the General Government."[96] But as the States were not to be abolished, he wondered at the attempts that were made to give powers inconsistent with their existence. Even moderate John Dickenson believed "the States never would nor ought to give up all authority over the Militia."[97] Delegates thought better of it and agreed to leave to the states the power to appoint militia officers.

To avoid reliance upon a standing army, therefore, delegates tried to provide for a more effective and uniform national militia. To do so it was necessary to transfer to the federal government a large measure of control over state militia. The states could still appoint officers and oversee the militia when it was not mobilized by the central government. The final language gave Congress power:

> To provide for calling forth the Militia to execute the Laws of the Union, suppress Insurrections and repel Invasions.
>
> To provide for organizing, arming, and disciplining the Militia, and for governing such Part of them as may be employed in the Service of the United States, reserving to the States respectively, the Appointment of the Officers, and the Authority of Training the Militia according to the discipline prescribed by Congress.

As the convention drew to a close several delegates had second thoughts about the proposed distribution of military power. Even men who had voted for these measures now became alarmed at the degree of military might vested in the new government. When a motion had been offered in August to limit the number of men in a peacetime army, George Mason had merely "hoped" there would be no standing army in peacetime, and he and Madison joined in rejecting it. A month later Mason was sufficiently apprehensive to propose his own cautionary language. "Being sensible that an absolute prohibition of standing armies in time of peace might be unsafe, and wishing at the same time to insert something pointing out and guarding against the danger of them," he moved to preface the clause granting Congress the authority to organize, arm, and discipline the militia with the words "And that the liberties of the people may be better secured against the danger of standing armies in time of peace."[98] Randolph seconded the motion and Madison spoke in favor of it, noting that "it did not restrain Congress from establishing a military force in time of peace if found necessary; and as armies in time of peace are allowed on all hands to be an evil, it is well to discountenance them by the Constitution, as far as will consist with the essential power of the Government on that head."[99] Gouverneur Morris objected on the ground that the motion set "a dishonorable mark of distinction on the military class of Citizen."[100] Pinckney and Bedford concurred. By this time a majority of delegates seemed impatient with amendments, and Mason's motion failed.

The great majority of delegates, some thirty-nine of fifty-five, signed the final draft. Mason, Randolph, and Gerry refused. Mason, author of the famous Virginia Bill of Rights, particularly objected to the absence of a federal declaration of rights, since "the laws of the general government being paramount to the laws and constitutions of the several States, the Declaration of Rights in the separate States are no security."[101] He pointed out, "There is no declaration of any kind, for preserving the liberty of the press, or the trial by jury in civil causes; not against the danger of standing armies in time of peace."[102]

Thus, the great distaste for a standing army notwithstanding, the proposed constitution provided the federal government with the power to create and maintain an army of unlimited size.[103] The passionate preference for a militia notwithstanding, the proposed constitution gave the federal government broad powers over state militia. There was no prohibition like that in the English Bill of Rights against standing armies in time of peace. Each was disturbing to a people suspicious of central power. Together they meant that the new government would dominate the nation's military force.

The debate over ratification proved long, passionate, and bitter. It took nearly a year before the required minimum of nine states ratified the constitution and ensured the new government a trial. Even then the crucial states of New York and Virginia had yet to join the union, and after they finally agreed, North Carolina and Rhode Island remained aloof.

As the dissenters at the convention had predicted, many Americans shared their misgivings about the extensive powers assigned the federal government, including its right to keep a peacetime army and its control over state militia. Both were sharply questioned. The Massachusetts ratification convention was warned that standing armies tended to increase in size and power. Thomas Dawes pointed out that Charles II and James II had enlarged the royal army until it "caused a great and just alarm through the nation; and accordingly when William III came to the throne, it was declared to be unconstitutional to raise or keep a standing army in time of peace, without the consent of the legislature."[104] He added that "most of our own state constitutions have borrowed this language from the English declaration of rights." General Thompson also cited the British attitude toward military power: "This section, I look upon it, is big with mischiefs. Congress will have power to keep standing armies. The great Mr. Pitt says standing armies are dangerous. Keep your militia in order—we don't want standing armies."[105] He ignored the failings of the militia during the Revolutionary War and repeated the traditional pieties: "Standing armies are a curse—take care of militia, they are virtuous men—soldiers in a standing army are the worst men—standing armies are never necessary . . . Britain never authorized the Parliament to pay an army for two years."[106]

During the Virginia deliberations identical objections were raised. Standing armies were described as "grand machines to suppress the liberties of the people . . . We ought, therefore, strictly to guard against the establishment of an army—whose only occupation would be idleness; whose only effort the introduction of vice and dissipation; and who would, at some future day, deprive us of our liberties, as a reward for past favors, by the introduction of some military despot."[107]

Fears about the creation of a standing army were compounded by the enhanced power the federal government would have over state militia. It might use that power to neglect the militia, to fail to arm or drill it. George Mason pointed out that some forty years earlier the English governor of Pennsylvania had planned to enslave Americans "by totally disusing and neglecting the militia."[108] Mason called upon the Virginia convention to "provide against the danger of having our militia, our real and natural strength, destroyed."

John Smiley raised similar alarms in the Pennsylvania convention. "I object to the power of Congress over the militia and to keep a standing army . . . the last resource of a free people is taken away."[109] He foresaw a variety of unpleasant possibilities: "Congress may give us a select militia which will, in fact, be a standing army—or Congress, afraid of a general militia, may say there will be no militia at all. When a select militia is formed, the people in general may be disarmed."[110] Patrick Henry told the Virginia convention that his "greatest objection" to the proposed government was "that it does not leave us the means of defending our rights, or of waging war against tyrants . . . Have we the means of resisting disciplined armies, when our only defence, the militia, is put into the hands of Congress?"[111] "I hope," Henry exhorted them, "before we part with this great bulwark, this noble palladium of safety, we shall have such checks interposed as will render us secure. The militia . . . is our ultimate safety. We can have no security without it."[112]

Defenders of the constitution repeated points made during the Constitutional Convention. In *The Federalist Papers* Alexander Hamilton assured readers there could never be government by an army, for the new constitution vested the power of raising armies in a representative assembly, and even that assembly could only approve the military budget for a two-year period.[113] As for federal power over the militia, Madison warned, as he had done at the convention, that if you limit the government's power "you give them a pretext for substituting a standing army."[114] In response to fears that the militia might not be properly armed George Nicholas asked the Virginia convention, "Will they be worse armed than they are now?"[115] In any event whatever the central government's military or other powers the people could protect their liberties because the population was, and would continue to be, armed. Sedgwick of Massachusetts, for example, found it "a chimerical idea to suppose that a country like this could ever be enslaved . . . Is it possible . . . that an army could be raised for the purpose of enslaving themselves or their brethren? or, if raised whether they could subdue a nation of freemen, who know how to prize liberty and who have arms in their hands?"[116] Noah Webster used the same argument: "Before a standing army can rule the people must be disarmed; as they are in almost every kingdom in Europe. The supreme power in America cannot enforce unjust laws by the sword; because the whole body of the people are armed, and constitute a force superior to any band of regular troops that can be, on any pretence, raised in the United States."[117]

The armed population was even seen as the safeguard of religious freedom. Zachariah Johnson told the Virginia convention their liberties would be safe because "the people are not to be disarmed of their weapons. They are left in full possession of them. The government is administered by the representatives of the people, voluntarily and freely chosen. Under these circumstances should any one attempt to establish their own system [of religion], in prejudice of the rest, they would be universally detested and opposed, and easily frustrated. This is the principle which secures religious liberty most firmly. The government will depend on the assistance of the people in the day of distress."[118] The federalists agreed with Blackstone that an armed population was the ultimate check on tyranny.

Persuasive as these reassurances seem, they do not, and did not, satisfy, for the federal government was in a position to control the power of the sword, particularly in the absence of a federal bill of rights. The need for a federal bill of rights subsumed all other issues. And on this subject opponents of the constitution received overwhelming support. Among its advocates were John Adams and Thomas Jefferson, those great architects of the American Revolution, both of whom were abroad during the deliberations in Philadelphia. In November 1787 Adams wrote to Jefferson: "What think you of a Declaration of Rights? Should not such a thing have preceded the Model?"[119] The following month Jefferson gave James Madison his opinion of the proposed constitution: "I will now add what I do not like. First the omission of a bill of rights providing clearly and without the aid of sophisms for freedom of religion, freedom of the press, protection against standing armies, restriction against monopolies, the eternal and unremitting force of the habeas corpus laws, and trials by jury in all matters of fact triable by the laws of the land and not by the law of Nations."[120] "Let me add," he continued, "that a bill of rights is what the people are entitled to against every government on earth, general or particular, and what no just government should refuse, or rest on inference."[121]

By early January 1788, over the vigorous objections of some citizens and the grave reservations of thousands of others, five states—Delaware, Pennsylvania, New Jersey, Georgia, and Connecticut—had ratified the constitution without insisting on amendments. Specific amendments had been proposed, but they failed to win approval. The Pennsylvania convention, for example, debated a list of fifteen amendments, one of which dealt with the right of the people to be armed, another with the militia. The amendment on the right to bear arms read:

> That the people have a right to bear arms for the defence of themselves and their own State, or the United States, or for the purpose of killing game; and no law shall be passed for disarming the people or any of them, unless for crimes committed, or real danger of public injury from individuals; and as standing armies in time of peace are dangerous to liberty, they ought not to be kept up; and that the military shall be kept under strict subordination to and be governed by the civil power.[122]

The Massachusetts convention was the first to submit a list of recommended amendments with its notice of ratification. That ratifying convention had been so evenly balanced between those for and against the constitution that the federalists agreed to amendments to secure ratification. Samuel Adams had proposed that the constitution "be never construed to authorize Congress to infringe the just liberty of the press, or the rights of conscience; or to prevent the people of the United States, who are peaceable citizens, from keeping their own arms; or to raise standing armies, unless when necessary for the defence of the United States, or of some one or more of them; or to prevent the people from petitioning, in a peaceable and orderly manner, the federal legislature, for a redress of grievances: or to subject the people to unreasonable searches and seizures."[123] But the nine amendments eventually proposed were rather haphazard, omitting, for example, guarantees for freedom of speech, the press, religion, and the right to bear arms, but reserving to the states all powers not delegated to the federal government.

The Massachusetts precedent of including suggested amendments along with ratification was copied by states that had not yet ratified. The New Hampshire convention, meeting hard on the heels of the Massachusetts convention, adopted the nine Massachusetts amendments and added three others: one to limit standing armies, a second to ensure the individual's right to have arms, and a third to protect freedom of conscience. The article on the right to keep arms read: "Congress shall never disarm any Citizen unless such as are or have been in Actual Rebellion."[124] Virginia drew up a list of forty amendments, many patterned after the Virginia Declaration of Rights. The Virginia arms amendment and similar declarations submitted by New York and North Carolina claimed that "the People have a right to keep and bear Arms" and that a militia composed of the body of the people "capable of bearing arms" is the proper and safe defence "of a free state."

Every state bill of rights had copied the English prohibition against maintenance of a standing army in time of peace without the consent of the legislature, and five of the eight states that proposed specific amendments urged the federal government to include a similar prohibition. Indeed, some wanted it more restrictive than the English right, and rather than a simple majority, asked that a two-thirds or even a three-fourths vote of members present in each house of Congress be required to approve a standing army in time of peace.[125]

Although the Constitution had been ratified by the required nine states without amendment, this was accomplished with the promise that the new Congress would add amendments to protect liberties and restrict federal powers.

When the first Congress of the United States convened on March 4, 1789, many congressmen believed that consideration of a bill of rights could be safely postponed, perhaps until their second session. Ironically, James Madison, who had advocated passage of the Constitution without such amendments, now pressed his colleagues to act.[126] When his remarks failed to produce any response, Madison drafted his own version of a bill of rights and interrupted his colleagues on June 8 to present it to them. He explained to Jefferson several days later that he had selected those rights for inclusion which were unexceptional and thus most likely to win approval.[127] He deliberately proposed amendments that would not detract from federal powers, among them a right for the citizenry to be armed.[128] His version of what would eventually become the Second Amendment stated: "The right of the people to keep and bear arms shall not be infringed; a well armed, and well regulated militia being the best security of a free country: but no person religiously scrupulous of bearing arms, shall be compelled to render military service in person."[129] He assumed that amendments protecting civil liberties would be most naturally accommodated within the body of the Constitution in the article which delineated the powers of Congress, section nine between the third and fourth clauses. The third clause forbade Congress from passing bills of attainder or *ex post facto* laws, the fourth referred to direct taxation.

It was another six weeks before Madison's amendments were discussed. The matter was then referred to a committee of three—Madison, John Vining of Delaware, and Roger Sherman of Connecticut. The committee was also to consider the numerous state proposals and report back to the House.

Nearly 200 years later, in 1987, a hitherto unknown draft for a bill of rights that Sherman apparently drew up for the consideration of the committee was found.[130] While Sherman's suggested list differs in many respects from the committee's final report, it is extremely interesting both for Sherman's suggestions and for the changes his colleagues made. Sherman does not specifically mention an individual right to keep and bear arms, although this may have been implied in his second article, which referred to "certain natural rights" retained by the people, among which he listed that of "pursuing . . . Safety." Blackstone had referred to the right of Englishmen to have weapons as a "natural right of resistance and self preservation."[131] The fifth of Sherman's eleven articles dealt with the militia but did not characterize it as "the best security" of a free country, or hint that it was preferable to a standing army. This article seems to have been intended to enhance somewhat the states' control of their militia.[132] Sherman proposed that when not in the service of the United States, the militia be subject to state law, albeit their organization and discipline remain under federal jurisdiction. His proposal read: "The militia shall be under the government of the laws of the respective States, when not in the actual Service of the united States, but such rules as may be prescribed by Congress for their uniform organization and discipline shall be observed in officering and training them, but military Service shall not be required of persons religiously scrupulous of bearing arms."

The committee clearly found Sherman's omission of a stated right to have weapons and his attempt to enhance state authority unsatisfactory. Its own arms amendment remained close to Madison's language. It failed to mention state powers over the militia but proclaimed and protected "the right of the people" to have weapons. The committee agreed upon the following amendment: "A well regulated militia, composed of the body of the people, being the best security of a free state, the right of the people to keep and bear arms shall not be infringed; but no person religiously scrupulous shall be compelled to bear arms."[133] The committee had amended Madison's article in several respects. In keeping with state proposals, the word "state" had been substituted for Madison's "country." "State" was a more precise term and, since a state was a polity, it could refer either to one state or to the United States. The language had also been tightened by reversing the reference to the militia and the right of the people to bear arms, perhaps intentionally putting more emphasis on the militia. Significantly, Madison's stipulation that the militia be well armed was omitted, but the committee added its own description of the militia as composed of the body of the people.

There were further delays before the House considered the committee report. When it did so, it agreed to Sherman's proposal that amendments be added at the end of the Constitution rather than imbedded within it. This has long been regarded as Sherman's major contribution. The amendments were approved and forwarded to the Senate, where senators "slashed out wordiness with a free hand."[134] The third and fourth articles on the House list, for instance, were combined into the present First Amendment. The article on the right to have arms was altered, tightened, and abbreviated to its modern form: "A well regulated Militia being necessary to the security of a free State, the right of the people to keep and bear Arms, shall not be infringed." The militia was now described not as "the best security" of a free state but as "necessary to the security" of a free state, an even stronger endorsement than Madison's original description. The phrase describing the militia as "composed of the body of the people" was dropped. Elbridge Gerry's fear that future Congresses might expand the religious exemption from militia service to include everyone seems to have convinced the Senate to drop that clause as well.[135]

Of even greater importance for an accurate understanding of the Senate's intentions are a suggested amendment and two proposals that the senators rejected. They turned down the recommendation of five states that standing armies in time of peace require explicit consent, and they denied a proposal to return to the states more power over their militia.[136] And like the Convention Parliament in 1689, the senators rejected a motion to add "for the common defense" after "to keep and bear arms."[137] The American Bill of Rights, like the English Bill of Rights, recognized the individual's right to have weapons for his own defence, rather than for collective defence. These decisions taken together make the task of deciphering the framers' intentions much surer. In this form, along with eleven other amendments, the Second Amendment was approved by Congress and sent to the state legislatures for ratification.

At each stage of its passage through Congress the arms amendment became less explicit. Doubtless congressmen felt no qualms about streamlining the language and omitting explanatory phrases because their constituents shared an understanding of the institutions and opinions behind it. But, in the long term, these understandings have vanished and brevity and elegance have been achieved at the cost of clarity. Modern writers, lacking the benefit of the historical tradition upon which the Second Amendment was based, have derived an astonishing variety of meanings from its single sentence. They argue, for example, that the purpose was only to preserve the states' powers over state militia; that the amendment merely protects the right of members of a militia—the National Guard of today—to be armed; and that the language "the right of the people to keep and bear arms" should not be interpreted to grant to any individual a right to own a weapon.[138] Lawrence Cress, for example, has maintained that the term "the people" in the Second Amendment means that a "collective" rather than an individual right is intended.[139] Yet this idiosyncratic definition founders because it cannot be reasonably applied to the First, Fourth, Ninth, and Tenth Amendments, where reference is also made to the right of "the people."[140] The Second Amendment was the product of Anglo-American attitudes, prejudices, and policies toward standing armies, militia, citizenship, and personal rights examined in this book. This history can enable us to recapture and clarify the intention of the framers.

The Second Amendment was meant to accomplish two distinct goals, each perceived as crucial to the maintenance of liberty. First, it was meant to guarantee the individual's right to have arms for self-defence and self-preservation. Such an individual right was a legacy of the English Bill of Rights. This is also plain from American colonial practice, the debates over the Constitution, and state proposals for what was to become the Second Amendment. In keeping with colonial precedent, the American article broadened the English protection. English restrictions had limited the right to have arms to Protestants and made the type and quantity of such weapons dependent upon what was deemed "suitable" to a person's "condition." The English also included the proviso that the right to have arms was to be "as allowed by law." Americans swept aside these limitations and forbade any "infringement" upon the right of the people to keep and bear arms.

These privately owned arms were meant to serve a larger purpose as well, albeit the American framers of the Second Amendment, like their English predecessors, rejected language linking their right to "the common defence." When, as Blackstone phrased it, "the sanctions of society and laws are found insufficient to restrain the violence of oppression," these private weapons would afford the people the means to vindicate their liberties.[141]

The second and related objective concerned the militia, and it is the coupling of these two objectives that has caused the most confusion. The customary American militia necessitated an armed public, and Madison's original version of the amendment, as well as those suggested by the states, described the militia as either "composed of" or "including" the body of the people.[142] A select militia was regarded as little better than a standing army.[143] The argument that today's National Guardsmen, members of a select militia, would constitute the *only* persons entitled to keep and bear arms has no historical foundation. Indeed, it would seem redundant to specify that members of a militia had the right to be armed. A militia could scarcely function otherwise. But the argument that this constitutional right to have weapons was exclusively for members of a militia falters on another ground. The House committee eliminated the stipulation that the militia be "well-armed," and the Senate, in what became the final version of the amendment, eliminated the description of the militia as composed of the "body of the people." These changes left open the possibility of a poorly armed and narrowly based militia that many Americans feared might be the result of federal control. Yet the amendment guaranteed that the right of "the people" to have arms not be infringed. Whatever the future composition of the militia, therefore, however well or ill armed, was not crucial because the people's right to have weapons was to be sacrosanct. As was the case in the English tradition, the arms in the hands of the people, not the militia, are relied upon "to restrain the violence of oppression."

The Constitution gave to the federal government broad authority over state militia. Was the Second Amendment meant to placate states fearful about this loss of control? In fact not one of the ninety-seven distinct amendments proposed by state ratifying conventions asked for a *return* of any control that had been allocated to the federal government over the militia. Sherman's proposal that some power be returned to the states was rejected by the drafting committee. In any event, the Second Amendment does nothing to alter the situation. Indeed, that was precisely the complaint of the anti-Federalist *Centinel* in a discussion of the House version of the arms article. The *Centinel* found that "the absolute command vested by other sections in Congress over the militia, are [sic] not in the least abridged by this amendment."[144] Had the intent been to reapportion this power some diminution of federal control would have been mandated. None was.

The clause concerning the militia was not intended to limit ownership of arms to militia members, or return control of the militia to the states, but rather to express the preference for a militia over a standing army. The army had been written into the Constitution. Despite checks within the Constitution to make it responsive to civil authority, the army was considered a threat to liberty. State constitutions that had a bill of rights had copied the English model and prohibited a standing army in time of peace without the consent of their state legislatures. Five states had urged such an amendment for the federal constitution. Some had suggested that a two-thirds or even a three-fourths vote of members of each house be required to approve a standing army in time of peace.[145] Indeed, George Mason had attempted to add such a proviso during the convention when he moved to preface the clause granting Congress authority to organize, arm, and discipline the militia with the words "And that the liberties of the people may be better secured against the danger of standing armies in time of peace."[146] A strong statement of preference for a militia must have seemed more tactful than an expression of distrust of the army. The Second Amendment, therefore, stated that it was the militia, not the army, that was necessary to the security of a free state. The reference to a "well regulated" militia was meant to encourage the federal government to keep the militia in good order.

The position of this amendment, second among the ten amendments added to the Constitution as a Bill of Rights, underscored its importance to contemporaries. It was no less than the safety valve of the Constitution. It afforded the means whereby, if parchment barriers proved inadequate, the people could protect their liberties or alter their government. It gave to the people the ultimate power of the sword. The *Philadelphia Federal Gazette* and *Philadelphia Evening Post* of Thursday, June 18, 1789, in an article later reprinted in New York and Boston, explained each of the proposed amendments to be sent to the states for ratification. The aim of the article that became the Second Amendment was explained this way: "As civil rulers, not having their duty to the people duly before them, may attempt to tyrannize, and as the military forces which must be occasionally raised to defend our country, might pervert their power to the injury of their fellow-citizens, the people are confirmed . . . in their right to keep and bear their private arms."[147]

The protection it granted was a blanket one. William Rawle, George Washington's candidate for the nation's first attorney general, described the scope of the Second Amendment's guarantee. "The prohibition," he wrote, "is general." "No clause in the constitution could by any rule of construction be conceived to give congress a power to disarm the people. Such a flagitious attempt could only be made under some general pretence by a state legislature. But if in any blind pursuit of inordinate power, either should attempt it, this amendment may be appealed to as a restraint on both."[148]

The Second Amendment brought the American Constitution into closer conformity with its English predecessor. In both cases, the intention was to guarantee citizens the means for self-defence and to ensure that when, in the course of time, it was necessary to raise standing armies, they would never pose a danger to the liberties of the people.

Afterword

The great ideals of liberty and equality are preserved against the assaults of opportunism, the expediency of the passing hour, the erosion of small encroachments, the scorn and derision of those who have no patience with general principles, by enshrining them in constitutions, and consecrating to the task of their protection a body of defenders.

JUSTICE BENJAMIN CARDOZO

THE right to be armed has not worn well, despite its enshrinement in the English and American bills of rights.[1] It is no longer a right of Englishmen.[2] The curious will still find it in the English Bill of Rights, but it has been so gently teased from public use that most Britons have no notion of when or how it came to be withdrawn. The American Second Amendment, on the other hand, is at the center of a noisy and emotional debate. It has been "infringed" by numerous laws and is under fierce assault. Many who believe it guarantees an individual right regard it as a dangerous anachronism, others insist that no individual right was ever intended. Two recent law review articles characterize it, respectively, as "embarrassing" and "terrifying," adjectives unlikely to be ascribed to any other right.[3] Given new historical evidence of the Second Amendment's original intent it is reasonable to ask how, if at all, this information should be applied. Americans, unsure whether banning weapons will make their lives more or less dangerous, can certainly question whether the purpose of its eighteenth-century authors is of other than academic interest. Although the demise of the English right and the significance of the Second Amendment's original intent are outside the scope of this essay, they deserve to be addressed.

The Englishman's right to be armed was in its heyday in the eighteenth and nineteenth centuries. Blackstone's pronouncement in 1765 that an armed public was essential to protect the constitution as well as the individual seems to have been readily and generally accepted. The Swiss author Jean DeLolme arrived in England the year Blackstone's *Commentaries* appeared, keen to understand the intricacies of the English constitutional system. Ten years later he produced *The Constitution of England,* a book brimming with admiration for the Englishman's rights, but realistic about their fragility. "All those privileges of the People, considered in themselves," were, in DeLolme's estimation, "but feeble defences against the real strength of those who govern. All those provisions, all those reciprocal Rights, necessarily suppose that things remain in their legal and settled course."[4] The problem was: "What would then be the resource of the People, if ever the Prince, suddenly freeing himself from all restraint, and throwing himself as it were out of the Constitution," attempted to force his will upon them? DeLolme found that England's answer was "resistance . . . the question has been decided in favour of this doctrine by the Laws of England."[5] This "resource" was actually guaranteed by a bill of rights that "expressly insured to individuals the right of publicly preferring complaints against the abuses of Government, and moreover, of being provided with arms for their own defence."[6] To DeLolme it was simple: "The power of the People is not when they strike, but when they keep in awe: it is when they can overthrow every thing, that they never need to move."[7] *The Constitution of England* appeared in numerous editions and earned its author Disraeli's praise as "England's Montesquieu."[8]

It is easy to defend popular liberties when "things remain in their legal and settled course," but far more difficult when anarchy, not absolutism, threatens. The French revolutionary wars were followed by a decline in real wages for workers in England. Their misery led to serious riots in Yorkshire and other industrial districts, and fears for public safety. Rioters were vigorously punished and public meetings restricted, but the tension continued. Then in August 1819 a large, peaceful crowd of working men and women assembled at St. Peter's Fields in Manchester to protest the Corn Laws that increased the price of bread and to demand the reform of Parliament. When the crowd refused to obey an order to disburse, the local magistrates seem to have panicked. The yeomanry were commanded to fire. A dozen people were killed and hundreds more were injured. The so-called Peterloo massacre caused public outrage and dismay, angry debate in Parliament, and repressive emergency legislation, including limitations on the right to keep and carry firearms. One meeting "to consider the best means of bringing the instigators and perpetrators of the late Manchester massacre to justice, and to embrace the subject of the necessity of Parliamentary Reform" was scheduled for November 15, 1819, at Habergham Eaves, near Burnley.[9] Although local magistrates warned the public to stay away, several thousand people turned out and, with music playing and banners flying, marched to the meeting site. Many marchers carried sticks. When a cry was raised during the meeting that soldiers were approaching, people "drew forth pikeheads which they had concealed, and some began to screw the pikeheads on staves. Some also produced pistols." After a second alarm the leaders dissolved the meeting. The magistrates had not interfered but, as the crowd disbursed, some of those who had pistols fired into the air.[10]

Several of the organizers were later arrested. They were charged initially with treason, but the charges were reduced to conspiring to assemble an unlawful meeting, attending an unlawful meeting, and causing people to go armed to a public meeting. Six of those arrested were convicted. A detailed record of their trial, *Rex versus George Dewhurst and Others,* has left us the arguments of opposing attorneys and the judge's finding about the legality of citizens' carrying arms and the separate, and thornier, issue of armed gatherings. The trial of these armed protesters, and Parliament's debates over a seizure of arms act, allow us to eavesdrop on discussions and judgments about the extent of the right to be armed at a time when that right seemed a threat to public safety.

The trial record reveals agreement about the individual's right to be armed for self-defence, but the Crown's attorney contended that while "people have a right to meet to discuss public grievances . . . by the law they cannot meet armed for the purpose of redressing or deliberating on any question."[11] The defence counsel, however, had "heard [of] the men of England having arms for their own protection," and quoted Blackstone, who, "speaking loudly and largely of the rights of the people of England," had designated this the fifth auxiliary right of the subject.[12] Counsel then launched into a stirring defence of the right to assemble, which is also applicable to the right to be armed.

> Gentlemen, many men would suppose it would be better if it had been no part of our Constitution, I can very readily believe. But our lot has been cast in a land where it has pleased our ancestors for now two centuries to go through a series of struggles and controversies of danger and of death for the acquisition of freedom . . . our ancestors were pleased rather to enjoy a condition of perilous freedom than a state of abject tranquillity in the condition of slaves. If with that glorious condition there be some qualification and some deduction, then I say only this . . . no institution is perfect, no condition absolute and without its fault; and if there be in the realm of England and the practice of our ancestors some hazard, difficulty, and danger, so I say also is there an inheritance of glory.[13]

Justice Bayley was uneasy with the quotation from Blackstone, presumably because of its revolutionary tenor, and the defence counsel retreated to the safer ground that "armament is lawful for self-defence."[14] The judge's summation to the jury provides an important clarification of the individual's right to be armed and the legality of armed crowds. Bayley cited the arms article from the Bill of Rights with its vague final clauses and asked: "But are arms suitable to the condition of people in the ordinary class of life, and are they allowed by law?" His answer gives the lie to those who would argue that the Englishman's right to be armed was more nominal than real.[15] Justice Bayley found that "a man has a clear right to arms to protect himself in his house. A man has a clear right to protect himself when he is going singly or in a small party upon the road where he is travelling or going for the ordinary purposes of business."[16] Indeed, weapons could be carried to a public meeting with one exception: "You have no right to carry arms to a public meeting, if the number of arms which are so carried are calculated to produce terror and alarm: and if you could be at liberty to carry arms upon an expectation that by possibility there might be an attack at the place, that would be an excuse for carrying arms in every instance when you went to a public meeting. Therefore I have no difficulty in saying persons are not warranted in carrying arms to a public meeting, if they are calculated to create terror and alarm."[17]

Parliament's own response to the disorders that autumn was swift passage of the so-called Six Acts, described by John Lord Campbell, then a barrister, as "the most obnoxious bills," "the latest violation of our free Constitution."[18] These included a ban on public meetings without licence, a high duty on newspapers intended to limit circulation, a prohibition against persons' practicing military drills without permission or carrying arms "under suspicious Circumstances," and the Seizure of Arms Act. The act to prevent unauthorized groups from armed drilling was an emergency measure still in force a century later, but it did not intrude upon a man's right to keep and use his own firearms.[19] The Seizure of Arms Act did.

This act empowered justices of the peace, on the testimony of a single witness, to issue warrants permitting a constable "to enter any place day or night," by force if necessary, to search for and seize weapons kept "for a purpose dangerous to the public peace."[20] It was up to the owner to "prove to the satisfaction of such Justice" that the weapons were not kept for a dangerous purpose. The act was limited to those industrial areas affected by the riots, but coverage could be extended by proclamation.

One would not expect vigorous defence of an armed citizenry when social upheaval seemed imminent, but the MPs' objections to the government bill were passionate and unyielding. Lord Rancliffe protested that similar bills in Ireland had served "but to open the door to the greatest oppression, and to rouse the most fiery passions of hatred and revenge. The atrocities perpetrated in that country under such an act as this . . . were such as no man could contemplate without horror."[21] In the Commons, T. W. Anson accused the government of exaggerating popular disorders and dangers "for the purpose of obtaining the concurrence of Parliament in measures hostile to the freedom, and repugnant to the feelings of Englishmen."[22] He took particular exception to the effect of the Seizure of Arms bill on individual self-defence: "The principles upon which it was founded, and the temper in which it was framed appeared to him to be so much at variance with the free spirit of their venerated constitution, and so contrary to that undoubted right which the subjects of this country had ever possessed—the right of retaining arms for the defence of themselves, their families, and property—that he could not look upon it without expressing his disapprobation and regret."[23] George Bennet objected to the bill "because he held that the distinctive difference between a freeman and a slave was a right to possess arms; not so much, as had been stated, for the purpose of defending his property as his liberty." "Neither could he do," he argued, "if deprived of those arms, in the hour of danger. It was a violation of the principles of a free government, and utterly repugnant to our constitution."[24]

Cynics might contend that this spirited defence of the public's right to be armed at a time of grave social unrest smacked more of political opportunism than constitutional sensitivities. That is why the comment of the government's spokesman, Lord Castlereagh, then foreign secretary, is so telling. He conceded "that the principle of the bill was not congenial with the constitution, that it was an infringement upon the rights and duties of the people, and that it could only be defended upon the necessity of the case."[25] Of course in his opinion "that necessity now existed; the security and general interests of the subject demanded the sacrifice."[26] The Seizure of Arms Act was to expire in two years, and Parliament allowed it to do so. The right of Englishmen to have arms had proved impressively resilient.

From the expiration of the Seizure of Arms Act to the twentieth century, "any person could purchase and keep in his possession a firearm without any restriction."[27] Belief in its utility for individual and constitutional defence remained firm, even after the creation of a professional police force in 1839. In 1850 the great Whig historian Thomas Macaulay maintained that it was "the security without which every other is insufficient."[28] Nearly forty years later James Paterson, in *Commentaries on the Liberty of the Subject and the Laws of England Relating to the Security of the Person,* was emphatic that "in all countries where personal freedom is valued, however much each individual may rely on legal redress, the right of each to carry arms—and these the best and the sharpest—for his own protection in case of extremity, is a right of nature indelible and irrepressible, and the more it is sought to be repressed the more it will recur."[29]

By the mid-twentieth century this right had vanished, and with it the attitude that undergirded it. Compare Paterson's stance with the sanctimonious tone of "America's Vigilante Values," a recent article in the *Economist.* The author, ignorant of his own nation's history, is astonished that "out of reverence for the constitution, America has always refused to countenance effective national controls on the possession of guns: a restraint on personal liberty that seems, in most civilised countries, essential to the happiness of others."[30] Or consider *Freedom, the Individual, and the Law,* purportedly the first book to "survey comprehensively" the state of civil liberties in Britain, which fails to mention any right to be armed or even a right to self-defence.[31] For its author, Harris Street, security means only national security, and disarmament, military disarmament.[32] Between Paterson and Street lay the First World War. While the reverberations of the French Revolution left the English right to keep arms intact, the repercussions of World War I and the Bolshevik Revolution did not.

The Englishman's right to have weapons had always depended upon what was "allowed by law." As long as Parliament refused to intrude upon that right, legal restrictions were minor.[33] At the beginning of the twentieth century, the only important firearms law was the Gun Licence Act of 1870, which required anyone who wished to carry a gun outside his home to purchase an excise licence for 10s. at a post office. This was actually a revenue measure. In 1893 and again in 1895 the House of Commons decisively rejected a stringent pistol control bill as "grandmotherly, unnecessary and futile."[34] The Pistols Act that eventually passed in 1903 merely prohibited the sale of pistols to minors and felons.[35] But in 1920, a century after passage of the Seizure of Arms Act, Parliament approved a comprehensive arms control measure that effectively repealed the right to be armed by requiring a firearm certificate for anyone wishing to "purchase, possess, use or carry any description of firearm or ammunition for the weapon."[36] The local chief of police was to decide who could obtain a certificate and to exclude anyone of intemperate habits, unsound mind, or "for any reason unfitted to be trusted with firearms." Beyond the latitude provided by the exclusion of anyone "for any reason unfitted to be trusted," the applicant had to convince the officer that he had a "good reason for requiring such a certificate." In the House of Lords the government spokesman conceded that "good reason" would be "determined by practice."[37] An Englishman refused a certificate could appeal to a court, but Irishmen were denied any appeal.

A firearms certificate specified not only the weapon but the precise quantity of ammunition an individual could purchase and hold at any one time. Each certificate was renewable every three years for a fee. The penalty for a violation of the act was a fine not exceeding £50—a substantial sum in 1919—or imprisonment with or without hard labour for a term not exceeding three months, or both.[38] While fitness requirements for pistol and rifle certificates were strict, those for shotguns for the English, though not the Irish, were more perfunctory. The act also included sweeping controls over the manufacture, import, transportation, and sale of weapons and ammunition.

The announced rationale for the dramatic shift in firearms policy was an increase in armed crime. Yet statistics for London show no such increase. True, guns were freely available and crime common. But the rate of *armed* crime was extraordinarily low.[39] Between 1878 and 1886, for instance, the average number of burglaries in London in which firearms were used was two cases per year. From 1887 to 1891 this had risen to 3.6 cases per year. Between 1911 and 1913 the average number of crimes of all types involving any sort of firearm in London—then the largest city in the world—was 45. And between 1915 and 1917 the average number of crimes in which firearms were used actually fell from 45 to 15, though this decline may be attributable to the government's extensive controls over firearms under the Defence of the Realm Act, and to many potential criminals being off in the war. But if an increase in armed crime was not the motive for the act, what was?

Confidential cabinet papers point to government fears not of crime but of disorder and even revolution. Reading these papers today, one finds the tone of Cabinet meetings in January and February of 1920 almost hysterical. The Cabinet secretary left one such meeting with his "head fairly reeling. I felt I had been in Bedlam. Red revolution and blood and war at home and abroad!"[40] He was skeptical about the danger and believed that the prime minister was as well, but some of the ministers were deeply concerned about sabotage and revolution.[41] There were real, if exaggerated, reasons for alarm. The Great War had been preceded by industrial unrest and had been waged with appalling ferocity. Demobilization brought back to Britain thousands of soldiers brutalized in a savage and senseless conflict.[42] The Bolshevik Revolution was in full swing, and 1920 would see the creation of the Communist Party of Great Britain and the Trades Union Congress. Wages were extremely low, and, in the midst of a rash of strikes, the government was threatened with a general strike.[43] Ireland was in a state of virtual civil war. Regulation 40B of the Defence of the Realm Act—the emergency measure which had given the government the power to impose stringent restrictions upon the manufacture, sale, and possession of firearms and ammunition—was due to expire on August 31, 1920.

The government laid out a strategy to protect itself. The home secretary had plans to raise a temporary force of 10,000 soldiers but was assured by the prime minister that they would be "of little use," and ministers discussed making weapons available "for distribution to friends of the Government."[44] At the same time, it was suggested that a bill was needed "for licensing persons to bear arms," a strategy which "has been useful in Ireland because the authorities know who were possessed of arms." In 1918 a secret Home Office committee had drafted legislation to control firearms and had urged its adoption before demobilization: "It is desirable that the arms which are being dispersed over the country by soldiers returning from the Front should be brought without delay under the system of control which we recommend."[45] The proposed legislation would help ensure order, but Shortt, the home secretary, warned the Cabinet that "there had always been objections" to control of firearms.[46] The government had little need for the act during the war, but its substantial powers under the Defence of the Realm Act were now due to expire.

The reaction of Parliament in 1920 to the government's arms control bill is in sharp contrast to the behaviour of Parliament a century earlier when the Seizure of Arms Act was passed. Both were post-war eras with social and industrial violence and the fear of revolution. But whereas in 1820 the government's harsh measures were hotly contested, limited in area, and temporary, the new bill was sweeping, permanent, and exposed a sea change in attitude. It is well beyond the scope of this study to pin down, if that is possible, the reason for this change of attitude. On the traditional litmus test of faith in the public—their right to be armed—the governors of the twentieth century betrayed an embarrassing loss of confidence. Or perhaps modern Britain had, as the author of the article in the *Economist* suggests, merely wished to become a more "civilised nation." The incredible loss of life in the Great War had led to a revulsion against violence. It is ironic but understandable that the very purpose of the right to be armed that Blackstone and generations after him had considered crucial to the maintenance of limited government—the ability of the people to rebel—had caused the government and the governing classes to lose their nerve and remove the right. They claimed, however, that in 1920 there were other, safer means to preserve popular control. Little thought was given to individual defence.

The manner in which the government attempted to slip its arms bill by Parliament betrays its anxiety about the reception it would receive, and how recent the shift in attitude toward the old right was. It was introduced to the House of Lords on March 31, where it met with no objections. The bill emerged somewhat strengthened and was sent on to the Commons. After its first reading in the Commons on June 1, 1920, it was scheduled for a second reading and full debate the following day. This was cancelled. Then, at 10:40 on the evening of June 8, the bill was brought back without warning and with two other bills scheduled for consideration in the few minutes remaining before adjournment.[47] Only a handful of those members present were given copies of the text. The home secretary, Mr. Shortt, introduced it as "quite a short Bill . . . which in all probability will commend itself to the House and be regarded as non-controversial."[48] The aim, he assured members, was to keep weapons from criminals and other dangerous persons, not to hamper "legitimate sport."[49] Shortt apparently left the impression that the bill would help deal with soldiers "who had become used to violence in the War" and threatened to become "a menace to the public."[50] The point was not lost. "After any great war," Major Barnes pointed out later in the debate, "there is a certain callousness with regard to life that needs to be dealt with." He noted that the previous firearms bill, the Pistols Act, was introduced in 1903 "after the South African War, and arose out of the necessities of the time."[51]

Shortt's point may have hit home but his strategy had failed. There was anger at the timing and manner of the debate and a variety of objections to the bill's contents. Interestingly, evidence of a new attitude toward the "ancient, indubitable right" on the part of both opponents and defenders of the bill surfaced in the debate. At the outset the government's motives were questioned. James Hogge suggested that the act might be applied to "grant the use of firearms to one class of people and absolutely deny it to another class."[52] James Kiley voiced the perennial argument that it would not reduce armed crime: "So far as burglars are concerned it will really have no effect. These men are dangerous, but there is nothing in this Bill which will adequately deal with them."[53] Only one member, Mr. Jameson, argued that ordinary people needed firearms for their personal protection. He took exception to the clause relating to Ireland because "for very many peaceful, law-abiding people it is a necessity of life almost that, if they are to remain in life, they shall have firearms with which to defend themselves against murderers and rebels . . . The danger is that if you pass a law like this it will be obeyed by the peaceable subject, but not by the murderers and criminals. Therefore, the latter will retain their arms while the murderee, if I may use the word, will be deprived of his arms."[54]

Lieutenant-Commander Kenworthy had a series of objections.[55] He found himself in agreement with "older" MPs that the new legislation was redundant; they need only enforce the 1903 Pistols Act. Then Kenworthy addressed the deeper issue: "There is a much greater principle involved than the mere prevention of discharged convicts having weapons. In the past one of the most jealously guarded rights of the English was that of carrying arms. For long our people fought with great tenacity for the right of carrying the weapon of the day . . . and it was only in quite recent times that was given up. It has been a well-known object of the Central Government in this country to deprive people of their weapons."[56] He pointed out that Henry VII managed to break the power of the nobility by gaining control of England's artillery. Kenworthy continued:

> I do not know whether this Bill is aimed at any such goal as that but, if so, I would point out to the right hon. Gentleman that if he deprives private citizens in this country of every sort of weapon they could possibly use, he will not have deprived them of their power, because the great weapon of democracy to-day is not the halberd or the sword or firearms, but the power of withholding their labour. I am sure that the power of withholding his labour is one of which certain Members of our Executive would very much like to deprive him. But it is our last line of defence against tyranny.[57]

He balked at granting the police the right to determine fitness for a certificate, considering it "contrary to English practice." The Pistols Act had placed that authority in the hands of a magistrate.

Major Earl Winterton leapt to the bill's defence and charged Kenworthy with holding "the most extraordinary theories of constitutional history and law."

> His idea is that the State is an aggressive body, which is endeavouring to deprive the private individual of the weapons which Heaven has given into his hands to fight against the State . . . Holding those views, and believing that it is desirable or legitimate or justifiable for private individuals to arm themselves, with . . . the ultimate intention of using their arms against the forces of the State, he objects to this Bill. There are other people who hold those views in this country, and it is because of the existence of people of that type that the Government has introduced this Bill.[58]

Kenworthy interrupted, "I do not think the Noble Lord wishes to misrepresent me . . . surely he understands that the very foundation of the liberty of the subject in this country is that he can, if driven to do so, resist, and I hope he will always be able to resist. You can only govern with the consent of the people."[59] The Earl refused to be drawn into "a long constitutional argument" but judged it "intolerable that, at this time, such a doctrine should be preached in this House as that it is desirable that people should arm themselves against the State."[60] He maintained that before the war the majority of Englishmen "had almost forgotten that there were such things as firearms and it was not necessary that the Home Secretary or the police should possess the powers which are necessary to-day." He backed away from the suggestion that "any attempt at armed insurrection is likely on the part of the great mass of the people of this country," but insisted that those "who wish to over-throw the State by violent means" must not be allowed to obtain fire-arms.[61]

Barnes then returned to the constitutional argument on behalf of the government. He judged "nothing more dangerous at the present time, or indeed at any time, than to lead the people of the country to believe that their method of redress was in the direction of armed resistance to the State."[62] "The time for that," he continued, "has gone."

> We have in our methods of election, in our access to Parliament, and in other ways, means of redress against the action of the State which in times past were not afforded, and some of us, looking back into history, may believe it was because at one time people were able to carry weapons and use them against the State that we are in the happy position in which we find ourselves to-day. We certainly owe much of our liberty to-day, and the fact that we do not need, and I hope never will need, to resort to armed resistance, to the fact that some 200 or 300 years ago there were people who found it necessary to take up arms against the State.[63]

Neither side argued against the need for popular control, although they found that control in different expedients. But Barnes seems to have been correct that there was "unanimous agreement on both sides of the House" that whenever the Executive tends to aggression, "whether it be against life and liberty or against property," the subject should have "free appeal to the Courts . . . and it is by giving him opportunity through Parliament and through the Courts to find redress that we shall most effectively turn his attention away from using weapons."[64] When the question was put the House divided, with 254 voting in favour of the bill and only 6 against.

For many years the legislation was liberally enforced. Perhaps for that reason Britons had little sense of its potential. It was refined in 1937 and in 1968 extended to include shotguns. Police policies and massive in-creases in fees in recent years have combined to reduce sharply the number of those holding firearms certificates. At the same time, however, armed crime has increased. The Firearms Control Act was not really necessary to prevent revolution and has failed to stop armed crime or eliminate illegally owned weapons.[65] But that is not really the point. The point is that a British parliament, fearful of mayhem and social upheaval, deprived the public of a right to be armed, hoping that the people's other rights—to petition Parliament and the courts and to strike—would prevent tyranny. One wonders what Blackstone would think. He took account of recourse to the courts and the right to petition Parliament, and still believed a right to be armed essential. Or Macaulay, who, writing after the Reform Act made elections more equitable and professional police had been established, still insisted that the right to be armed was the "security without which every other is insufficient."

Are Britons sufficiently protected without the dangerous option of armed insurrection? Are individual Britons able to defend themselves and their families without recourse to firearms? Great Britain's modest level of violent crime has not skyrocketed and, since 1920, things have remained "in their legal and settled course." In DeLolme's words, the people have not needed "to move." Let us hope the decision taken in 1920 is never put to the test, and that other "democratic contrivances," other "quarantine measures against that ancient plague, the lust for power," can achieve the same end.[66]

Should the Second Amendment to the American Constitution be permitted to go the way of the English right to be armed, as a dangerous relic of another era? In fact, it cannot be legislated out of existence in the same way. The American Congress is not sovereign, our Constitution is. The Constitution has a clear procedure for altering its contents—amendment. If the government and people in their wisdom come to the conclusion that no need for the right of the people to be armed exists, or that such a right does more harm than good, then amendment is the course that should be followed. While it is unconstitutional to legislate a right out of existence, this particular right is threatened with misinterpretation to the point of meaninglessness.[67] Granted, this is a far easier method of elimination than amendment, being much quicker and not requiring the same rigid consensus or forthright discussion of its constitutional relevancy. But it is also the way of danger. For to ignore all evidence of the meaning and intent of one of those rights included in the Bill of Rights is to create the most dangerous sort of precedent, one whose consequences could flow far beyond this one issue and endanger the fabric of liberty.

Should the Second Amendment be altered or eliminated through amendment? Before that is considered it is imperative to grant the founders of the American Constitution, whose wisdom in so much else has borne the test of time, the courtesy of considering why they included this right. Their original intent is of not only academic but immediate interest. What does the right actually mean, and why did they consider it essential? Are standing armies still a threat to a twentieth-century world? Do the people need a right and a means to revolution? Will other rights suffice? Are individuals still in need of personal weapons, "and these the best and the sharpest," for protection "in case of extremity?"[68] I am not an advocate but a historian and ask merely for a decent respect for the past. We are not forced into lockstep with our forefathers. But we owe them our considered attention before we disregard a right they felt it imperative to bestow upon us.

Abbreviations · Notes · Index

Abbreviations

Add. MSS	British Library, Additional Manuscripts
BL	British Library
Calendar SP Venetian	*Calendar of State Papers and Manuscripts, Relating to English Affairs, Existing in the Archives and Collections of Venice and in Other Libraries of Northern Italy*
CJ	*Journals of the House of Commons*
CSPD	*Calendar of State Papers, Domestic Series*
HMC	*Historical Manuscripts Commissions Reports*
LJ	*Journals of the House of Lords*
PC	Privy Council Registers (PRO)
PRO	Public Record Office, London
SP	State Papers Domestic (PRO)
Wing	*Short-title Catalogue of Books Printed in England, Scotland, Ireland, Wales, and British America and of English Books Printed in Other Countries, 1641–1700*, ed. Donald Wing, 2nd ed. (New York, 1972–1988)

Notes

Preface

1. Thomas Macaulay, *Critical and Historical Essays, Contributed to the Edinburgh Review,* vol. 1 (Leipzig, 1850), pp. 154, 162.
2. William Blackstone, *Commentaries on the Laws of England,* 4 vols., 1st ed. (London, 1765–1769, repr. Chicago, 1979), 1:136.
3. Ibid., p. 139.

1. A People Armed

1. For a sound summary of English society during the seventeenth century, see Keith Wrightson, *English Society: 1580–1680* (London, 1982). Unfortunately, Wrightson fails to deal with issues involving the use of weapons by the common people.
2. See "The Duty of an Officer," f. 1, Add. MS 33,265, BL.
3. Michael Dalton, *The Country Justice: Containing the Practice of the Justices of the Peace out of Their Sessions* (London, 1697), pp. 308, 356. This book was first published in 1618.
4. The requirement to raise a "hue and cry" dates from at least the thirteenth century. A writ of 1252 explained that upon the raising of the cry neighbours were to turn out with weapons they were bound to keep. See Frederick Pollock and Frederic Maitland, *The History of English Law,* 2 vols., 2nd ed. (Cambridge, 1968), 2:578–579. The quotation from Richard Burn's popular eighteenth-century guidebook for justices illustrates the longevity of this requirement. See Richard Burn, *The Justice of the Peace and Parish Officer,* 2 vols. (London, 1753), 1:16–20.
5. Anchitel Grey, *Debates in the House of Commons from the Year 1667 to the Year 1694,* 10 vols. (London, 1763), 1:109. The quotation is from the debate held on March 10, 1667/8.
6. The requirement that householders stand watch can be traced to an ordinance of 1233. The system was consolidated in the Statute of Winchester, 1285. See Pollock and Maitland, *History of English Law,* 1:565–566. For

evidence of its enforcement beyond the seventeenth century, see Burn, *Justice of the Peace,* 2:512.

7. S. A. Peyton, ed., *Minutes of Proceedings in Quarter Sessions Held for the Parts of Kesteven in the County of Lincoln, 1674–1695,* 2 vols., Lincolnshire Record Society, vols. 25, 26 (Lincoln, 1931), 1:lx.

8. H. Jenkinson and D. L. Powell, eds., *Surrey Quarter Sessions Records, Order Book, and Sessions Rolls, 1666–68,* Surrey Record Society (1951), pp. 177–178, 181, 190, 194, 208, 210, 232, 246, 251. Note that those refusing came from every sector of the community and included labourers, watermen, craftsmen, and gentlemen.

9. *Lincolnshire Quarter Sessions,* 1:lx, note 3.

10. "The Security of Englishmen's Lives . . .", *State Tracts: Being a Further Collection of Several Choice Treatises Relating to Government from the Year 1660 to 1689* (London, 1692), p. 225. See, for example, Oliver Cromwell, Speech to Parliament, September 17, 1656; Griffith Williams, Bishop of Ossory, "Vindiciae Regum; or, The Grand Rebellion . . ." (Oxford, 1643), Wing W2675, pp. 82–83.

11. Pollock and Maitland, *History of English Law,* 1:421 and 421–422, note 4.

12. F. W. Maitland, *The Constitutional History of England,* ed. H. A. L. Fisher (Cambridge, 1968), p. 162; Pollock and Maitland, *History of English Law,* 1:421.

13. 1 Edward III, c.5. Translation from Maitland, *Constitutional History,* p. 277.

14. See A. Hassell Smith, "Militia Rates and Militia Statutes, 1558–1663," in *The English Commonwealth, 1547–1640: Essays in Politics and Society Presented to Joel Hurstfield,* ed. Peter Clark et al. (Leicester, 1979), pp. 93–110.

15. Lindsey Boynton, *The Elizabethan Militia* (London, 1967), pp. 16, 91.

16. Sir John Dalrymple, writing in the eighteenth century, overstated aristocratic influence over the militia, but he was probably expressing a common notion when he warned, "The feudal militias which, at the command of their Lords flocked to the standard of the King, were ready at the same command to turn their swords against him." John Dalrymple, *Memoirs of Great Britain and Ireland,* 3 vols., 2nd ed. (London, 1771), 1:7–8.

17. For an excellent account of the military revolution that took place during the seventeenth century, see Michael Roberts, "The Military Revolution, 1560–1650," in Orest Ranum, ed., *Searching for Modern Times* (New York, 1969), 1:220–230.

18. Roberts, *Military Revolution,* p. 230.

19. Magna Carta, 1215, art. 51, reprinted in *Magna Carta and the Idea of Liberty,* ed. James C. Holt (New York, 1972), p. 180. And see C. G. Cruickshank, *Elizabeth's Army,* 2nd ed. (Oxford, 1966), p. 5; Lois G. Schwoerer, *"No Standing Armies!": The Antiarmy Ideology in Seventeenth-Century England* (Baltimore, 1974), chap. 1.

20. On this issue, see Conrad S. R. Russell, "Monarchies, Wars, and Estates in England, France, and Spain, c.1580–c.1640," *Legislative Studies Quarterly,* VII, 2 (May 1982), pp. 205–220.

21. 33 Henry VIII, c.9 (1541).
22. 3 Hen. VIII, c.3. And see G. Sharp, *Tracts, concerning the Antient and Only True Legal Means of National Defence, by a Free Militia* (London, 1782), p. 12; Cruickshank, *Elizabeth's Army*, pp. 103–104.
23. George Roberts, *The Social History of the People of the Southern Counties of England in Past Centuries* (London, 1856), pp. 118, 123.
24. Ibid., p. 123.
25. In 1621, Sir James Parrett fretted about the decline in numbers of armed retainers kept by the great lords and the woeful state of the county militia arsenals: "Those gentlemen whose grandfathers kept 16 or 17 lusty serveing men and but one or two good silver boules to drinke in, into their grandchildren fallen from Charity to impiety keep scarce 6 men and greate Cubards of plate to noe purpose . . . In two shyres not a barrell of Gunnpowder to bee seene." Wallace Notestein, F. H. Relf, and H. Simpson, eds., *Commons Debates, 1621*, 7 vols. (New Haven, 1935), 6:318. And see R. Johnson, "Relations of the Most Famous Kingdomes and Commonwealths" (London, 1630), cited by Boynton, *Elizabethan Militia*, p. 28.
26. *Commons Debates, 1621*, 6:318; 4 & 5 Philip and Mary, c.2, and 4 & 5 Philip and Mary, c.3; 2 James I, c.25.
27. Smith, "Militia Rates and Militia Statutes," pp. 99–102. There were a number of proposals in Parliament for a revised militia assessment, but no new militia act until the eve of the Civil War.
28. For nearly nine years, from 1604 to 1613, decline and inaction became the rule. According to the Earl of Hertford, lord lieutenant of the Somerset and Wiltshire militia during this period, the "long vacation and rest" caused militia regiments to forget their former discipline. Along with the militia, the armaments industry experienced a rapid decline, with armourers and gunmakers claiming that their numbers had slipped from thirty-five in Elizabeth's day to only five in 1607. Boynton, *Elizabethan Militia*, p. 212. Stagnation was not uniform, and the Northamptonshire division and Bristol militia seemed to have maintained a good level of preparedness (pp. 213, 219). And see Anthony Fletcher, *Reform in the Provinces: The Government of Stuart England* (New Haven, 1986), especially chap. 9 and pp. 308–310, for a discussion of the militia.
29. In his article "Militia Rates and Militia Statutes," p. 94, Smith argues that the reason for the failure of Charles's exact militia was not that too much was asked but that the rating system produced a sense of grievance that undermined the efficiency of the militia.
30. Boynton, *Elizabethan Militia*, p. 268. For a discussion of Charles I's efforts to improve the militia, and the difficulties he encountered, see Boynton, chap. 8. Despite the King's efforts, for example, by 1634 failure to send the government the usual certificates of muster results had become so general that twenty-one counties had sent none at all for three consecutive years (p. 271). Also see Fletcher, *Reform of the Provinces*, pp. 286–316, on the militia under the first two Stuarts. Fletcher points out that, in the period prior to the Civil War, "it was the lack of a statutory basis for the deputies' actions which was the critical element in the situation" (p. 309).

31. Robert Ward, *Animadversions of Warre* (London, 1639), p. 152.
32. J. G. A. Pocock, *The Political Works of James Harrington* (Cambridge, 1977), pp. 18–19.
33. Schwoerer, *"No Standing Armies!"* p. 18; Felix Raab, *The English Face of Machiavelli: A Changing Interpretation, 1500–1700* (London, 1964), p. 102.
34. Sir Walter Raleigh, *The Works of Sir Walter Raleigh,* ed. T. Birch, 8 vols. (Oxford, 1829), 3:22.
35. Sir Thomas More, *Utopia,* trans. and ed. Robert M. Adams (New York, 1975), p. 71.
36. The early Statute of Northampton, 2 Edward III, c.3, which stated that no man "go nor ride armed by night or day in fairs, markets, nor in the presence of the justices or other ministers, nor in no part elsewhere," was clearly a sweeping restriction. It was designed to prevent the terrorizing of peaceable citizens and government officials and the robbery of markets. However, it does not appear to have been enforced in the seventeenth century. See Chapter 6 for James II's unsuccessful efforts to use this law in Knight's case.
37. See 33 Henry VIII, c.6. The act's preamble stated that "malicious and evil disposed persons" were riding "in the King's highways and elsewhere, having with them cross-bows, and little hand-guns . . . to the great peril and fear of the King's most loving subjects." The preamble also included an admission that English armies would, henceforth, employ firearms as well as longbows.
38. 2 & 3 Edward VI, c.14, "An Act against the shooting of Hail Shot."
39. H. H. Copnall, ed., *Nottingham County Records: Notes and Extracts . . . of the Seventeenth Century* (Nottingham, 1915), p. 92.
40. Dalton, *The Country Justice,* p. 93.
41. Cruickshank, *Elizabeth's Army,* pp. 110–112; *CSPD*, vol. 7, Addenda 1566–1579, vol. 14, pp. 78–81.
42. Cruickshank, *Elizabeth's Army,* p. 116.
43. J. R. Jones, *The Revolution of 1688 in England* (London, 1972), p. 77, note 2. Much has been made of the restrictions on Catholics, but by the mid-seventeenth century members of that faith constituted a relatively small portion of the English population, probably no more than one in fifty.
44. John Hawkins, *Life of Johnson* (London, 1787), p. 606.
45. William Nelson, *The Laws of England Concerning the Game* (London, 1727), preface.
46. William Blackstone, *Commentaries on the Laws of England,* 4 vols., 1st ed. (London, 1765–1769, repr. Chicago, 1979), 2:414.
47. William S. Holdsworth, *A History of English Law,* 7 vols. (Boston, 1924), 4:505.
48. Blackstone, *Commentaries,* 2:411. Holdsworth, in *A History of English Law,* argued that game statutes which proceeded on the principle merely that game should be preserved made offences against them misdemeanours,

whereas those which aimed to suppress disorder tended to make an offence a felony, that is, a capital crime. This is a crude yardstick and not completely correct. See Holdsworth, *A History of English Law*, 4:506.

49. Cited by E. P. Thompson, *Whigs and Hunters: The Origin of the Black Act* (New York, 1975), p. 58.

50. See Douglas Hay, "Poaching and Game Laws on Cannock Chase," in *Albion's Fatal Tree: Crime and Society in Eighteenth-Century England*, ed. Hay et al. (London, 1975), p. 212. Hay points out that higher property qualifications for hunting, by reducing the number of those allowed to hunt, created a community of interest between vast numbers of farmers and their labourers, who frequently poached together and, if caught, supported one another's alibis.

51. C. Kirby and E. Kirby, "The Stuart Game Prerogative," *The English Historical Review* 46 (1931), p. 243.

52. Ibid., pp. 242–243.

53. D. G. H. Allan, "The Rising in the West, 1628–1631," *Economic History Review* 5 (1952), p. 78; Philip A. Pettit, *The Royal Forests of Northamptonshire: A Study in Their Economy, 1558–1714*, Northamptonshire Record Society, vol. 23 (1968), pp. 168–182, and tables 22, 23, and 24.

54. Eric Kerridge, "The Revolts in Wiltshire against Charles I," *Wilts Arch & Nat Hist. Mag.*, 57 (1958–1959), p. 72.

55. For the subsequent information on forest enclosures and riots, I am chiefly indebted to Allan, "Rising in the West," and Kerridge, "Revolts in Wiltshire."

56. Buchanan Sharp, *In Contempt of All Authority: Rural Artisans and Riot in the West of England: 1586–1660* (Berkeley, 1980), p. 89.

57. J. Charles Cox, *The Royal Forests of England* (London, 1905), p. 200. Inhabitants of Egham, Surrey, banded together in 1641 in groups of 80 to 100 to destroy the deer, and when the Restoration of Charles II in 1660 seemed likely to result in the reestablishment of the forest in Surrey, they marched out again. See E. P. Thompson, *Whigs and Hunters*, p. 55.

58. William Menzies, *The History of Windsor Great Park and Windsor Forest* (London, 1864), p. 13. I am indebted to Menzies for much of the material on Windsor and New Lodge.

59. Pettit, *Forests of Northamptonshire*, p. 93.

2. Bearing Arms through War and Revolution

1. Proclamation, August 12, 1642.

2. C. H. Firth, ed., *The Memoirs of Edmund Ludlow, Lieutenant General of the Horse in the Army of the Commonwealth of England, 1625–1672*, 2 vols. (Oxford, 1894), 1:14.

3. Counties were ordered to "lend" their militia equipment to the Crown and to provide the army with carts and horses free of charge. Districts through which the Crown's troops marched were left to shoulder the costs of billeting and purveyance.

4. Strafford to Sir George Radcliffe, 1640, BL, Beaumont Papers, Add. MSS C. 259/149.

5. Edward Hyde, Earl of Clarendon, *History of the Rebellion and Civil Wars in England,* ed. W. Dunn Macray, 6 vols. (Oxford, 1888), 1:100, note.

6. Ibid., p. 377.

7. Ibid., pp. 376–377.

8. Ibid., p. 377.

9. See John Forster, *The Debates on the Grand Remonstrance, November and December 1641* (London, 1861), p. 232, note.

10. S. R. Gardiner, ed., *The Constitutional Documents of the Puritan Revolution: 1625–1660,* 3rd ed., rev. (London, 1968), p. 211.

11. Clarendon, *History of the Rebellion,* 1:397; J. M. Lloyd Thomas, ed., *The Autobiography of Richard Baxter: Being the Reliquiae Baxterianae* (London, 1925), p. 33; Lucy Hutchinson, *Memoirs of the Life of Colonel Hutchinson,* ed. Julius Hutchinson (London, 1968), p. 75.

12. Robin Clifton, "Fear of Popery," in Conrad Russell, ed., *The Origins of the English Civil War* (New York, 1973), p. 158. In this atmosphere panics were sparked by the flimsiest of evidence. Word that a Jesuit boasted that "there would be many fatherless children in London very shortly" excited serious concern, and the announcement that two little girls in Colchester had seen suspicious strangers who might be Irish arsonists sent that city into an uproar (p. 158).

13. Ibid., pp. 160–161; Mary Coate, "Exeter in the Civil War and Interregnum," *Devon and Cornwall Notes and Queries,* 18, 8 (October 1935), pp. 340–341.

14. Clarendon, *History of the Rebellion,* 2:60–61.

15. For a full discussion of the tribulations of the royal recruiters, see Joyce Malcolm, *Caesar's Due: Loyalty and King Charles, 1642–1646* (London, 1983), especially chap. 2. See Ronald Hutton, *The Royalist War Effort: 1642–1646* (London, 1982), for a different point of view on royalist recruitment and administration during the Civil War.

16. "True Intelligence from Lincolne-shire" (London, 1642), Wing M., P. 67, p. 4.

17. In addition to Malcolm, *Caesar's Due,* chap. 2, see Clarendon, *History of the Rebellion,* 2:347; "Speciall Passages and certain Informations from severall places . . . ," no. 6 (London, 1642), Thomason Tracts E.118, pp. 45, 48; "The Latest Remarkable Truths from Worcester, Chester, Salop . . ." (London, 1642), in J. A. Atkinson, ed., *Tracts Relating to the Civil War in Cheshire, 1641–1659,* Chetham Society, n.s. 65 (1909), app. B, p. 238; J. R. Phillips, *Memoirs of the Civil War in Wales and the Marches, 1642–1649,* 2 vols., 1st ed. (London, 1874), 2:13; "Some special passages from Hull, Alanby, and Yorke: truly informed Munday the first of August 1642" (London, 1642), Thomason Tracts E.108(33), p. 4; "A Private Letter, from an Eminent Cavalier . . . to His Mighty Honoured Friend in London; Freely Relating the Present State of His Majesties Forces" (London, 1642), Thomason Tracts E.116(32), p. 6.

18. Ian Roy, "The Royalist Army in the First Civil War, 1642–1646" (Oxford, D. Phil., 1963), pp. 313–315; M. D. G. Wanklyn, "The King's Armies in the West of England, 1642–6" (Manchester, M.A., 1966), pp. 100–101.

19. Ralph Hopton, *Bellum Civile: Hopton's Narrative of His Campaign in the West, 1642–1644, and Other Papers*, ed. C. E. H. Chadwyck-Healey, Somerset Record Society, 18 (1902), p. 25.

20. J. W. Burrows, *The Essex Regiment: The Essex Militia* (Southend-on-Sea, 1929), p. 98.

21. See C. H. Firth and R. S. Rait, eds., *Acts and Ordinances of the Interregnum, 1642–1660*, 3 vols. (London, 1911), 1:370, 494.

22. Charles I, "A Proclamation against the spoyling and loosing of Armes by the Souldiers of His Majesties Army, for the keeping of them fixt, and bringing all Armes hereafter into His Majesties Magazines," March 10, 1643, James F. Larken, ed., *Stuart Royal Proclamations*, 2 vols. (Oxford, 1983), 2:871–873.

23. D. H. Pennington and I. A. Roots, eds., *The Committee of Stafford, 1643–1645*, Staffs. Hist. Coll., 4th ser., 1 (Manchester, 1957), p. 4.

24. Oliver Heywood, *Autobiography and Diaries of Oliver Heywood*, ed. J. H. Turner, 4 vols. (Brighouse, 1881), 1:96, and cited by Brian Manning, *The English People and the English Revolution* (London, 1976), p. 218.

25. For further information on the club movement, see Malcolm, *Caesar's Due*, pp. 212–227; J. S. Morrill, *The Revolt of the Provinces: Conservatives and Radicals in the English Civil War, 1630–1650* (New York, 1976).

26. Colonel Massey to Sir Samuel Luke, March 22, 1645, in J. Webb and T. W. Webb, eds., "A Military Memoir of Colonel John Birch," Camden Soc., 7 (1873), pp. 216–217, and H. G. Tibbutt, ed., *The Letter-books of Sir Samuel Luke, 1644–1645*, Bedfordshire Hist. Rec. Soc., 42 (1963), p. 485; R. Scrope and T. Monkhouse, eds., *State Papers Collected by Edward, Earl of Clarendon*, 3 vols. (Oxford, 1767–1786), 2:188–189.

27. C. V. Wedgwood, *The King's War, 1641–1647* (London, 1973), p. 428.

28. For two studies of the conflicts between the majority in Parliament and the New Model Army, see Mark Kishlansky, *The Rise of the New Model Army* (Cambridge, 1979), and David Underdown, *Pride's Purge: Politics in the Puritan Revolution* (Oxford, 1971).

29. For an analysis of how English government and society coexisted with the Interregnum army, see H. M. Reece, "The Military Presence in England, 1649–1660" (Oxford, D. Phil., 1981).

30. Ibid., p. 125.

31. Ibid., p. 134. Although Reece states that these magazines were "often collected from county forces at the end of the war," the citations he provides do not touch on this contention.

32. See *CSPD, 1649–50*, pp. 109, 112, 127, 199, 205.

33. See *Acts and Ordinances of the Interregnum*, 2:397. For a detailed analysis of the Militia Act of 1650, see Chapter 3.

34. Jeremy G. A. Ive, "The Local Dimensions of Defence: The Standing Army and Militia in Norfolk, Suffolk, and Essex, 1649–1660" (Cambridge,

Ph.D., 1986), p. 213. Ive presents one of the most complete studies to date of the militia during the Interregnum. *CSPD, 1648–49,* pp. 8, 9, 25, 44, 72, 327.

35. Ive, "Local Dimensions of Defence," p. 201.
36. *Acts and Ordinances of the Interregnum,* 2:397–402.
37. Ibid., p. 397.
38. See D. W. Rannie, "Cromwell's Major-Generals," *English Historical Review* 10 (1895), especially pp. 474–475.
39. Ibid., p. 475.
40. See Ive, "Local Dimensions of Defence," pp. 246–250.
41. Evelyn P. Shirley, *Some Account of English Deer Parks* (London, 1867), pp. 46–47; *CSPD, 1661,* p. 67.
42. *Acts and Ordinances of the Interregnum,* 1:915–916.
43. Ibid., 2:548.
44. *CSPD, 1653–54,* pp. 115–120.
45. See, for example, T. Birch, ed., *A Collection of State Papers of John Thurloe, Esq., Secretary First to the Council of State and Afterwards to the Two Protectorates,* 7 vols. (London, 1742), especially vol. 3, pp. 88, 95, 108, 163. A newsletter of January 6, 1654/5, referred to a plot in which "many hundreds of pistolls were brought downe hence [from Scotland] by carriers, and [sent] . . . to disafected persons in the country." The gunsmith's house from which these came was searched, the report continues, and some 4000 "fixed armes" found. Royalist correspondence does not confirm such a report. See C. H. Firth, ed., *The Clarke Papers: Selections from the Papers of William Clarke,* vol. 3, Camden Society (London, 1899), p. 17.
46. See David Underdown, *Royalist Conspiracy in England, 1649–1660* (New Haven, 1960).
47. Captain George Bishope to Secretary Thurloe, Bristol, February 17, 1654, *Thurloe State Papers,* 3:161.
48. *CSPD, 1655,* p. 77.
49. Ibid.
50. For a good account of the major-generals, see Rannie, "Cromwell's Major-Generals"; *Thurloe State Papers,* 4:333–334, 379.
51. Rannie, "Cromwell's Major-Generals," pp. 489–490.
52. Firth, *Clarke Papers,* p. 66.
53. Ibid., p. 67.
54. James Harrington, *The Political Works of James Harrington,* ed. J. G. A. Pocock (Cambridge, 1977), p. 145. Machiavelli, for one, had made a similar point many years before. See Quentin Skinner, *The Foundations of Modern Political Thought,* 2 vols. (Cambridge, 1978), 1:173–175.
55. See Pocock, *Harrington Works,* pp. 54–55, 58, 70.
56. Ibid., pp. 131–132, 139.
57. G. P. Gooch, *English Democratic Ideas in the Seventeenth Century,* 2nd ed. (New York, 1959), pp. 254–256.
58. Ibid., pp. 271–272.

59. Ibid., p. 272. Harrington's ideas influenced those Englishmen who opposed William's maintenance of a large, peacetime army late in the seventeenth century. See Chapter 7.
60. Hutchinson, *Memoirs of Colonel Hutchinson*, p. 299.
61. *Acts and Ordinances of the Interregnum*, 2:1317–1319.
62. Braye MSS, *HMC 10th Report*, app. 6, p. 211; O. Ogle, W. H. Bliss, W. D. MacRay, and F. J. Routledge, eds., *Calendar of the Clarendon State Papers Preserved in the Bodleian Library*, 4 vols. (Oxford, 1869–1932), 4:260, 275.
63. Edmund Waringe to Fleetwood, July 23, 1659, Bridgnorth, *Calendar Clarendon State Papers*, 4:295.
64. Margaret M. Verney, *Memoirs of the Verney Family*, 4 vols. (London, 1892–1899), reprint New York, 1970, 3:448.
65. Ibid., pp. 448–449.
66. Ibid., p. 449, note 1.
67. See *Calendar Clarendon State Papers*, 4:299–309. A letter dated August 21, 1660, in the State Papers seems to support the contention that royalists had been buying up arms in quantity, albeit with some risk. The letter certifies that Richard Arscott, during Sir George Booth's rising, "bought 300 case of pistols for the gentry of Devon to be employed in the King's service—which arms he brought out of Exon. with the hazard of his life." SP 29/11, f. 13.
68. Captain Waring to President of Council of State, August 3, 1659, Shrewsbury, *Calendar Clarendon State Papers*, 4:309.
69. C. H. Firth, *Cromwell's Army*, 4th ed. (London, 1962), p. 381.

3. The Dissidents Disarmed

1. E. S. deBeer, ed., *Memoirs Illustrative of the Life and Writings of John Evelyn*, 6 vols. (London, 1955), 3:246. Three recent monographs that take a close look at the period immediately following Charles's return are J. R. Jones, *Charles II: Royal Politician* (London, 1987); Ronald Hutton, *The Restoration: A Political and Religious History of England and Wales, 1658–1667* (Oxford, 1985); and Paul Seaward, *The Cavalier Parliament and the Reconstruction of the Old Regime, 1661–1667* (Cambridge, 1989).
2. Bennet to King, April 1662, MS Clarendon 77/150–153, Bodleian Library; Samuel Pepys, *Diary of Samuel Pepys*, ed. Henry B. Wheatley, 8 vols. (London, 1913), 7:17; Edward Hyde, Earl of Clarendon, *The Life of Edward Earl of Clarendon*, 3 vols. (Oxford, 1827), 1:315. Hutton writes that few regimes "have fallen in the estimation of their subjects as dramatically as the restored monarchy did." Hutton, *Restoration*, p. 185.
3. Ayloffe to Leveson, London, June 5, 1660, Duke of Sutherland MSS, *HMC 5th Report*, p. 184.
4. Clarendon, *Life*, 2:117. Some of the Crown's more obvious opponents, however, had been disarmed in April 1660 in the wake of Lambert's escape

from the Tower. See Richard L. Greaves, *Deliver Us from Evil: The Radical Underground in Britain, 1660–1663* (Oxford, 1986), pp. 27–29.

5. On the topic of Charles's intentions, Davies wrote, "Probably he never formulated even in his own mind any precise theory of government but relied on expedients to meet situations as they arose." G. Davies, "Charles II in 1660," *Essays on the Later Stuarts* (Westport, Conn., 1975), p. 35. J. R. Jones agrees that Charles concentrated "almost entirely on short-term tactics" to achieve "mainly defensive objectives." Jones, *Charles II,* p. 1. In his recent book on the army of Charles II, John Childs argues that Charles never meant to govern with an army but wanted only "to secure his throne and his own position in relation to Parliament and not to overawe the Lords and Commons." John Childs, *The Army of Charles II* (London, 1976), p. 14. For an interesting assessment of the potential for absolutism in this period, see John Miller, "The Potential for 'Absolutism' in Later Stuart England," *History,* 69 (1984), pp. 187–207.

6. SP 29/1/81, PRO. On Charles II's attitude toward absolute kingship, Ailesbury noted in his memoirs that Charles had once told him some councillors "to flatter him gave him how to set up to govern at his will. 'Nonsense,' he replied, 'A King of England that is not a slave to five hundred Kings [meaning the lower house] is great enough.'" Thomas Bruce, Earl of Ailesbury, *Memoirs of Thomas Earl of Ailesbury,* 2 vols., Roxburghe Club (London, 1890), 1:22.

7. "Two Treatises addressed to the Duke of Buckingham," Lansdowne MS 805, f. 75, BL.

8. (Henry Coventry) to Mr. Kirton (Hyde), London, May 4, 1660, *CSPD, 1660–61,* p. 11.

9. During a debate on the Militia Bill, William Pierrepont moved to cast it out "because there was martial law provided in it; which, he said, would be a strange grievance laid upon the people." Sir Heneage Finch said that whoever brought in martial law deserved to be made the first example of it, and that they could never consent to bring themselves to be "wards of an army." Sir Walter Erle added that he never knew any bill that entrenched so far upon the subject's privilege as this did. William Cobbett, ed., *The Parliamentary History of England from the Earliest Period to the Year 1803,* 36 vols. (London, 1808–1820), 4:145. John Stephens warned that the House of Commons "ought to take heed of putting an iron yoke about their own necks." Edward Dyer, "Politics and Ideology in the English Revolution, 1641–1663" (Harvard, Ph.D., 1979), p. 371. Also see Mordaunt to Hyde, May 4, 1660, *CSPD, 1660–61,* p. 12.

10. Clarendon, *Life,* 1:335; *CJ,* 8:5–6.

11. Newport to Leveson, June 9, 1660, Duke of Sutherland MSS, *HMC 5th Report,* p. 153.

12. See, for example, SP 29/11, ff. 146–174, PRO. But see Hutton, *Restoration,* p. 129, where he claims that deputy-lieutenants and officers of the militia had mixed political backgrounds.

13. See Langdale to Nicholas, January 3, 1661, *CSPD, 1660–61* p. 466.

14. SP 29/11, ff. 146–174, PRO; "Instructions to Lords Lieutenant, Whitehall, 1660," Egerton MS 2542, f. 512, BL; "Earl of Devonshire Lord Lieutenancy Papers," Add. MS 34,306, ff. 18, 19, BL.

15. See 13 Car. II, c.6.

16. See "Instructions of Lords Lieutenant, Whitehall, 1660," Egerton MS 2542, BL. "Earl of Devonshire Lord Lieutenancy Papers," Add. MS 34,306, ff. 18, 19, BL; "Earl of Westmorland Letter Book, 1660–1665," Add. MS 34,222, f. 9. Cromwell had organized a special volunteer militia to aid his major-generals, but unlike Charles's volunteers, these men were paid. Their pay came from the proceeds of a tax on wealthier "malignants." See J. R. Western, *The English Militia in the Eighteenth Century* (London, 1965), p. 8; D. W. Rannie, "Cromwell's Major-Generals," *English Historical Review* 10 (1895), p. 475.

17. SP 29/1, f. 81, PRO. Seaward found evidence that the government planned in 1661 to obtain Parliament's approval for a "select militia" along the lines of that raised by Cromwell's major-generals, a force of volunteer horsemen regionally based. This plan was later set aside. Seaward, *Cavalier Parliament*, pp. 143–144.

18. William, Earl of Exeter, to Nicholas, August 26, 1660, SP 29/11, f. 52, PRO.

19. The first Derbyshire muster after the Restoration divided into "trayned soldiers" and "private soldiers": Scarsdale Hundred: 84 trayned, 94 private; High Seat Hundred: 80 trayned, 79 private; Hundred of Wirkesworth: 47 trayned, 47 private (total 431). Add. MS 34,306, ff. 1–5, BL. Lincolnshire muster of cavalry, April 1664: 6 troops Trained Bands, 360 men; 5 troops Volunteers, 400 men. MS Clarendon 92, f. 143, Bodleian. In Kent the Earl of Winchelsea listed eleven troops of volunteer horse in October 1660. Stowe MS 744, f. 51, BL.

20. See, for example, note 16.

21. Winchelsea to Dering, October 4, 1660, Stowe MS 744, f. 49, BL.

22. "Some Propositions concerning the Trained Bands," Egerton MS, f. 526, BL.

23. Winchelsea to Dering, September 29, 1660, Stowe MS 744, f. 52, BL.

24. Langdale to Nicholas, January 3, 1661, *CSPD, 1660–61*, p. 466.

25. Westmorland to Nicholas, August 7, 1662, "Westmorland's Letter Book," Add. MS 34,222, f. 32, BL.

26. "Diary of Seymour Bowman, M.P., 1660," Salway MS dep., ff. 9, 39, Bodleian.

27. "A Letter from a Person of Quality to his friend in the Country," *State Tracts: Being a Collection of Several Treatises relating to the Government* (London, 1693), p. 55.

28. *CJ*, 8:142–143.

29. Ibid., p. 161.

30. Ibid., p. 163.

31. Ibid., p. 167.

32. See Statute of Northampton (1328), 2 Edward III, c.3. This declared that

no man should "go nor ride armed by night or day in fairs, markets nor in no part elsewhere upon pain." It was enacted during a time of extreme disorder, and there is no evidence it was enforced during the seventeenth century.

33. Carlton to Leveson, London, September 1, 1660, Duke of Sutherland MS, *HMC 5th Report*, p. 168. And see *HMC Le Fleming MSS*, p. 24; SP 29/29, f. 45, PRO.

34. H. C. Foxcroft, *Life and Letters of Sir George Savile, Bart., First Marquis Halifax*, 2 vols. (London, 1898), 2: 376.

35. "His Majesties Gracious Speech together with the Lord Chancellor's to both Houses of Parliament . . . Saturday, 29 December 1660," SP 29/24/96, PRO; and see Edmund Ludlow, *The Memoirs of Edmund Ludlow, Lieutenant-General of the Horse in the Army of the Commonwealth of England, 1625–1672*, ed. C. H. Firth, 2 vols. (Oxford, 1894), 2:329.

36. Council to Devonshire, December 14, 1660, "Correspondence of Lord Cavendish, Earl of Devonshire as Lord Lieutenant of Derbyshire," Add. MS 34,306, f. 6, BL.

37. Morrice to Downing, cited by Seaward, *Cavalier Parliament*, p. 146. Seaward provides further information on the government's disclosures and finds "the attempt to manipulate parliamentary opinion . . . quite evident" (pp. 144–146). For details of plots against the government between 1660 and 1663, see Greaves, *Deliver Us from Evil*.

38. PC 2/55, f. 71, PRO.

39. Add. MS 34,306, f. 6, BL. And see Dalrymple, *Memoirs*, 1:25.

40. King to Lords Lieutenant, December 19, 1660, Add. MS 34,306, f. 6, BL; Ludlow, *Memoirs*, 2:329 and 329, note 1. See James Walker, "The Yorkshire Plot, 1663," *Yorks, Arch. J.*, 31 (1934), pp. 348–359. There is uncertainty about whether dangerous plots were really being hatched or merely fabricated. Of those of 1663 and 1664, Walker writes: "Evidence that risings were being organized all over England does not exist" (p. 355). Whatever the truth of the matter, the government was genuinely concerned and did use the rumours of plots to tighten its control. In 1664 Clarendon referred to "the reproach of the late times, of contriving plots only to commit men to prison against whom there was any prejudice." See Clarendon, *Life*, 2:279.

41. SP 29/24, f. 96, PRO.

42. SP 29/24, f. 43, PRO. For evidence of such fears, see, for example, Newport to Leveson, September 22, 1660, *HMC 5th Report*, app., p. 153; Delaville to Grey, January 10, 1660/1, *CSPD, 1660–61*, p. 470.

43. Delaville to Grey, January 10, 1660/1, *CSPD, 1660–61*, p. 470.

44. W. Cobbett and T. B. Howell, eds., *A Complete Collection of State Trials and Proceedings for High Treason and Other Crimes and Misdemeanors from the Earliest Period to the Year 1783*, 21 vols. (London, 1816), 6:67, note. The Fifth Monarchists had attempted to overthrow the regime of Oliver Cromwell and somehow "escaped beyond expectation."

45. Ibid., p. 69, note.

46. Pepys, *Diary*, entry for January 10, 1661. And see Evelyn, *Diary*, 3:266.

47. *LJ*, 11:243.

48. See W. G. Johnson, "Post-Restoration Non-Conformity and Plotting, 1660–1675" (Manchester, M.A., 1967). Articles of impeachment drawn up against Clarendon in 1667 charged that "he set on foot a plot at a committee of Lords and Commons merely on purpose to move the King to set up a standing army." Milward, *Diary*, p. 100.

49. Privy Council orders, January 8, 1660/1, January 22, 1660/1.

50. Council to Lords Lieutenant, January 8, 1660/1, Add. MS 34,222, f. 15, BL.

51. Add. MS 34,222, f. 17, BL.

52. Johnson, "Post-Restoration Non-Conformity," p. 85.

53. Capt. John Butler to Monck, January 22, 1660/1, PC 2/55, f. 520, PRO.

54. March 29, 1661, PC 2/55, f. 189, PRO.

55. "Proclamation Prohibiting the seizing of any Persons, or Searching Houses without Warrant except in time of Actual Insurrections," January 17, 1660/1, 669, f. 26(49), BL.

56. Council to Lords Lieutenant, January 22, 1660/1, Add. MS 34,306, f. 9.

57. See, for example, Add. MS 34,222, f. 18, Council to Lords Lieutenant, March 4, 1660/1, giving permission to discharge Quakers from prison, excepting only "ringleaders of faction amongst them."

58. *LJ*, 9:241–243.

59. Clarendon, *Life*, 2:97.

60. 13 Car. II, c.6. For an excellent analysis of the thorny problem of militia assessment that any permanent militia statute would have to resolve, see A. Hassell Smith, "Militia Rates and Militia Statutes, 1558–1663," *The English Commonwealth: 1547–1640*, ed. Peter Clark et al. (Leicester, 1979), pp. 93–110.

61. Mark Thomson, *A Constitutional History of England, 1642–1801* (London, 1938), p. 160. And see Joseph R. Tanner, *English Constitutional Conflicts of the Seventeenth Century, 1603–1689* (Cambridge, 1928), p. 224. Western wrote on this point: "The militia system established by the acts of 1661–3 gave the king the shadow but only a little of the substance of power." *Eighteenth Century Militia*, p. 16. And see Anthony Fletcher, *Reform in the Provinces: The Government of Stuart England* (New Haven, 1986), especially p. 321. Fletcher writes that, despite the concession to the King in 1661, the "real significance" of the militia acts of 1661, 1662, and 1663 lay elsewhere. "The king won a victory of principle but the country gentry obtained the substance of power." Hassell Smith, however, argues that the militia acts of 1662 and 1663 "provided a sound militia system which could be misused by the Crown." Smith, "Militia Rates and Militia Statutes," p. 110.

62. Henry Coker was threatened by some victims with litigation for his militia activities in Wiltshire, despite the fact that he had acted according to orders. He believed he was saved by the Militia Act of 1661. See Western, *English Militia*, p. 11.

63. Council to Lords Lieutenant, August 19, 1661, Add. MS 34,306, f. 12, BL.

64. Lords Lieutenant to Deputies, August 21, 1661, Add. MS 34,306, f. 12, and see f. 14, BL.
65. Add. MS 34,222, f. 19, BL.
66. William Holcroft, "Notebooks and Papers of William Holcroft of Walthamstow", D/DCV1, f. 2, Essex Record Office.
67. Deputy Lieutenants to Lords Lieutenant, October 11, 1661, Add. MS 34,222, f. 19, BL.
68. Milward to Lords Lieutenant, January 11, 1660/1, Add. MS 34,306, f. 9, BL.
69. Milward to Lords Lieutenant, November 25, 1661, Add. MS 34,306, f. 17, BL.
70. PC 2/55/367, 187, PRO. The order was dated September 4, 1661.
71. CJ, 8:334.
72. BM 1851, c.8 (133), (134), (135), BL.
73. CJ, 8:338–339.
74. This proclamation was reissued on June 22, 1664; November 3, 1664; November 18, 1665; and June 10, 1670.
75. Francesco Giavarino to Doge and Senate, December 15, 1662. *Calendar SP Venetian, 1661–64*, p. 221.
76. Bennet to King, April 1662, MS Clarendon 76/150–153, Bodleian. Bennet was a hard-line royalist who was always ready to advance the King's power and an enemy to Clarendon. He was created Lord Arlington in 1665.
77. *LJ*, 11:471, May 19, 1662.
78. Northampton to King, Coventry, August 18, 1662, MS Clarendon 77, ff. 236–237, Bodleian. The new militia act required officers to swear that they did not believe it lawful "upon any pretence whatsoever" to take up arms against the King.
79. Brereton to Lord Norwich, September 9, 1662, MS Clarendon 77, f. 380, Bodleian.
80. *CSPD, 1661–62*, pp. 423–424.
81. Add. MS 34,222, ff. 24–26, BL.
82. Westmorland to Vane, July 21, 1662, MS Clarendon 77/66a, Bodleian.
83. Northampton to King, August 18, 1662, MS Clarendon 77/236–237, Bodleian.
84. Samuel Pepys was, by the autumn of 1662, skeptical of Crown alarms about plots. On Sunday, October 26, he recorded in his diary: "All this day, soldiers going up and down the towne, there being [an] alarme and many Quakers and others clapped up; but I believe without any reason. Only they say in Dorsettshire there hath been some rising discovered." And see note 48.
85. *LJ*, 11:455.
86. James Macpherson, ed., *Original Papers, Containing the Secret History of Great Britain, from the Restoration, to the Accession of the House of Hannover to which are Prefixed Extracts from the Life of James II As Written by Himself: 1660–1714*, 2 vols. (London, 1775), 1:9.
87. Pepys, *Diary*, January 22, 1661/2, 2:165–166.
88. Hutton, *Restoration*, p. 289.

4. The Gentleman's Game

1. J. L. DeLolme, *The Constitution of England; or an Account of the English Government* (New York, 1792), p. 164.
2. David Ogg, *England in the Reign of Charles II*, 2nd ed. (Oxford, 1972), p. 159.
3. P. J. Cook, "Property and Prerogative in Game: The Legal Background to the History of the English Game and Forest Laws" (Birmingham, L.L.M., 1975), p. 58.
4. See *CSPD, 1662*, pp. 431, 491; Evelyn F. Shirley, *Some Account of English Deer Parks* (London, 1867), p. 48.
5. SP 29/10/2; Egerton MS 2542, f. 428, BL.
6. Shirley, *Deer Parks*, p. 51. And see SP 29/11, ff. 89, 106, 107, 125, 127, 133, 137; Egerton MS 2542, f. 422, BL.
7. Cook, "Game Laws," p. 169.
8. SP 29/11/125.
9. King to Vice-Chancellor, August 15, 1660, SP 29/10/151; King to Robert Lord Bruce, September 10, 1660, *CSPD, 1660–61*, p. 262; King to Countess of Carlisle, December 19, 1660, SP 29/24/1.
10. E. P. Thompson, *Whigs and Hunters: The Origin of the Black Act* (New York, 1975), p. 40.
11. *CJ*, 1662, p. 429; Ogg, *Reign of Charles II*, pp. 56–59.
12. Ogg, *Reign of Charles II*, p. 58.
13. See J. P. Kenyon, *The Stuart Constitution, 1603–1688* (Cambridge, 1966), p. 498; Alan Harding, *A Social History of English Law* (London, 1966), p. 267.
14. See in particular the detailed analysis of this issue in Anthony Fletcher, *Reform in the Provinces: The Government of Stuart England* (New Haven, 1986).
15. Ibid., pp. 321–322.
16. J. H. Plumb, *The Growth of Political Stability in England, 1675–1725* (London, 1967), p. 20. Fletcher concludes on this subject: "From the 1660s, then, the deputies and justices were firmly in command of their own shires." Fletcher, *Reform in the Provinces*, p. 358.
17. William Cobbett, ed., *The Parliamentary History of England from the Earliest Period to the Year 1803*, 36 vols. (London, 1806–1820), 4:145.
18. *LJ*, 11:456–457.
19. Ibid., p. 456.
20. Joseph Williamson, cited by J. C. R. Childs, "The Army and Society in Restoration England" (University of London, Ph.D., 1973), pp. 384–385.
21. Godfrey Davies, "Charles II in 1660," *Essays on the Later Stuarts* (Westport, Conn., 1975), p. 35.
22. Ogg, *Reign of Charles II*, p. 292.
23. Samuel Pepys, *Diary of Samuel Pepys*, ed. Henry B. Wheatley, 8 vols. (London, 1913), 7:37.
24. "History of Henry Gregory, Rector of Middleton Stoney, Oxfordshire, 1662–1681," Add. MS 19,526, f. 57, BL.

25. Anchitel Grey, *Debates in the House of Commons from the Year 1667 to the Year 1694,* 10 vols. (London, 1763), 2:395. On the subject of the general anxiety over a royal standing army, John Childs writes: "There was little evidence to suggest that Charles ever planned to rule with an army at the expense of Parliament, but history and the nature of the armed forces gave the Commons cause for suspicion." However, he added, "Parliament's sensitivity about the army was not a fantasy," since there was the danger three times within twenty-five years that the army, increased because of warfare, would not disband. See John Childs, *The Army of Charles II* (London, 1976), pp. 219–220.
26. Pepys, *Diary,* 4:47.
27. Grey, *Debates in House of Commons,* 2:393.
28. See Childs, *The Army of Charles II,* especially pp. 213–217.
29. *CJ,* 8:500.
30. Edward Hyde, Earl of Clarendon, *The Life of Edward Earl of Clarendon,* 3 vols. (Oxford, 1827), 2:211.
31. Ibid., pp. 219–220.
32. Clarendon, *Life,* 2:220; Hemsworth to Rewe, November 17, 1663, De L'Isle and Dudley MSS, *HMC,* 6:519–520.
33. Pepys, *Diary,* 7:17.
34. *CSPD, 1671,* pp. 93–94.
35. Grey, *Debates in House of Commons,* 1:337.
36. Clarendon, *Life,* 1:315.
37. John Evelyn wrote of the surviving English fleet, "I beheld that sad spectacle, namely more than halfe of that gallant bulwark of the Kingdome miserably shattered, hardly a Vessall intire, but appearing rather so many wracks and hulls, so cruely had the Dutch mangled us." John Evelyn, *The Diary of John Evelyn,* ed. E. S. deBeer, 6 vols. (Oxford, 1955), 3:441. And see Ogg, *Reign of Charles II,* p. 301.
38. Evelyn, *Diary,* 3:441.
39. Ogg, *Reign of Charles II,* p. 312.
40. Ibid., pp. 291–292.
41. Evelyn, *Diary,* 3:477, and see 451–454, 464.
42. Ibid., p. 464; John Milward, *The Diary of John Milward: September 17th, 1666 to May 8th, 1668,* ed. Caroline Robbins (Cambridge, 1938), p. 13.
43. Cited by D. T. Witcombe, *Charles II and the Cavalier House of Commons, 1663–1674* (Manchester, 1966), p. 55.
44. J. R. Western, *The English Militia in the Eighteenth Century: The Story of a Political Issue, 1660–1802* (London, 1965), p. 44.
45. *CSPD, 1665–66,* pp. 489–490, 475–476, 561. And see Western, *Eighteenth-Century Militia,* pp. 44–45.
46. *CSPD, 1667,* pp. 172, 179–183, 189. And see Western, *Eighteenth-Century Militia,* p. 45. Pepys reported in July 1667 the rumour that the King was raising a land army, the Duke of York was enthusiastic about it, and the intent was to have a government like that of France. See Pepys, *Diary,* 7:17, 37.

47. See, for example, Western, *Eighteenth-Century Militia,* pp. 45–48.
48. Ibid., p. 47. Also see Fletcher, *Reform in the Provinces,* p. 322, where he argues that from 1663 on "Parliament . . . precluded a standing army by accepting the device of a standing militia." Members agreed with the concept of a standing militia, but by 1667 questioned the select nature of the personnel.
49. Western, *Eighteenth-Century Militia,* p. 47.
50. See Milward, *Diary,* pp. 113–114.
51. Clarendon, *Life,* 2:449. On Clarendon's opposition to an army, see James S. Clarke, *The Life of James the Second,* 2 vols. (London, 1816), 1:390–391; T. H. Lister, *Life and Administration of Edward, First Earl of Clarendon,* 3 vols. (London, 1837–1838), 2:65–66.
52. Cited by Witcombe, *Charles II and House of Commons,* p. 65.
53. Milward, *Diary,* pp. 83–84. Parliament also wanted to consider "wherein the militia is defective and how it may be amended" (p. 175).
54. Grey, *Debates of House of Commons,* 1:56, 112; 2:17; Milward, *Diary,* pp. 215–218.
55. Add. MSS 11,610, ff. 59–60, BL; Legh MSS, *HMC 3rd Report,* p. 269; LeFleming MSS, *HMC 5th Report,* pp. 38, 40.
56. Milward, *Diary,* pp. 11–12.
57. Ibid., pp. 111, 122, 138–141.
58. Grey, *Debates of House of Commons,* 1:215, note.
59. Andrew Marvell, *The Poems and Letters of Andrew Marvell,* ed. H. M. Margoliouth, 2 vols., 3rd ed. (Oxford, 1971), 2:315.
60. Ibid., pp. 316–317.
61. Cited by Witcombe, *Charles II and House of Commons,* p. 101. And see Grey, *Debates in House of Commons,* 1:246–247 and note.
62. Marvell, *Letters,* 2:317; Grey, *Debates in House of Commons,* 1:247.
63. Lord Wharton, cited by Douglas R. Lacey, *Dissent and Parliamentary Politics in England, 1661–1689* (New Brunswick, N.J., 1969), p. 61.
64. Ibid. It has been argued that even as the new Conventicle Act was brought forward, there was a notable change in thought in the House of Commons, that "perhaps for the first time, the leading speakers in both Houses were on the side of toleration." See Frank Bate, *The Declaration of Indulgence, 1672* (London, 1908), p. 66.
65. Marvell, *Letters,* 2:317–318.
66. Ibid.
67. Although this part of the treaty was kept secret, there were rumours that the King was receiving French money. See Clarke, *Life of James II,* 1:442; Lyttleton to Hatton, October 7, 1671, in E. M. Thompson, ed., *Letters Addressed to Christopher, First Viscount Hatton, 1601–1704,* Camden Society, 2 vols. (London, 1878), 1:72.
68. *CJ,* 9:181.
69. Grey, *Debates in House of Commons,* 1:336–337.
70. Ibid., pp. 334, 336–337.
71. Ibid., p. 334.

72. *Calendar SP Venetian, 1671–72*, p. 14.

73. 22 Car. II, c.1, "Act to prevent malicious Maiming and Wounding" (1671).

74. John Kenyon, *The Popish Plot* (London, 1972), p. 15. Bate, *Declaration of Indulgence*, pp. 74–75.

75. "Newsletters to Sir Willoughby Aston," Add. MS 36,916, f. 217, BL.

76. *CJ*, 9:219–237. The House may have been "thin" at this time, that is, many members may already have returned to their homes and the large number named to the committee may have been necessary in order to have a reasonable number of members in attendance at meetings. A newsletter dated March 21, 1671, reported that only thirty-eight members of the Commons attended the session that afternoon. Add. MS 36,916, f. 215, BL.

77. 22&23 Car. II, c.25 (1671).

78. 12 Car. II, c.10, "An Act to prevent the unlawful Coursing, Hunting, or Killing of Deer" (1661).

79. C. and E. Kirby, "The Stuart Game Prerogative," *The English Historical Review* 46 (1931), pp. 251–252.

80. C. Kirby, "English Game Law Reform," in *Essays in Modern English History in Honour of Wilbur C. Abbot* (Cambridge, Mass., 1941), p. 348.

81. The emphasis is my own.

82. William Blackstone, *Commentaries on the Laws of England*, 4 vols., 12th ed. (London, 1793–1795), 4:175. It is interesting to note that while inflation had greatly expanded the size of the electorate, as well as the numbers of those able to hunt, the 40s. standard for voting had not been altered since it was established in 1430.

83. See 13 Ric. II, c.13, "None shall hunt but they which have a sufficient living."

84. See 3 Jac., c.13 (1605); 7 Jac., c.13 (1609).

85. Witcombe, in *Charles II and the Cavalier House of Commons*, p. 140, completely overlooks passage of the Game Act in summing up the session of 1671. But see J. P. Kenyon, *The Stuart Constitution, 1603–1688* (Cambridge, 1966), p. 494.

86. G. M. Trevelyan, *English Social History* (New York, 1965), p. 279. Although Trevelyan and others refer to the "game acts" of the Restoration, in fact only the act of 1671 made any real alteration.

87. Christopher Hill, "Reformation to Industrial Revolution," in *The Restoration*, ed. Joan Thirsk (London, 1976), p. 29.

88. Sidney and Beatrice Webb, *English Local Government from the Revolution to the Municipal Corporations Act*, 9 vols. (London, 1906), 1:598; Hill, "Reformation to Industrial Revolution," p. 29. Derek Hirst sees the increasingly "draconian" game laws of the Restoration period as part of a social reaction of the upper classes against the meaner sort. See Derek Hirst, *Authority and Conflict: England, 1603–1658* (Cambridge, Mass., 1986), p. 358. The power of a single justice of the peace to decide game offences was in accord with a trend that began at the Restoration to authorize magistrates to exercise summary jurisdiction. See J. M. Beattie,

Crime and the Courts in England: 1660–1800 (Oxford, 1986), pp. 17, 269, 315.

89. P. B. Munsche, *Gentlemen and Poachers: The English Game Laws, 1671–1831* (Cambridge, 1981), p. 19. Also see pp. 16–19.
90. Trevelyan, *English Social History,* p. 279.
91. See Cook, "Game Laws," pp. 33–34; Kirby, "Stuart Game Prerogative."
92. Anxiety had been growing over the influence of Catholics at Court, the Crown's toleration of the religion, and the Catholic menace to the kingdom. In 1670 rumours began to circulate that James, Duke of York, had converted to Catholicism. Shortly after the Game Bill was first read the Duchess of York died, and there was great indignation when it was rumoured that she had called for a priest on her deathbed. See Witcombe, *Charles II and House of Commons,* p. 122. Her conversion may not have caused the submission of the Game Bill, but it may have added urgency to its passage as an independent means for the Protestant gentry to disarm Catholics. Munsche, in *Gentlemen and Poachers,* p. 213, note 41, found evidence that the Game Act was used to punish those whose real crime was non-attendance at church. No doubt one motive for passage of the Game Act was the same reason that, according to an observer in 1662, the post of justice of the peace was sought after, for "the honour of being trusted and the pleasure of being feared. . . ." See Hill, "Reformation to Industrial Revolution," p. 29.

5. Enforcement of Arms Restrictions

1. J. R. Western, *Monarchy and Revolution: The English State in the 1680's* (London, 1972), p. 144.
2. John Miller, "The Militia and the Army in the Reign of James II," *The Historical Journal,* XVI, 4 (1973), p. 675.
3. *CSPD, 1660–61,* p. 484.
4. Bellingham to D. Fleming, August 25, 1666, LeFleming MSS, *HMC 12th Report,* part 7, p. 41.
5. Charles II to Lords Lieutenant, November 24, 1666, Add. MS 11,610, ff. 59–60, BL.
6. D. Fleming to Braithwaite, Layburne West, January 25, 1667, LeFleming MSS, *HMC 12th Report,* part 7, p. 44.
7. Elizabeth M. Halcrow, ed., *Charges to the Grand Jury at Quarter Sessions, 1660–1677, by Sir Peter Leicester,* Chetham Society (Manchester, 1953), p. 51.
8. W. G. Johnson, "Post-Restoration Nonconformity and Plotting, 1660–1675" (Manchester, M.A., 1967), p. 29.
9. "Account of State of Lincolnshire under Earl of Lyndsay, Lord Lieutenant, April 1664," MS Clarendon 92, f. 143, Bodleian Library.
10. See W. LeHardy, ed., *Hertfordshire County Records, Calendar of the Sessions Books,* 9 vols. (Hertford, 1905–1939), vol. 6.; S. C. Ratcliffe and H. C. Johnson, eds., *Quarter Sessions Indictment Book, Easter 1631 to*

Epiphany 1674, Warwick County Records, vol. 6 (Warwick, 1941); Ratcliffe and Johnson, eds., *Quarter Sessions Records, Easter 1674 to Easter 1682,* Warwick County Records, vol. 7 (Warwick, 1946).

11. H. H. Copnall, ed., *Nottingham County Records, Notes and Extracts . . . of the Seventeenth Century* (Nottingham, 1915), p. 92.

12. J. C. Jeaffreson and W. LeHardy, eds., *Middlesex County Records, Middlesex Sessions Rolls, 1625–1688,* vol. 3 (London, 1888; repr. 1974), p. 40.

13. Ratcliffe and Johnson, *Warwickshire Quarter Sessions Indictment Book,* p. 48.

14. LeHardy, *Hertfordshire Sessions Books,* p. 102; Ratcliffe and Johnson, *Warwickshire Quarter Sessions Indictment Book,* p. 157.

15. J. W. Willis-Bund, *Worcester County Records: Quarter Session Rolls,* vol. 1, part 1, Worcestershire Historical Society (1899–1900), p. 228.

16. Halcrow, *Charges to Grand Jury.*

17. Copnall, *Nottingham County Records,* p. 92.

18. 6 & 7 William III, c.13.

19. Margaret Verney, ed., *Memoirs of the Verney Family,* 4 vols. (London, 1892–1899), 4:282.

20. Thomas Andrew Green, *Verdict According to Conscience: Perspectives on the English Criminal Trial Jury, 1200–1800* (Chicago, 1985), traces the long history of juries refusing to convict defendants because they believed the punishment was too harsh.

21. John Evelyn, *The Diary of John Evelyn,* ed. E. S. deBeer, 6 vols. (Oxford, 1955), January 21, 1664. And see Verney, *Memoirs,* 4:291, 314–315, 317.

22. Joan Parkes, *Travel in England in the Seventeenth Century* (Oxford, 1925), p. 154. Also see J. L. Rayner and G. T. Crook, eds., *The Complete Newgate Calendar,* 5 vols. (London, 1926), 1:172.

23. See John Milward, *The Diary of John Milward, September 17th, 1666 to May 8th, 1668,* ed. Caroline Robbins (Cambridge, 1938), pp. 111, 122, 138–141.

24. Verney, *Memoirs,* 4:286.

25. Anthony Wood, *The Life and Times of Anthony Wood, Antiquary of Oxford, 1632–95, Described by Himself,* ed. A. Clark, 5 vols. Oxf. Hist. Soc. (Oxford, 1891–1900), vol. 2, February 7, 1677.

26. Verney, *Memoirs,* 4:316.

27. Rayner and Crook, *Newgate Calendar,* 1:180.

28. Ibid., p. 147.

29. See Howard L. Blackmore, *British Military Firearms, 1650–1850* (London, 1961), p. 27; Robert Held, *The Age of Firearms,* rev. ed. (Northfield, Ill., 1970), p. 87.

30. Samuel Pepys, *Diary of Samuel Pepys,* ed. Henry B. Wheatley, 8 vols. (London, 1913), 2:176, 262–263, 268, 286–287, 290–291.

31. MS Clarendon 92, f. 143, Bodleian Library.

32. Ibid. And see George Roberts, *The Social History of the People of the Southern Counties of England in Past Centuries* (London, 1856), pp. 208–209; Willis-Bund, *Worcestershire Quarter Sessions Rolls,* p. 448. Richard Burn, in *The Justice of the Peace and Parish Officer,* states that a foot

soldier in the militia of Charles II was paid 2s. 6d. per day, far more than the 18d. stated in the manuscript from the Clarendon State Papers cited here. If Burn is correct, a foot soldier could have purchased a new musket in less than five days of active service. Richard Burn, *The Justice of the Peace and Parish Officer,* 2 vols. (London, 1755), 2:148.

33. See Alex W. Bealer, *The Art of Blacksmithing,* rev. ed. (New York, 1979), p. 381.

34. Parkes, *Travel,* p. 166.

35. John Clavel, "Recantation of an Ill Ledde Life," cited by Parkes, *Travel,* p. 175.

36. Verney, *Memoirs,* 4:353.

37. Pepys, *Diary,* 2:320.

38. William Blizard, *Desultory Reflections on Police: With an Essay on the Means of Preventing Crimes and Amending Criminals* (London, 1785), p. 36.

39. Verney, *Memoirs,* 4:130.

40. Thomas Bruce, Earl of Ailesbury, *Memoirs of Thomas, Earl of Ailesbury,* 2 vols., Roxburghe Club (London, 1890), 1:29.

41. "Letter Book of Thomas Belasyse, Viscount Fauconberg, Lord Lieutenant of North Riding of Yorkshire, 1665–1684," Add. MSS 41,254, f. 13, BL.

42. John Kenyon, *The Popish Plot* (London, 1972), pp. 108–109.

43. Ibid., p. 109. Also see Anchitel Grey, *Debates in the House of Commons from the Year 1667 to the Year 1694,* 10 vols. (London, 1763), 1:109.

44. Grey, *Debates,* 1:348.

45. William Blackstone, *Commentaries on the Laws of England,* 4 vols., 1st ed. (London, 1765–1769, repr. Chicago, 1979), 4:409.

46. See William LeHardy, ed., *Hertfordshire Sessions Books* (Hertford, 1930), vol. 6; J. C. Jeaffreson and William LeHardy, eds., *Middlesex Sessions Rolls* (London, 1888, 1892), vols. 3, 4; H. H. Copnall, ed., *Nottingham County Records: Notes and Extracts . . . of the Seventeenth Century* (Nottingham, 1915); S. A. Peyton, ed., *Minutes of the Proceedings in Quarter Sessions Held for the Parts of Kesteven in the County of Lincoln, 1674–1695,* 2 vols., Lincoln Rec. Soc. Publ., 25–26 (Lincoln, 1931). Note that the Lincolnshire series does not begin until 1674.

47. See S. C. Ratcliffe and H. C. Johnson, eds., *Warwick County Records: Quarter Sessions Indictment Book* (1631–1674), Warwick County Records, vol. 6 (Warwick, 1941); Ratcliffe and Johnson, eds., *Warwick County Records: Quarter Sessions Records* (1674–1682), Warwick County Records, vol. 7 (Warwick, 1946); Ratcliffe and Johnson, eds., *Warwick County Records: Quarter Sessions Records* (1682–1690), vol. 8 (Warwick, 1953); *Warwick County Records: Quarter Sessions Records* (1690–1696), vol. 9.

48. William LeHardy, ed., *County of Buckingham Calendar to the Sessions Records,* 4 vols. (Aylesbury, 1933), 1:137.

49. P. B. Munsche, *Gentlemen and Poachers: The English Game Laws, 1671–1831* (Cambridge, 1981), p. 214, note 45.

50. Ibid.

Notes to Pages 87–95

51. Ibid., pp. 84–85.

52. P. B. Munsche, "The Game Laws in Wiltshire, 1750–1800," in J. S. Cockburn, ed., *Crime in England, 1550–1800* (Cambridge, 1977), p. 218; Douglas Hay, "Poaching and the Game Laws on Cannock Chase," in D. Hay, ed., *Albion's Fatal Tree: Crime and Society in Eighteenth-Century England* (London, 1975), p. 200.

53. John Mordant, *The Complete Steward*, cited by Munsche, "Game Laws in Wiltshire," p. 217.

54. See Hay, "Poaching and the Game Laws," pp. 195, 241.

55. "Notebook and Papers of William Holcroft of Walthamstow, Justice of the Peace and Verderer of the Forest of Waltham, 1661–1688," MSD/DCV1 and D/DCV2–5, Essex Record Office.

56. E. H. Bates-Harbin and M. C. B. Dawes, eds., *Quarter Sessions Records for the County of Somerset, 1607–1677*, Somerset Rec. Soc., 34 (1919), p. 178.

57. King to George Legge, March 5, 1671, SP 29/288, f. 29, PRO.

58. Cited by E. P. Thompson, *Whigs and Hunters: The Origin of the Black Act* (New York, 1975), p. 60.

59. See Onslow MSS, *HMC 14th Report*, part 9, pp. 485–486.

60. PC 2/63, p. 392, PRO.

61. PC 2/63, pp. 395, 401, 404, PRO.

62. See Munsche, *Gentlemen and Poachers*, p. 81.

63. 3 Will. & Mar., c.10, 1691.

64. Evelyn Curtis, *Crime in Bedfordshire, 1660–1688*, Leaflet 4 (Elston Moot Hall, 1956), p. 19.

65. Munsche, *Gentlemen and Poachers*, pp. 213–214, note 41.

66. Kenyon, *Popish Plot*, pp. 108–109.

67. House of Lords MSS, *HMC 11th Report*, app. 2–3, pp. 70–71.

68. Western, *Monarchy and Revolution*, p. 144.

69. Ibid., pp. 144–145. It is possible that on occasion arms confiscated before the Rye House Plot were not returned. However, after that event it was government policy not to return such weapons.

70. Evelyn, *Diary*, 4:409.

71. Ibid., pp. 411–412.

72. Ibid., p. 416.

6. James II and Control of Firearms

1. John Miller argues that the initiative for the confiscation of borough charters and their alteration to give the Crown more control came from the Tories, not the Crown. See John Miller, *James II: A Study in Kingship* (London, 1978), p. 113.

2. See David Ogg, *England in the Reign of Charles II*, 2nd ed. (Oxford, 1972), pp. 338, 370.

3. James Welwood, *Memoirs of the Most Material Transactions in England*

for the Last Hundred Years [to 1688], ed. F. Maseres (London, 1820), p. 113.

4. "The Several Debates of the House of Commons Pro et Contra, Relating to the Establishment of the Militia, Disbanding the New-Raised Forces . . . November 1685" (London, 1689), pp. 6–7. William Temple, *The Works of Sir William Temple,* ed. S. Hamilton, 4 vols. (London, 1814), 2:577–579. The Parliament of 1680 explained: "The issue of our most deliberate thoughts and consultations, that for the Papists to have their hopes continued, that a Prince of that religion shall succeed in the throne of these kingdoms, is utterly inconsistent with the safety of your Majesty's person, the preservation of the Protestant religion, and the prosperity, peace, and welfare of your Protestant subjects."

5. See Lionel K. J. Glassey, *Politics and the Appointment of Justices of the Peace: 1675–1720* (Oxford, 1979), pp. 42–57. Glassey writes, "The view that the county benches were controlled by Tory justices by 1685 is substantially correct" (p. 55). Ogg, *England in the Reign of Charles II,* pp. 623–624. Tories aided in consolidating power within boroughs in their own and the Crown's hands. See John Miller, *The Glorious Revolution* (London, 1983), p. 3.

6. See Onslow MSS, *HMC 14th Report,* part 9, pp. 484–485.

7. See Robin Clifton, *The Last Popular Rebellion: The Western Rising of 1685* (London, 1984), p. 282.

8. J. R. Western, *Monarchy and Revolution: The English State in the 1680's* (London, 1972), p. 124. For an excellent, detailed account of the army under Charles II, see John Childs, *The Army of Charles II* (London, 1976).

9. John Lowther, Viscount Lonsdale, *Memoir of the Reign of James II* (York, 1808), p. 4.

10. John Evelyn, *The Diary of John Evelyn,* ed. E. S. deBeer, 6 vols. (Oxford, 1955), 4:437.

11. Miller, *The Glorious Revolution,* pp. 4, 9.

12. There is an incident recorded in the Verney *Memoirs* that is particularly illuminating in regard to James's intentions. On October 20, 1680, during the exclusion controversy, Lord Fairfax was walking in St. James Park when the then Duke of York saw him "and so came to him and took him by ye hand and said to him, Well my Lord I see you are all com up to doe what you can against me; I am ye more sory for ye occasion, replied that Lord, but we are all resolved to assert ye properties of our nation and ye Prodistant Religion; and His Royal Higness replyd again, I will give you all ye asshurance you can ask that I will not disturb your propertie." Margaret Verney, ed., *Memoirs of the Verney Family,* 4 vols. (London, 1892–1899), 4:265.

13. J. G. Simms, *Jacobite Ireland: 1685–1691* (London, 1969), pp. 16–17.

14. King to Archbishop of Armagh, Earl of Granard, Lords Justices of Ireland, March 27, 1685, *CSPD, 1685,* pp. 110–114.

15. See John Childs, *The Army, James II, and the Glorious Revolution* (Manchester, 1980), p. 60.

16. King to Archbishop of Armagh, Earl of Granard, Lords Justices of Ireland, March 27, 1685, *CSPD, 1685*, pp. 110–114.
17. Sunderland to Lords Justices of Ireland, May 30, 1685, *CSPD, 1685*, p. 174; King to Lords Justices of Ireland, June 9, 1685; together with Sunderland to Lords Justices of Ireland, June 6, 1685, *CSPD, 1685*, p. 187.
18. Granard to Sunderland, Carrickfergus, July 6, 1685, *CSPD, 1685*, p. 252.
19. Childs, *The Army, James II, and the Glorious Revolution*, p. 62.
20. Ibid.
21. Clarendon to Sunderland, Dublin, January 19, 1685/6 in S. W. Singer, ed., *The Correspondence of Henry Hyde, Earl of Clarendon, and of His Brother, Laurence Hyde, Earl of Rochester*, 2 vols. (London, 1828), 1:216.
22. Simms, *Jacobite Ireland*, p. 25. Tyrconnel insisted that religion was of no consequence in these alterations, but he instructed Catholic bishops to have parish priests send them lists of all their male parishioners capable of bearing arms. He cashiered 400 to 500 Protestants from a single regiment on the ground that they were beneath the proper height and replaced them with Catholics who were even shorter. He is said to have ordered Lord Roscommon, in the presence of several other officers, "upon his allegiance to admit no men into the vacancies he had made in the Duke of Ormond's regiment but Roman Catholics." Clarendon, *Correspondence*, 1:501–502. See Thomas Macaulay, *History of England*, 5 vols., Chicago, 2:135, 137. Childs believed that James's methods in Ireland of purging Protestant officers and ridding the English army of all but its most devoted Protestants "caused sufficient ill-will and suspicion among a small number of officers to ruin his whole design." Childs, *The Army, James II, and the Glorious Revolution*, pp. 62, 113. Also see Miller, *James II*, p. 218.
23. See Childs, *The Army, James II, and the Glorious Revolution*, pp. 62–66.
24. See R. H. George, "Parliamentary Elections and Electioneering in 1685," *Trans. Royal Historical Soc.*, 4th ser., vol. 19 (1936), pp. 167–195; Western, *Monarchy and Revolution*, pp. 78–81.
25. Narcissus Luttrell, *A Brief Historical Relation of State Affairs from September 1678 to April 1714*, 6 vols. (Oxford, 1857), 1:341. And see Gilbert Burnet, *Bishop Burnet's History of His Own Time*, 2 vols. (London, 1840), 2:402. According to a letter in the Frankland-Russell-Astley Collection, many gentlemen declined even to stand for Parliament. See Mrs. Frankland-Russell-Astley MSS, HMC (1900), pp. 59–60.
26. See J. R. Western, *The English Militia in the Eighteenth Century* (London, 1965), p. 63; Duke of Rutland MSS, *HMC 12th Report*, vol. 2, p. 86.
27. John Miller, "Catholic Officers in the Later Stuart Army," *English Historical Review*, vol. 88, no. 346 (1973), p. 36; Evelyn, *Diary*, 4:442–443; Burnet, *History*, 2:402. The makeup of the Parliament was a great triumph for the King.
28. *LJ*, vol. 14, p. 10. And see Western, *Monarchy and Revolution*, p. 108.
29. Miller, *James II*, pp. 136–137.

30. See Maurice Ashley, *James II* (London, 1977), p. 165, for an account of the revenues voted to James II.
31. Ibid.
32. Cited by Childs, *The Army, James II, and the Glorious Revolution*, p. 106.
33. Miller, "Catholic Officers," pp. 42, 46, 47.
34. David Ogg, *England in the Reigns of James II and William III* (Oxford, 1955), p. 148. For a good account of the Monmouth rising, see Peter Earle, *Monmouth's Rebels* (London, 1977).
35. Macaulay, *History*, 1:531. In his autobiography Sir John Bramston claims that Monmouth had 16,000 men, only 7000 of whom were armed, figures that seem too high. Sir John Bramston, *The Autobiography of Sir John Bramston of Skreens*, ed. Lord Braybrooke, Camden Soc. (1845), p. 185.
36. Bramston, *Autobiography*, p. 185.
37. Ibid., p. 205.
38. Burnet, *History*, 2:424.
39. Childs, *The Army, James II, and the Glorious Revolution*, p. 19.
40. Cited by Miller, *James II*, p. 143.
41. F. C. Turner, *James II* (New York, 1948), p. 284, argues that the Catholic officers had no prior experience, but John Childs points out that many Catholic officers had served abroad. See Childs, *The Army of Charles II* (London, 1976), pp. 26–29, 132–133, 175.
42. Bramston, *Autobiography*, p. 210.
43. Burnet, *History*, 2:424.
44. Childs, *Army of Charles II*, p. 232. And see Miller, "Catholic Officers," p. 38.
45. For details of this debate I have drawn upon Bramston, *Autobiography*, pp. 210–217.
46. Ibid., p. 212; Childs, *The Army, James II, and the Glorious Revolution*, p. 12.
47. Miller, *James II*, p. 148.
48. Cited by James S. Cockburn, *A History of the English Assizes, 1558–1714* (Cambridge, 1972), p. 258.
49. *CSPD, 1686–87*, p. 432.
50. Earle, *Monmouth's Rebels*, p. 263. And see Anthony Fletcher, *Reform in the Provinces: The Government of Stuart England* (New Haven, 1986), p. 344. Fletcher provides a careful study of the militia during this period.
51. Burlington to Rochester, Yorkshire, July 16, 1685, Clarendon, *Correspondence*, 1:147–148.
52. See, for example, *CSPD, 1685*, pp. 103, 145, 191, 312, 316, 390, 398, 401–402, 417.
53. Beaufort to Sunderland, April 5, 1686, *CSPD, 1686–87*, p. 94.
54. Sunderland to Beaufort, May 1, 1686, *CSPD, 1686–87*, p. 118.
55. London Newsletter, June 10, 1686, *CSPD, 1686–87*, p. 164.
56. See *CSPD, 1686–87*, pp. 308, 313, 349; *Modern Reports; or Select Cases Adjudged in the Courts of King's Bench, Chancery, Common Pleas, and*

Exchequer, since the Restoration of Charles II, vol. 3 (London, 1700), p. 117.

57. Sunderland to Burlington, December 6, 1686, *CSPD, 1686–87,* p. 314.
58. For example, a Roman Catholic had been appointed lord lieutenant of Cambridgeshire in October 1686.
59. Cited by P. B. Munsche, *Gentlemen and Poachers: The English Game Laws, 1671–1831* (Cambridge, 1981), p. 81.
60. *HMC 10th Report,* app. 1, part 1, p. 135.
61. Miller finds the idea that James aimed at absolutism "unconvincing" but admits that "contemporaries were sure that James II wished to make himself absolute." *Glorious Revolution,* p. vii.
62. Louis XIV had a standing army of between 80,000 and 100,000 men during the 1680's to control a population of some 20,000,000 subjects, while James II had an army of 20,000 to control a population of some 5,500,000 persons. The French had a ratio of 1 soldier to every 225 civilians, the English a ratio of 1 soldier to every 275. See Childs, *The Army, James II, and the Glorious Revolution,* p. 103.
63. Ibid.
64. Ibid., p. 101.
65. Ibid., p. 91. And see pp. 85–87, 94.
66. Ibid., p. 94.
67. Ibid., pp. 86–87.
68. Edmund Bohun, cited by Childs, *The Army, James II, and the Glorious Revolution,* p. 104. Childs refers to many instances of troopers killing civilians and finds James's army a badly disciplined force (p. 95).
69. Western, *Monarchy and Revolution,* p. 121.
70. Lonsdale, *Memoir,* p. 18.
71. J. H. Plumb, *The Growth of Political Stability in England, 1675–1725* (London, 1967), p. 60.
72. Bramston, *Autobiography,* p. 304.
73. See Macaulay, *History,* 2:305–306.
74. John Kenyon, *Stuart England* (London, 1978), p. 239.
75. For the account of the recall of the Anglo-Dutch regiments, I have relied upon J. R. Jones, *The Revolution of 1688 in England* (London, 1972), pp. 180–182.
76. Luttrell, *State Affairs,* 1:440.
77. Lonsdale, *Memoir,* p. 31; Luttrell, *State Affairs,* 1:448.
78. Luttrell, *State Affairs,* 1:464.
79. *London Gazette,* October 18, 1688.
80. Cited by Ogg, *James II and William III,* p. 217.
81. Bramston, *Autobiography,* p. 325.
82. *Ibid.*
83. Cited by Western, *Monarchy and Revolution,* p. 273.
84. Barillon, cited by Ogg, *James II and William III,* p. 169.
85. *London Gazette,* November 24, 1688.
86. Luttrell, *State Affairs,* 1:484–485.

87. Western, *Monarchy and Revolution*, p. 121.
88. Burnet, *History*, 2:397.

7. Arms for Their Defence

1. Unless otherwise noted, the comments cited in this and the next paragraph are from "Grey's Debates," in *A Parliamentary History of the Glorious Revolution*, ed. David Lewis Jones (London, 1988), p. 125–133.
2. Anchitel Grey, *Debates in the House of Commons from the Year 1667 to the Year 1694*, 10 vols. (London, 1763), 9:30; "Anonymous Account of Convention Proceedings, 1688," Rawlinson MS D1079, f. 4, Bodleian Library, Oxford (the Marquis of Halifax may be the author); Robert Frankle, "The Formulation of the Declaration of Rights," *Historical Journal*, 17 (1974), p. 267.
3. *CJ*, 1:666. This statement was made in Parliament in 1621.
4. Somers MS, in *Miscellaneous State Papers from 1501 to 1726*, ed. Philip Yorke, Earl of Hardwicke, 2 vols. (London, 1778), 2:415.
5. Gilbert Burnet, *Bishop Burnet's History of His Own Time*, 2 vols. (London, 1840), 2:522.
6. See Lois Schwoerer, *The Declaration of Rights, 1689* (Baltimore, 1981), especially p. 152.
7. See Somers MS, *Miscellaneous State Papers*, 2:407–418, for this debate.
8. Erle MS 4/4, Churchill College, Cambridge.
9. Rawlinson MS D1079, f. 10.
10. *CJ*, 1688–1693, 10:21–22.
11. At first, items requiring new legislation were retained in the report in a separate section. However, the following day the Somers committee proposed that the formulation naming William and Mary as king and queen be attached to the list of ancient rights, and that the list of reforms needing new legislation be separated from that document. The "heads of grievances" now became a declaration of rights.
12. Schwoerer, *Declaration of Rights*, p. 36.
13. *CJ*, 10:25.
14. Ibid., p. 29.
15. J. R. Western, *Monarchy and Revolution: The English State in the 1680's* (London, 1972), p. 339. Conversely, J. H. Plumb argues that, since the "sanctions clauses" of the Bill of Rights specified that "there was to be no standing Army and Protestant gentlemen were to be allowed arms, the right of rebellion is implicit." See J. H. Plumb, *Growth of Stability in England, 1675–1725* (London, 1967), p. 64.
16. See, for example, Chapter 8 and Joyce Lee Malcolm, "The Right of the People to Keep and Bear Arms: The Common Law Tradition," *Hastings Constitutional Law Quarterly*, vol. 10, no. 2 (Winter 1983), pp. 288–289.
17. See Frankle, "Formulation of Declaration of Rights."
18. Thomas Macaulay, *The History of England from the Accession of James II*, 5 vols., Chicago, 2:592. G. M. Trevelyan agreed that the Declaration

"introduced no new principle of law" and was "a mere recital of those existing rights of Parliament and of the subject, which James had outraged, and which William must promise to observe." See G. M. Trevelyan, *The English Revolution, 1688–1689* (Oxford, 1938, repr. Oxford, 1968), pp. 79–80.

19. David Hume, *The History of England from the Invasion of Julius Caesar to the Abdication of James the Second, 1688,* 6 vols. (New York, 1880), 6:362.
20. Schwoerer, *Declaration of Rights,* pp. 283–284.
21. Ibid., p. 100.
22. See, for example, G. D. Newton and F. E. Zimring, "Firearms and Violence in American Life: A Staff Report Submitted to the National Commission on the Causes and Prevention of Violence," U.S. Printing Office (1969), p. 255; Lee Kennet and James Anderson, *The Gun in America* (Westport, Conn., 1975), pp. 25–27.
23. "Proposals of William, Prince of Orange, 1688," *State Tracts: Being a Further Collection of Several Choice Treatises Relating to Government from the Year 1660 to 1689* (London, 1692), p. 441.
24. For this debate see William Cobbett, ed., *The Parliamentary History of England from the Earliest Period to the Year 1803,* 36 vols. (London, 1808–1820), 5:182–184.
25. Ibid., p. 344. This is the same Sir William Williams cited above who argued that the laws must be preserved before the throne was filled. Apparently, he was satisfied with the declaration of a right to have arms and was content to await a more secure time to revise the Militia Act.
26. *CJ,* 10:621. Western notes that an amendment offered to the measure would have allowed all who had taken the oaths of allegiance and supremacy to arm themselves in time of invasion or rebellion. See Western, *Monarchy and Revolution,* p. 340, note 1.
27. Mutiny Act, 1689, 1 Will. & Mar., c.5. This act was passed before the new Coronation Oath Act, 1 Will. & Mar., c.6.
28. The Mutiny Act seems to have failed this first test, since no Mutiny Act was passed from 1697 until 1702. See Jennifer Carter, "The Revolution and the Constitution," in *Britain after the Glorious Revolution, 1689–1714,* ed. Geoffrey Holmes (London, 1969), pp. 43–44. Lois G. Schwoerer, *"No Standing Armies!": The Antiarmy Ideology in Seventeenth-Century England* (Baltimore, 1974), p. 151. This book is an excellent history of the antiarmy sentiment. See especially chap. 8.
29. Cited by Forrest McDonald, *Novus Ordo Seclorum: The Intellectual Origins of the Constitution* (Lawrence, Kansas, 1985), p. 74.
30. John Trenchard, "An Argument Shewing that a Standing Army Is Inconsistent with a Free Government, and Absolutely Destructive to the Constitution of the English Monarchy" (London, 1697), pp. 114–115.
31. Ibid., p. 115. Harrington wrote, "Wherever the Balance of a Government lys, there naturally is the Militia of the same" and argued that it was "the Sword in the hands of her Citizens" that made Rome great. "There is no other [system]," he warned, "that dos not hazard all." See James Har-

rington, "The Art of Lawgiving," in John Toland, ed., *The Oceana and Other Works of James Harrington, Esq., with an Exact Account of His Life* (London, 1727), pp. 388, 454, and *Oceana*, p. 100.

32. Trenchard, "Standing Armies," pp. 112, 115.

33. William may have played a part in encouraging Parliament to pass a new game act. According to Bishop Burnet, when not attending to business, William was an avid hunter, which "put him on a perpetual course of hunting, to which he seemed to give himself up, beyond any man I ever knew." Burnet, *History of His Own Time*, 2:438–439.

34. Thomas Coventry and Samuel Hughes, *An Analytical Digested Index to the Common Law Reports from the Time of Henry III to the Commencement of the Reign of George III*, 2 vols. (Philadelphia, 1832), 2:1303.

35. Richard Burn, *The Justice of the Peace and Parish Officer*, 2 vols. (London, 1755), 1:442–443; *Modern Reports; or Select Cases Adjudged in the Courts of King's Bench, Chancery, Common Pleas, and Exechequer, since the Restoration of Charles II*, vol. 10 (London, 1741), p. 26.

36. For this debate see Narcissus Luttrell, *The Parliamentary Diary of Narcissus Luttrell, 1691–1693*, ed. Henry Horwitz (Oxford, 1972), p. 444.

37. *CSPD, 1690–91*, pp. 14–15.

38. *Rex and Regina versus Alsop, Modern Reports*, vol. 4 (London, 1703), pp. 49–51.

39. *Bowkley versus William & al.* Edward Lutwyche, *Reports*, trans. Nelson (London, 1718), p. 484.

40. A. H. A. Hamilton, *Quarter Sessions from Queen Elizabeth to Queen Anne* (London, 1878), p. 269.

41. Anthony Fletcher, in *Reform in the Provinces: The Government of Stuart England* (New Haven, 1986), p. 360, discusses this dependency. Indeed, even the authors of these books were sometimes uncertain which statutes were continued and which were repealed.

42. See 5 Ann, c.14.

43. Joseph Chitty, *A Treatise on the Game Laws, and on Fisheries*, 2nd ed. (London, 1826), p. 83 and 83, note c.

44. Burn, *The Justice of the Peace*, 1:443.

45. John Strange, *Reports of Adjudged Cases in the Courts of Chancery, King's Bench, Common Pleas and Exchequer*, 2 vols. (London, 1755), 2:1096; Burn, *Justice of the Peace*, 1:442–443.

46. Joseph Sayer, *Reports of Cases Adjudged in the Court of King's Bench Beginning Michaelmas Term, 25 Geo. II, England Trinity Term, 29 & 30 Geo. II, 1751–1756* (London, 1775), pp. 15–17.

47. William Blackstone, *Commentaries on the Laws of England*, 4 vols., 1st ed. repr. (Chicago, 1979), 1:136.

48. Ibid., p. 139.

49. See Cobbett, *Parliamentary History*, 21:655–656.

50. See ibid., p. 691–692, for Richmond's comments.

51. Ibid., p. 691.

52. Ibid., p. 726.

53. Ibid., p. 727.

54. See ibid., pp. 728–746, for the debate and vote.
55. Granville Sharp, *Tracts, Concerning the Antient and Only True Legal Means of National Defence, by a Free Militia* (London, 1782), pp. 17–18, 27.
56. T. A. Critchley, *The Conquest of Violence: Order and Liberty in Britain* (London, 1970), pp. 67–68.
57. Ibid.
58. J. R. Western, *The English Militia in the Eighteenth Century: The Story of a Political Issue, 1660–1802* (London, 1965), p. 73.
59. Critchley, *Conquest of Violence,* p. 68.
60. William Blizard, *Desultory Reflection on Police: With an Essay on the Means of Preventing Crimes and Amending Criminals* (London, 1785), pp. 59–60.
61. Blackstone, *Commentaries on the Laws of England,* ed. Edward Christian, 4 vols., 12th ed. (London, 1793–1795), 2:441.

8. The Second Amendment and the English Legacy

1. Ben R. Miller, sec. 3, "The Legal Basis for Firearms Controls," *Report to the American Bar Association,* 22 (1975), p. 22.
2. Ibid., p. 26.
3. See Joyce Lee Malcolm, "The Right of the People to Keep and Bear Arms: The Common Law Tradition," *The Hastings Constitutional Law Quarterly,* vol. 10, no. 2 (Winter 1983), especially pp. 286–289; Sanford Levinson, "The Embarrassing Second Amendment," *The Yale Law Journal,* vol. 99 (1989); Don B. Kates, Jr., "Handgun Prohibition and the Original Meaning of the Second Amendment," *Michigan Law Review,* vol. 82, no. 2 (November 1983); Robert E. Shalhope, "The Ideological Origins of the Second Amendment," *The Journal of American History,* vol. 69, no. 1 (December, 1982); David T. Hardy, "The Second Amendment and the Bill of Rights," *The Journal of Law and Politics,* vol. 4, no. 1 (Summer 1987); Lawrence Cress, "An Armed Community: The Origins and Meaning of the Right to Bear Arms," *The Journal of American History,* vol. 71, no. 1 (June 1984); Shalhope and Cress, "The Second Amendment and the Right to Bear Arms: An Exchange," *The Journal of American History,* vol. 71, no. 3 (December 1984). Stephen P. Halbrook, *That Every Man Be Armed: The Evolution of a Constitutional Right* (Albuquerque, 1984), a survey of Second Amendment history, particularly of value for the period after the ratification of the Second Amendment, should be used with caution for English common law history. See Joyce Lee Malcolm, "That Every Man Be Armed," *The George Washington Law Review,* vol. 54, nos. 2 and 3 (January and March 1986), pp. 452–464. Also see Stephen P. Halbrook, *A Right to Bear Arms: State and Federal Bills of Rights and Constitutional Guarantees* (Westport, Conn., 1989); Lee Kennet and James Anderson, *The Gun in America* (Westport, 1975). Earlier works of interest are George D. Newton and Franklin E. Zimring, "Firearms and Violence in American

Life: A Staff Report Submitted to the National Commission on the Causes and Prevention of Violence" (Washington, 1969); John Levin, "The Right to Bear Arms: The Development of the American Experience," *Chicago-Kent Law Review,* vol. 148 (1971); Roy Weatherup, "Standing Armies and Armed Citizens: An Historical Analysis of the Second Amendment," *Hastings Constitutional Law Quarterly,* vol. 2 (1975).

4. See, for example, Malcolm, "Right of the People to Keep and Bear Arms," pp. 285–289.

5. Newton and Zimring, "Firearms and Violence in American Life," p. 255; Kennet and Anderson, *The Gun in America,* pp. 25–27.

6. Weatherup, "Standing Armies and Armed Citizens," pp. 973–974.

7. Ibid. Weatherup also denied that the complaints in the Declaration of Rights that James II had disarmed Protestants were to be taken literally.

8. Among the fine historical and constitutional works on this era of American history are Gordon S. Wood, *The Creation of the American Republic: 1776–1787* (Chapel Hill, 1969); Forrest McDonald, *Novus Ordo Seclorum: The Intellectual Origins of the Constitution* (Lawrence, Kansas, 1985); Donald S. Lutz, *Popular Consent and Popular Control: Whig Political Theory in the Early State Constitutions* (Baton Rouge, 1980); Jackson Turner Main, *The Anti-Federalists: Critics of the Constitution, 1781–1788* (Chapel Hill, 1961); Robert Allen Rutland, *The Birth of the Bill of Rights: 1776–1791* (Chapel Hill, 1955). Those that treat the subjects of the militia, army, and Second Amendment include James Kirby Martin and Mark Edward Lender, *A Respectable Army: The Military Origins of the Republic, 1763–1789* (Arlington Heights, 1982); John Shy, *A People Numerous and Armed: Reflections on the Military Struggle for American Independence* (New York, 1976); and John Phillip Reid, *In Defiance of the Law: The Standing-Army Controversy, the Two Constitutions, and the Coming of the American Revolution* (North Carolina, 1981).

9. Alexis de Tocqueville, *Democracy in America,* ed. J. P. Mayer, trans. George Lawrence (Garden City, 1969), p. 32.

10. Cited by Weatherup, "Standing Armies and Armed Citizens," p. 975, note 33; *Blankand v. Galdy,* 1693, discussed by Thomas Barnes in *English Legal System Carryover to the Colonies,* p. 16. And see George Lee Haskins, *Law and Authority in Early Massachusetts: A Study in Tradition and Design* (New York, 1960), pp. 4–8. More specifically, English law was applicable either as it existed on the date of settlement in settled colonies or as it existed on the date the first colonial assembly met in the case of conquered colonies. See *Cambell v. Hall.* In the first volume of *Commentaries,* Blackstone distinguished between uninhabited countries where "all the English laws are immediately there in force" once Englishmen settle, and conquered countries that have laws of their own. In this last case the King may alter or change those laws. He placed "our American plantations" in the latter category. See William Blackstone, *Commentaries on the Laws of England,* 4 vols., 1st ed., repr. (Chicago, 1979), 1:304–305. Colonial charters that provided for common law include the charters of Mas-

sachusetts (1626); Rhode Island (1663); Connecticut (1662); New York (1664); New Jersey (charter date unknown); Pennsylvania (1681); Delaware (1701); Maryland (1701); Virginia (1606); North Carolina (1663); South Carolina (1712); and Georgia (1732).

11. See Kermit Hall, *The Magic Mirror: Law in American History* (Oxford, 1989), pp. 11–12.

12. The growth of the population in England's American colonies was phenomenal. The population in 1670 of approximately 85,000 persons had quadrupled by 1713 and quadrupled again by 1754 to some 1,500,000 persons. See Samuel Eliot Morison, *The Oxford History of the American People,* 3 vols. (New York, 1972), 1:196. On the charters see, for example, the Charter of Virginia, 1606, *The Federal and State Constitutions, Colonial Charters, and Other Organic Laws of the States, Territories, and Colonies,* ed. F. Thorpe (1909); Charter of Connecticut, Charles II, *The Public Records of the Colony of Connecticut,* ed. J. Hammond Trumbull et al., 15 vols. (Hartford, 1852–1890), 1:7.; Charter of Massachusetts Bay, William & Mary, *Acts and Resolves of the Province of Massachusetts Bay* (Boston, 1869), vol. 1, p. 14.

13. See McDonald, *Novus Ordo Seclorum,* pp. 12–13.

14. David S. Lovejoy, *The Glorious Revolution in America* (New York, 1972), p. 378.

15. Hall, *Magic Mirror,* p. 13.

16. Part of the impetus to limit slavery in Georgia, for example, was the need to increase the number of armed free men in the frontier population.

17. See, for example, *The Book of the General Lawes and Libertyes Concerning the Inhabitants of the Massachusetts Bay,* (1st ed. Boston, 1648; photo. repr. 1975), pp. 39–42; *The Public Records of the Colony of Connecticut; Records of the Colony of Rhode Island and Providence Plantations in New England,* ed. J. Bartlett, 10 vols. (Providence, 1856–1865).

18. Fred Anderson compares the Massachusetts militia to "an all-purpose military infrastructure: a combination of home guard, draft board, and rear-echelon supply network." Fred Anderson, *A People's Army: Massachusetts Soldiers and Society in the Seven Years' War* (Chapel Hill, 1984), p. 27.

19. *Laws of Colony of New Plymouth, 1623,* repr. in *The Compact with the Charter and Laws of the Colony of New Plymouth* (Boston, 1836), p. 31.

20. "An Act Preventing Negroes from Bearing Arms" (1640), *The Old Dominion in the Seventeenth Century: A Documentary History of Virginia, 1606–1689,* ed. W. Billings (Chapel Hill, 1975), p. 172.

21. *Records of Colony of Rhode Island,* 1:94.

22. *The Statutes at Large: Being A Collection of All the Laws of Virginia from the First Session of the Legislature, in the Year 1619,* ed. William Waller Hening (New York, 1823), 1:127, nos. 24, 25, 27, 28; 1:174, Act 51 (1631–1632).

23. *Records of Colony of Connecticut,* 8:380.

24. *The Colonial Records of the State of Georgia* (Atlanta, 1904–1910), vol. 1, XIX, pt. 1, pp. 137–139.

25. See "Governor Nicholls' Answer to the Severall Queries Relative to the Planters in the Territories of His Royal Highness the Duke of Yorke in America," *Documents Relative to the Colonial History of the State of New York,* ed. E. B. O'Callaghan and B. Fernow, 15 vols. (Albany, 1853–1887), 1:88; *Massachusetts General Laws,* p. 35.

26. See Halbrook, *That Every Man Be Armed,* pp. 56–57.

27. See Robert Cottrol and Raymond T. Diamond, "The Second Amendment: Toward an Afro-Americanist Reconsideration," *The Georgetown Law Journal,* vol. 80, no. 2 (December, 1991), pp. 323–324.

28. *Massachusetts General Laws,* p. 28. And see *Laws of Colony of New Plymouth,* p. 63.

29. Morison, *The Oxford History of the American People,* 1:159.

30. "An Act for the Safeguard and Defence of the Country against the Indians," 28 Car. II, cited by Halbrook, *That Every Man Be Armed,* p. 56.

31. There is an instance in 1652 where Massachusetts apparently did require such participation. See Winthrop Jordan, *White over Black: American Attitudes toward the Negro, 1550–1812* (Chapel Hill, 1968), p. 71.

32. Lorenzo J. Greene, *The Negro in Colonial New England* (New York, 1968), p. 127. Also see Jordan, *White over Black,* p. 71.

33. A. L. Higginbotham, *In the Matter of Color: Race and the American Legal Process: The Colonial Period* (New York, 1978), p. 32.

34. *Old Dominion in the Seventeenth Century,* p. 172; Higginbotham, *In the Matter of Color,* p. 32.

35. See Higginbotham, *In the Matter of Color,* pp. 201–215.

36. *Colonial Records of Georgia,* XIX, pt. 1, pp. 76–77.

37. See J. R. Western, *The English Militia in the Eighteenth Century: The Story of a Political Issue, 1660–1802* (London, 1965), for a general discussion of the problems facing the English militia. The Mutiny Act remained of only twelve-month duration into the twentieth century.

38. See Michael Roberts, *The Military Revolution* (Belfast, 1956).

39. 1 Will. & Mar., sess. 2, c.2; 1 Will. & Mar., c.5. And see Thomas Alan Critchley, *The Conquest of Violence: Order and Liberty in Britain* (London, 1970), p. 68; Western, *English Militia,* p. 73. Reid finds English magistrates sometimes reluctant to use the army to quell riots. See Reid, *In Defiance of the Law,* pp. 233–234, app. p. 235.

40. Bernard Bailyn, *The Ideological Origins of the American Revolution* (Cambridge, Mass., 1967), p. 43.

41. See John Trenchard, "An Argument Shewing that a Standing Army Is Inconsistent with a Free Government, and Absolutely Destructive to the Constitution of the English Monarchy" (London, 1697), pp. 112, 115.

42. Howard cited Bacon's comment: "Take away from the king the absolute power to compel men to take up arms, otherwise than in case of foreign invasion; power to compel men to go out of their countries to war, to charge men for the maintenance of wars, power to make them find arms at his pleasure, and lastly power to break the peace, or do ought that may tend thereto; certainly the power of the militia that remaineth, though

never so surely settled in the king's hand, can never bite this nation." See Simeon Howard, "A Sermon Preached to the Ancient and Honorable Artillery Company in Boston" (Boston, 1773), repr. in *American Political Writing during the Founding Era: 1760–1805*, eds. Charles S. Hyneman and Donald Lutz, 2 vols. (Indianapolis, 1983), 1:200 and note.

43. Edwin S. Corwin, *The "Higher Law" Background of American Constitutional Law*, 1st ed. 1928 (Ithaca, 1974), p. 85. The shrewd Philadelphia printer who produced the first American edition of the full work in 1771–1772 had 1400 advance orders. See p. 85, note 126.

44. Locke was third, with less than half the citations of Blackstone; Machiavelli was twenty-eighth; and Harrington was thirty-fifth. Donald Lutz, "The Relative Influence of European Writers on Late Eighteenth-Century American Political Thought," *The American Political Science Review*, 78 (March 1984), table 3, p. 194.

45. Blackstone, *Commentaries*, 1:136–139. Blackstone identified these five auxiliary rights:

   1. The constitution, powers, and privileges of Parliament

   2. The limitation of the King's prerogative

   3. The right to apply to the courts of justice for redress of injuries

   4. The right of petitioning the King or either house of Parliament

   5. The right of subjects to have arms for their defence, suitable to their condition and degree, and such as are allowed by law.

46. Ibid., 1:140.

47. Ibid., 1:395.

48. Ibid., 1:395, 400.

49. Katharine Chorley, *Armies and the Art of Revolution*, repr. (Boston, 1973), p. 216. For further information on the transmission of the English antiarmy attitude to America, see Reid, *In Defiance of the Law*.

50. See 30 Geo. II, c.25 (1757), 2 Geo. III, c.20 (1761), 4 Geo. III, c.17 (1763). The quotation is from the act of 1761. And see C. M. Clode, *The Military Forces of the Crown: Their Administration and Government*, 2 vols. (London, 1869), 1:42.

51. Howard, "Sermon," Hyneman and Lutz, *American Political Writing*, 1:199.

52. Cited by Reid, *In Defiance of the Law*, pp. 5–6, from *Gazette and Post-Boy*, April 30, 1770, p. 1, col. 2.

53. *Boston Evening Post*, February 6, 1769, repr. in *Boston under Military Rule, 1768–1769, as Revealed in A Journal of the Times*, ed. Oliver Morton Dickerson (Boston, 1936), p. 61.

54. *New York Journal Supplement*, April 13, 1769, *Boston under Military Rule*, p. 79.

55. See Richard C. Perry and John C. Cooper, *Sources of Our Liberties:*

Documentary Origins of Individual Liberties in the United States Constitution and Bill of Rights (Chicago, 1959), p. 288, statement from the Continental Congress.

56. See John C. Miller, *Origins of the American Revolution* (Boston, 1943), pp. 173–176.

57. Ibid., pp. 173–176.

58. Articles of Confederation, article 6.

59. See Halbrook, *Right to Bear Arms,* for a somewhat different interpretation of provisions for a right to bear arms and militia concerns in the first state constitutions.

60. *The Papers of George Mason: 1725–1792,* ed. Robert A. Rutland, 3 vols. (Chapel Hill, 1970), 1:288. See Halbrook, *Right to Bear Arms.*

61. "Declaration of Rights and Fundamental Rules of the Delaware State," 1776.

62. *Debates and Proceedings in the Convention of the Commonwealth of Massachusetts, Held in the Year 1788,* eds. Bradford K. Pierce and Charles Hale (Boston, 1856), pp. 198–199.

63. Constitution of New Hampshire, 1783, pt. I, "The Bill of Rights."

64. Constitution of Massachusetts, 1780, pt. I, "A Declaration of Rights."

65. Constitution of Pennsylvania, 1776, chap. I, "A Declaration of the Rights of the Inhabitants of the State of Pennsylvania."

66. *Mason Papers,* 1:288. The emphasis is my own.

67. Constitution of the State of New York, 1791, article 40.

68. See Constitution of Pennsylvania, 1776, and Constitution of Delaware, 1776.

69. Constitution of Massachusetts, 1780, article 17, article 1.

70. Samuel Adams, "The Rights of the Colonists," November 20, 1772, repr. in *Old South Leaflets,* ed. Edwin D. Mead, vol. 7, no. 173.

71. Adams went on to declare that "all persons born in the British American Colonies are, by the laws of God and nature and by the common law of England exclusive of all charters from the Crown, well entitled, and by acts of the British Parliament are declared to be entitled, to all the natural, essential, inherent and inseparable rights, liberties, and privileges of subjects born in Great Britain or within the realm." Ibid., p. 4.

72. *The Debates in the Several State Conventions on the Adoption of the Federal Constitution,* ed. Jonathan Elliot, 5 vols., 2nd ed. (Philadelphia, 1863), 3:451. The belief that rights existed in nature before they were declared was drawn in large part from English legal theory. As Philip Livingston wrote in 1774, even Magna Carta did not create liberties, it merely proclaimed and affirmed them. "Legal rights" were "those rights which we are entitled to by the eternal laws of right reason." Such rights were independent of positive law and stood as a measure of its legitimacy. "The Other Side of the Question" (New York, 1774), cited by Bailyn, *Ideological Origins,* pp. 188–189.

73. *The Papers of James Madison,* eds. Charles F. Hobson and Robert A. Rutland, 15 vols. (1962–1979), 12:203.

74. Constitution of New Jersey, 1776.
75. Rhode Island, like Connecticut, simply retained its royal charter. See Elliot, *State Debates*, 3:317. Such arguments did not persuade residents of Massachusetts, who turned down the first constitution offered to them because it contained no bill of rights. In "The Essex Result," an essay urging citizens of the Commonwealth to reject that first constitution, the second of eighteen objections read: "That a bill of rights, clearly ascertaining and defining the rights of conscience, and that security of person and property, which every member of the State hath a right to expect from the supreme power thereof, ought to be settled and established previous to the ratification of any constitution for the State." Hynaman and Lutz, *American Political Writing*, 1:481.
76. Constitution of New Hampshire, 1783, article 10.
77. Draft of address by Mr. Wilson, "Notes on the Federal Convention," James Madison Papers, series 7, container 2, Library of Congress.
78. Morris to Moss Kent, January 12, 1815, Max Farrand, ed., *The Records of the Federal Convention of 1787*, 3 vols. (New Haven, 1911), app. A, 315, pp. 420–421.
79. Ibid. He added, "We flattered ourselves, that the constitutional restriction on the use of militia, combined with the just apprehension of danger to liberty from a standing army, would force those entrusted with the conduct of national affairs, to make seasonable provision for a naval force."
80. James Madison, *Notes of Debates in the Federal Convention of 1787*, ed. Adrienne Koch (Athens, Ohio, 1966), p. 484.
81. Farrand, *Records of Federal Convention*, app. A, 211, p. 319.
82. Madison, *Notes*, p. 478.
83. Ibid.
84. Ibid.
85. Ibid., pp. 481–482.
86. Ibid., p. 482.
87. Ibid., pp. 481–482.
88. This was of particular concern during the Virginia ratification debates. See Elliot, *State Debates*, 3:380.
89. The Articles of Confederation, article 6.
90. Few needed General Pinckney's reminder that on at least one occasion during the Revolutionary War "a dissimilarity in the militia of different States had produced the most serious mischiefs." Madison, *Notes*, p. 483. Pinckney was convinced that "the States would never keep up a proper discipline to the militia." According to Edmund Randolph, "the Militia were every where neglected by the State Legislatures, the members of which courted popularity too much to enforce a proper discipline." See Madison, *Notes*, pp. 483, 515.
91. Madison, *Notes*, p. 516.
92. Ibid., p. 478.
93. Madison defended this grant of power: "If resistance should be made to the execution of the laws, it ought to be overcome. This could be done

only two ways; either by regular forces, or by the people. By one or the other it must unquestionably be done. If insurrections should arise, or invasions should take place, the people ought unquestionably to be employed to suppress and repel them, rather than a standing army. The best way to do these things, was to put the militia on a good and sure footing, and enable the government to make use of their services when necessary . . . ." And Randolph asked, "What remedy then could be provided?— Leave the country defenceless? In order to provide for our defence, and exclude the dangers of a standing army, the general defence is left to those who are the objects of defence. It is left to the militia who will suffer if they become instruments of tyranny. The general government must have power to call them forth when the general defence requires it." Farrand, *Records of Federal Convention,* app. A, 211, p. 319.

94. See Articles of Confederation, article 7.
95. Madison, *Notes,* p. 513.
96. Ibid., p. 516. And see p. 483.
97. Ibid., p. 483.
98. Ibid, p. 639.
99. Ibid.
100. Ibid.
101. Farrand, *Records of Federal Convention,* 2:637.
102. Ibid., p. 640. In a letter to Thomas Jefferson during the ratification debates, Mason explained his objections to the proposed constitution. He began with the military arrangements, "particularly the almost unlimited Authority over the Militia of the several States; whereby, under Colour of regulating, they may disarm, or render useless the Militia, the more easily to govern by a standing Army; or they may harass the Militia, by such rigid Regulations, and intollerable Burdens, as to make the people themselves desire its Abolition." See Michael Kammen, ed., *The Origins of the American Constitution: A Documentary History* (New York, 1986), p. 112.
103. See the Constitution of the United States, article 1, section 7; article 2, section 2.
104. *Debates and Proceedings in the Convention of the Commonwealth of Massachusetts, Held in the Year 1788,* eds. Bradford K. Pierce and Charles Hale (Boston, 1856), pp. 198–199.
105. Ibid., p. 180.
106. Ibid., pp. 313–314. Another delegate vowed, "Had I an arm like Jove I would hurl from the globe those villains that would dare attempt to establish in our country a standing army . . . What occasion have we for standing armies? We fear no foe. If one should come upon us, we have a militia, which is our bulwark." Jonathan Eliot, ed., *The Debates in the Several State Conventions on the Adoption of the Federal Constitution,* 5 vols., 2nd ed. (Philadelphia, 1863), 2:137.
107. Elliot, *State Debates,* 3:611.
108. Ibid., 3:380.
109. John Smiley, Pennsylvania Convention, December 6, 1787, in *Documen-*

tary History of the Ratification of the Constitution, eds. Kaminski and Saladino (1981), 2:509.

110. Ibid.

111. If the new army became a threat to liberty, how, Henry demanded, "are you to punish them? Will you order them to be punished? Who shall obey these orders? . . . Your militia is given up to Congress . . . They will therefore act as they think proper: all power will be in their own possession." Elliot, *State Debates,* 3:47–48, 51–52.

112. Ibid., 3:385.

113. Alexander Hamilton, *The Federalist Papers,* no. 24.

114. Elliot, *State Debates,* 3:383.

115. Ibid., pp. 390–391.

116. Ibid., 2:97.

117. Noah Webster, "An Examination into the Leading Principles of the Federal Constitution," 1787, in *Pamphlets on the Constitution of the United States, Published during Its Discussion by the People, 1787–1788,* ed. Paul Leicester Ford (Brookline, 1888), p. 56.

118. Elliot, *State Debates,* 3:646.

119. Cited by Rutland, *Birth of the Bill of Rights,* p. 132.

120. Jefferson to Madison, December 20, 1787, Paris, in Kammen, *Origins of the American Constitution,* pp. 90–91.

121. Kammen, *Origins of the American Constitution,* pp. 133–134.

122. *Pennsylvania and the Federal Constitution, 1787–1788,* p. 422.

123. *Debates and Proceedings in Massachusetts,* p. 86.

124. *Documentary History of the Constitution of the United States, 1787–1870,* 3 vols. (Washington, 1894), 2:143.

125. Ibid., 2:143, 191, 269, 314; Elliot, *Debates in the State Conventions,* 2:406.

126. Madison may have been acting out of political expediency, or Jefferson may have persuaded him to champion a bill of rights. Jefferson had written to Madison shortly after the session began: "There is a remarkable difference between the character of the Inconveniences which attend a Declaration of Rights and those which attend the want of it. The inconveniences of the Declaration are that it may cramp government in its useful exertions, but the evil of this is shortlived, moderate and reparable. The inconveniences of the want of a Declaration are permanent, afflicting and irreparable: they are in constant progression from bad to worse." Jefferson to Madison, March 15, 1787, Paris, Madison papers, series 1, reel 3, Library of Congress. In his address to the House on the subject, however, Madison remained unenthusiastic about a bill of rights, though he was prepared to become its advocate. He "always conceived," he informed members, "that in a certain form and to a certain extent, such a provision was neither improper nor altogether useless." *Papers of James Madison,* 12:203. And see Madison to Jefferson, October 17, 1788, in Kammen, *Origins of the Constitution,* pp. 367–371, and Jefferson's reply, March 15, 1789, pp. 376–378. Madison wrote to Randolph in April that he believed the

concurrence of his colleagues "will proceed from a spirit of conciliation rather than conviction." Madison to Randolph, April 12, 1789, cited by Rutland, *Birth of Bill of Rights,* p. 201. This seems to have been the case. John Marshall recalled later that, since "in almost every convention" which approved the constitution "amendments to guard against the abuse of power were recommended," it was "in compliance with a sentiment thus generally expressed, to quiet fears thus extensively entertained, amendments were proposed by the required majority in congress, and adopted by the states." *Barron v. Baltimore,* repr. in *Cases on Constitutional Law,* ed. J. B. Thayer, 2 vols. (Cambridge, Mass., 1895), 1:452.

127. Madison to Jefferson, June 13, 1789, cited by Rutland, *Birth of Bill of Rights,* p. 209.

128. See Donald Lutz, "The State Constitutional Pedigree of the U.S. Bill of Rights," *Publius,* vol. 22, no. 2 (Spring 1992), pp. 19–45.

129. *Papers of James Madison,* 12:201. This language may not be precise. There is no existing handwritten draft of Madison's suggested rights. The only version of his speech presenting them to Congress is that printed in the Congressional Register, and this was prepared by a shorthand reporter whose skills were hampered by excessive drink. Madison himself is said to have condemned, the Register as exhibiting "the strongest evidences of mutilation and perversion." See Herbert Mitgang, "Handwritten Draft of a Bill of Rights Found," *New York Times,* July 29, 1987, sec. A, p. 1, col. 4; sec. C, p. 21, col. 3.

130. Roger Sherman, draft of amendments to constitution, July 1789, ser. 1, vol. 11, James Madison Papers, Library of Congress.

131. Blackstone, *Commentaries,* 1:139.

132. The Constitution, in Article 1, Section 8, gave Congress the power "to provide for organizing, arming, and disciplining the Militia and for governing such Part of them as may be employed in the Service of the United States."

133. August 17, 1787, *Annals of Congress,* 1:750.

134. Rutland, *Birth of Bill of Rights,* p. 215.

135. "The Right to Keep and Bear Arms: Report of the Subcommittee on the Constitution of the Committee on the Judiciary, United States Senate, Ninety-Seventh Congress, Second Session," Government Printing Office (Washington, 1982), p. 6.

136. *Documentary History of the Constitution,* 2:143, 191, 269, 314; Elliot, *State Debates,* 2:406; Halbrook, *That Every Man Be Armed,* p. 80, note 166.

137. Halbrook, *That Every Man Be Armed,* p. 81, note 167.

138. See Malcolm, "Right of the People to Keep and Bear Arms," pp. 288–289.

139. Cress, "An Armed Community," p. 31.

140. See Levinson, "Embarrassing Second Amendment," p. 645.

141. Blackstone, *Commentaries,* 1:139.

142. See the proposals of Virginia, New York, North Carolina, and Rhode Island, in *Documentary History of the Constitution,* 2:380, 191, 269, 314.

143. See John Smiley, *Documentary History of the Ratification,* 2:509.

144. "Centinel, Revived," no. 24, *Independent Gazetteer,* September 9, 1789, p. 2, col. 2, and cited by Halbrook, *That Every Man Be Armed,* p. 80.

145. *Documentary History of the Constitution,* 2:143, 191, 269, 314; Elliot, *State Debates,* 2:406.

146. Madison, *Notes,* p. 639.

147. *Philadelphia Federal Gazette* and *Philadelphia Evening Post,* June 18, 1789, no. 68, vol. 2, p. 2, repr. by *New York Packet,* June 23, 1789, p. 2, col. 1–2, and by *Boston Centenial,* July 4, 1789, p. 1, col. 2.

148. William Rawle, *A View of the Constitution of the United States of America,* 2nd ed. (Philadelphia, 1829), pp. 125–126.

Afterword

1. Benjamin N. Cardozo, *The Nature of the Judicial Process* (New Haven, 1921), pp. 92–93.

2. This means not that firearms are unobtainable in Great Britain, but that there is no right to have them.

3. Sanford Levinson, "The Embarrassing Second Amendment," *The Yale Law Review,* vol. 99, no. 3 (December 1989); David C. Williams, "Civic Republicanism and the Citizen Militia: The Terrifying Second Amendment," *The Yale Law Review,* vol. 101, no. 3 (December 1991).

4. Jean L. DeLolme, *The Constitution of England; or an Account of the English Government* (New York, 1792), p. 227. This book was first published in London in 1775 and subsequently appeared in numerous editions.

5. Ibid.

6. Ibid., p. 228.

7. Ibid., p. 232.

8. See *Dictionary of National Biography,* ed. L. Stephen and S. Lee, 63 vols. (London, 1885–1900).

9. *The King vs George Dewhurst and Others,* John Macdonell, ed., *Reports of State Trials,* new series, vol. 1, pp. 529–608.

10. *Rex v. Dewhurst,* p. 538.

11. Ibid.

12. Ibid., p. 576.

13. Ibid., p. 578–579.

14. Ibid., p. 580.

15. This phrase seems to have been first used by Justice Joseph Story and frequently repeated. See Joseph Story, *Commentaries on the Constitution of the United States,* 2 vols. (Boston, 1833; 5th ed. 1891), 2:678.

16. *Rex v. Dewhurst,* pp. 601–602.

17. Ibid., p. 602.

18. John Lord Campbell, *Lives of the Lord Chancellors and Keepers of the Great Seal of England,* 7th ed. (New York, 1878), vol. 9, pp. 131–132. Campbell was active in the Commons in law reform and served as solicitor-general and attorney-general.

19. "An Act to Prevent the Training of Persons to the Use of Arms, and to the Practice of Military Evolutions and Exercise," 60 Geo. III, c.1 (1819).

20. The mere keeping of weapons was not sufficient to authorize the search. There had to be some information that an ill purpose was intended. That information, however, might only be the assertion of a single witness. See "An Act to authorise Justices of the Peace, in certain disturbed Counties, to seize and detain Arms collected or kept for purposes dangerous to the Public Peace; to continue in force until the Twenty fifth Day of March One thousand eight hundred and twenty two," 1 George IV, c.2.

21. T. C. Hansard, *The Parliamentary Debates from the Year 1803 to the Present Time,* 41 vols., December 14, 1819, 41:1126.

22. Ibid., p. 1128.

23. Ibid.

24. Ibid., pp. 1130–1131.

25. Ibid., p. 1136. Castlereagh also pointed to the bills passed to disarm the Scots in 1715, 1745, and 1812. On those occasions, however, there was open rebellion in Scotland with foreign aid. See pp. 1136, 1139. Note also that after a long debate on the constitutional implications of the bill, Mr. George Canning, then a senior member of the government and later prime minister, admitted the constitutional right but pointed to the allowance made for circumstances: "I am perfectly willing to admit the right of the subject to hold arms according to the principles laid down by the Honour-able and Learned Gentleman [Mr. Anson], having stated it on the authority of Mr. Justice Blackstone. The doctrine so laid down, I am willing to admit, is no other than the doctrine of the British Constitution. The Bill of Rights, correctly quoted and properly construed, brings me to the construction of the Bill which, in fact, recognises the right of the subject to have arms, but qualifies that right in such a manner as the necessity of the case requires."

26. Ibid., p. 1136.

27. This statement of fact was made by the Earl of Onslow in introducing the government's firearms bill in the House of Lords on April 27, 1920. See *Parliamentary Debates,* House of Lords, new series, 39:1025.

28. Thomas Macaulay, *Critical and Historical Essays, Contributed to the Ed-inburgh Review* (Leipzig, 1850), pp. 154, 162.

29. James Paterson, *Commentaries on the Liberty of the Subject and the Laws of England Relating to the Security of the Person,* 2 vols. (London, 1877), 1:441.

30. *The Economist,* June 20–26, 1992, p. 17.

31. Harris Street, *Freedom, the Individual and the Law,* 2nd ed. (Bristol, 1963), p. 10.

32. Ibid., pp. 191, 205.

33. "An Act to amend the Law relating to Firearms and other Weapons and Ammunition, and to amend the Unlawful Drilling Act, 1819," 10 & 11 Geo. V, c.43. And see Colin Greenwood, *Firearms Control: A Study of Armed Crime and Firearms Control in England and Wales* (London, 1972), p. 25.

34. Greenwood, *Firearms Control,* p. 25.
35. The Pistols Act of 1903, 3 Edward VII, c.18, did not apply to Ireland and, according to the Earl of Onslow, "A person there can purchase and keep in his possession any number of pistols of any size or description, without even going through the formality of buying a gun licence." See *Parliamentary Debates,* 39:1026. For a brief account of the parliamentary debates on the pistol control bills of 1893 and 1895, see Greenwood, *Firearms Control,* pp. 23–25.
36. "An Act to amend the Law relating to Firearms and other Weapons and Ammunition, and to amend the Unlawful Drilling Act, 1819," 10 & 11 Geo. V, c.43.
37. *Parliamentary Debates,* 39:1030.
38. These penalties were substantially greater in Ireland, which was in a virtual state of civil war at the time. Imprisonment could be for two years, there was no provision for appeal, and additional powers of arrest and search were conferred upon police constables in dealing with persons suspected of being in possession of firearms.
39. I am indebted to Colin Greenwood, author of *Firearms Control,* for the crime statistics that follow.
40. Thomas Jones, *Whitehall Diary,* ed. Keith Middlemas, 3 vols. (Oxford, 1969), 1:97.
41. The Cabinet discussions are from Jones, *Whitehall Diary,* 1:97–102.
42. Prior to World War I there was growing anxiety about pistol-wielding anarchists and the dangers of rapid-firing revolvers, but the statistics fail to reflect any real increase in armed crime.
43. Of these strikes, the first was that of the metropolitan police in August 1918. Their wages had fallen so low that many officers' families were actually destitute.
44. According to Jones's notes, he believed that the Prime Minister merely "played the role of taking the revolution very seriously." There were suspicions that the panic "was a War Office dodge for increasing the number of army recruits." When the Prime Minister pointed out that the eight battalions intended for the plebiscitary areas had been detained at home, the Home Office secretary's demand for the 10,000 men was dropped. See Jones, *Whitehall Diary,* 1:99.
45. Indeed, their first recommendation was that military firearms and ammunition that belonged to the government should on demobilization be returned to store and remain under *"complete and permanent Government control."* Military firearms that belonged to officers or enlisted men were to be prevented from being thrown upon the market. "Report of Committee on the Control of Firearms," #5514, 1918, par. 16, Cambridge Institute of Criminology.
46. The Committee was chaired by Sir Ernley Blackwell, Under Secretary of State for the Home Department, and included the former Commissioner of the Prison Service and representatives from the metropolitan police, the county and borough police, the Board of Customs, the Board of Trade, the

War Office, and the Irish Office. It met in secret and its reports were never published.

47. See *The Parliamentary Debates: Official Report,* House of Commons, 5th series, 1920, 130:361–370, 655–686.
48. Ibid., 130:361. When discussion resumed on the bill on June 10, the government was accused of having "attempted to force it through the House at a late hour." See 130:656–657.
49. Ibid., 130:361–362.
50. Ibid., p. 657.
51. Ibid., p. 672.
52. Ibid., pp. 364–365.
53. Ibid., p. 369.
54. Ibid., 133:86.
55. See Ibid., 130:656–665.
56. Ibid., p. 658.
57. Ibid., pp. 658–659.
58. Ibid., pp. 662–663.
59. Ibid., p. 663.
60. Ibid.
61. Ibid., pp. 664–665.
62. Ibid., p. 670.
63. Ibid., p. 671. And see p. 674.
64. Ibid., p. 671.
65. There are now fewer than 50,000 pistols in legitimate hands in England and Wales. According to Colin Greenwood, since the end of World War II a quarter of a million illegally held pistols have been confiscated by the police, and the annual numbers confiscated continue to increase. The number of illegal pistols confiscated in London over a four-year period exceeded the number of legally held pistols. I wish to thank Mr. Greenwood for making the results of his studies available to me.
66. Friedrich Wilhelm Neitzsche, in *The Viking Book of Aphorisms,* ed. W. H. Auden and Louis Kronenberger (New York, 1966), p. 310.
67. See Levinson, "The Embarrassing Second Amendment."
68. Paterson, *Commentaries on the Liberty of the Subject,* 1:441.

Index

Index

Index

Index

Englishman, as peacekeeper, 1–2; collective responsibility, 2–3; militia service, 9; right to be armed, 136
Erle, Thomas, 116–117
Essex, 21, 48, 88, 111
Evelyn, John, 31, 32, 61, 62, 82, 93, 96
Exclusion controversy, 95
Exeter, William, Earl of, 37
Exeter, 45, 83
Ex parte Grossman, 137

Fairfax, Sir Thomas, 22, 64, 82
Falkland, Lord. *See* Cary, Anthony
Federalist Papers, The (Alexander Hamilton), 156
Fifth Monarchists, 29, 43–44
Finch, Heneage, 116
Firearms: statutes and regulations, 6, 9–10, 17–18, 21, 42–43, 45–46, 48, 87, 104, 122–123, 139–141; restrictions on, 9–13, 140–141, 166, 170; quantity, 20; sale of, 21; ban on importation, 43; registration, 43; violations, 79–83, 105–106; cost of, 83–84; enforcement of restrictions, 103
Firearms Control Act (1920): debate on, 172–175; amended, 175
Forest law, 14–15, 56
Forest of Ayles Holt, 89
Forest of Groveley, 90
Forest of Waltham, 88
Forest of Woolmer, 89
Freedom, the Individual, and the Law (Harris Street), 170
French and Indian War, 144
French revolutionary wars, 166, 170

Gage, Thomas, 144, 145
Game, royal prerogative, 74, 75
Game acts, 25; (1389), 13, 72; (1485), 13; (1604), 13, 72, 90; (1605), 13; (1609), 13, 71; (1651), 25, 73; (1654); 26; (1661), 70, 73; (1671), 12, 13, 54, 56, 65, 69–76, 77, 86, 105–106, 116, 120, 125, 127, 128, 129; enforcement of, 86–92, 103; William and Mary (1691), 91, 125, 128; (1692), 126, 128; Ann (1706), 128, 129; George I (1717), 90; property

qualifications in, 12; violations of, 79–80
Gamekeepers, 87–88, 89, 90, 91; creation of, 70, 75
Game park, 55
Garroway, William, 64, 113
General Revenue Act, 144
George III, 143, 146
Georgia, 138, 141, 149, 158
Gerry, Elbridge, 152, 153, 161
Gillingham Forest, 14
Glasgow, 99
Glorious Revolution, 128, 138
Gloucester, Henry, Duke of, 40
Gloucester, 51
Gordon, Lord George, 130
Gordon riots, 130–134
Grand Remonstrance, 18
Gray, Thomas, 83
Great Fire, 62
Grenville, John, Earl of Bath, 111
Gun Licence Act (1870), 170
Gunpowder monopoly, 11, 17, 18
Gunsmiths, 28, 92; rates of, 83

Hamilton, Alexander, 156
Hancock, John, 145
Harrington, James, 27, 125
Henrietta Maria, 110
Henry, Patrick, 150, 156
Henry VII, 174; Game Act of 1485, 13
Henry VIII, 6, 9–10; 1541 act, 87, 120, 128, 132
Hereford, 22
Herick, Sir William, 88
Hertfordshire, 80, 86
High Commission, Court of, 107, 110
Highwaymen, 84
Hind, Captain, 82
Hinton, Lord, 133
Hogge, James, 173
Holcroft, William, 48, 88–89
Holdep, Gilliard, 88, 89
Holdsworth, William, 12
Holt, Sir John, Judge, 82
Holt, Sir Robert, 68
Hopton, Sir Ralph, 20
Hounslow Heath, 107, 111
Howard, Simeon, 142, 144
Hue and cry, 2

Index

Index

Index

Index